Winds WITHDRAWN
of
Change

Challenges Confronting
Journalism Education

FREE PRESS. FREE SPEECH. FREE SPIRIT.

Winds *of* Change
Challenges Confronting
Journalism Education

By Betty Medsger

©1996 The Freedom Forum
1101 Wilson Boulevard
Arlington, Virginia 22209

703/528-0800
www.freedomforum.org

ISBN #0-9655091-0-9

Betty Medsger

A former reporter with *The Washington Post, The* (Philadelphia) *Evening Bulletin* and *The* (Johnstown, Pa.) *Tribune-Democrat*, Betty Medsger is also an investigative journalist who has worked in broadcasting, photojournalism and books. She is a former professor and chair of the Department of Journalism at San Francisco State University and a former representative of journalism education administrators to the Accrediting Council on Education in Journalism and Mass Communications.

Cover illustration by Steve McCraken for The Freedom Forum

This book is dedicated
to the memory of
two journalists who were also journalism educators:

Lynn Kidder (1950-96)
Oakland Tribune reporter;
lecturer, Department of Journalism,
San Francisco State University

H. Roger Tatarian (1916-95)
Vice president and editor-in-chief,
United Press International;
professor, Department of Mass Communication
and Journalism,
Fresno State University

They loved journalism.
They were dedicated
to practicing journalism at its best
and to preparing the next generation
of journalists.

Universities should recruit best teachers to prepare students for journalism careers

Charles L. Overby

The central skills of an excellent journalist — the ability to systematically gather, analyze and communicate information — are also central to higher education. They should be respected as such. But, too often, that has not been the case. Too many educators view the teaching of traditional journalism as a second-rate undertaking. Too many journalists view educators as out of touch with the profession. But if journalism education is to survive, it needs a close relationship between the practitioners and the teachers.

The Freedom Forum commissioned a major report on journalism education by Betty Medsger, who has good credentials as a news professional and as a journalism educator. She had the freedom to pursue the story as she saw it. This report tells what she found.

A few headlines:

■ Journalism core values need to be emphasized. That means more emphasis on the teaching of writing, editing and the history, law and ethics of journalism.

■ The pendulum has swung too far in favoring advanced degrees over professional experience in hiring and promoting journalism educators.

■ There is too much gloom and doom imparted by journalism educators about the future of newspapers and television news.

As budget-conscious university administrators look for ways to consolidate programs and save money, they too often look for a convenient way to lump everything from journalism to speech pathology under one roof. It is probably counterproductive to fight that trend. But let's not pretend that it is all journalism or that all resources devoted to things besides journalistic core values are helping to prepare future journalists.

The Freedom Forum has a mission to work with journalism educators, wherever they are found in the university, and to strengthen their ability to emphasize journalistic core values in their teaching and their writing.

The standard for assessing journalism instruction should be simple: How much emphasis and how many resources are being allocated to teaching writing/reporting and editing and the study of journalism history, law and ethics? There also should be more recognition of top professors who teach these core values. The argument that focusing on journalism basics reduces journalism schools to trade schools is nonsense. Nobody calls law schools trade schools. Their faculties often lead the profession and showcase the best thinking in the field. There is no good reason journalism educators should be different.

In that regard, the battle over who is hired and promoted to teach journalism — real journalism — seems to have been a losing one for news professionals. I am aware of many situations where editors with years of distinguished service were turned down in favor of candidates with less distinguished service but with advanced degrees. Students were the losers because those editors would have been great teachers. They had been teaching in their newsrooms for years.

Journalism students need core journalism courses to go along with a broad liberal-arts education. Journalism administrators need to recruit the best teachers for those core courses, without regard to advanced degrees.

Fueling the conflict between academics and news professionals is the belief among many professors that traditional news outlets are dinosaurs. Historically, that is without basis. There is no record of one medium forcing another out of business. Media that have adapted to changes have always survived and thrived. As we prepare for a multimedia future, the focus should be on students and how to prepare them for meaningful journalism careers. Educators and editors need to talk together about the best ways to make that happen.

For more than four decades, The Freedom Forum has been a partner with educators and journalists to strengthen journalism education. This report furthers that partnership. As it is read and discussed, The Freedom Forum will sponsor forums around the country to focus attention on this important issue. We look forward to your comments.

Charles L. Overby
President and Chief Executive Officer
The Freedom Forum

Communication courses proliferate while journalism education gets harder to find

Félix Gutiérrez

Students have to look harder to find a journalism education these days. It may be hidden under such names as mass communication or information sciences or it may have disappeared altogether into generic communicator courses.

As print, broadcast and electronic media continue to grow, more students are studying the importance of media and news in our society. Many hope to build careers in the field. But finding the courses and professors that will lead them in that direction has become more of a task.

The problem is not finding communication studies on campus. It is figuring out where journalism best fits into the curriculum. That was not much of a problem for earlier generations of students and professionals. Aspiring reporters and editors could find the courses they needed in departments with "journalism" in their name.

Today it is easier than ever to find college and university courses in communication, mass communication, media studies, information sciences and a host of fields in and around the news. The number of graduates receiving bachelor's degrees in various communication fields grew 1,500%, from 3,131 to 52,799, in the 25 years between 1966 and 1991, according to a 1995 study by Ohio State Professor Lee B. Becker and graduate student Joseph D. Graf. But not all the communication programs prepare students for careers in journalism.

While the proliferation of departmental names accurately represents a field that is both expanding and converging — as new media are created and as established media find new partnerships — it is also confusing for students seeking careers in the news and for the news organizations looking to connect with them.

The Freedom Forum's commitment to journalism education and students preparing for newsroom careers spans more that four decades. For nearly two decades that effort has been a primary commitment of Executive Vice President Gerald M. Sass, who has worked with journalists and educators to shape an ambitious range of initiatives to advance students, faculty members and professionals committed to journalism education. This partnership has continued as colleges and universities reassess the role and place of journalism in their curricula.

It was with an eye toward helping professors and professionals shape the future of journalism education that The Freedom Forum asked Betty Medsger, a journalist and journalism education administrator, to invest more than a year studying the winds of change affecting the field. In pursuing this assignment she enjoyed the academic freedom to pursue the inquiry in the directions that appeared to be most productive. Her findings and recommendations are presented in this report, which was published with the editorial and production support of Rod Sandeen, Maurice Fliess and Patty Casey of The Freedom Forum News and Public Information Department.

The findings, conclusions and recommendations are those of the author. We hope they will provide a basis for spirited and lively dialogue on the future of journalism education in the nation's colleges and universities. You are invited to read this report with a eye toward being part of that discussion, and we invite your comments.

Félix Gutiérrez
Senior Vice President, The Freedom Forum
Executive Director, Pacific Coast Center

Table of Contents

Methodology   1

CHAPTER 1: **Introduction**   5

CHAPTER 2: **Competing visions**   9

The intellectual skills of journalism
vs. generic communication

CHAPTER 3: **Who are new journalists?**   27

How they were educated and why
they love journalism but may leave it

CHAPTER 4: **Doctoral degree essential**   41

Journalism educators' expertise, confusion
and desire for change

CHAPTER 5: **Takeover of journalism education**   53

How journalism education has been submerged
during the last half of the 20th century

CHAPTER 6: **Conclusions**   65

Recommendations for the improvement
of journalism education

Appendix   71

Survey of Journalism Educators   73
Survey of Newsroom Recruiters and Supervisors   92
Survey of New Journalists   111
Voices   139
   Educators   140
   News Professionals   155
University Policies   167

Bibliography   179

Methodology

The Freedom Forum commissioned the Roper Center at the University of Connecticut to scientifically survey three distinct groups in journalism and journalism education to assess the strengths and weaknesses of journalism education in developing future journalists:

- **New journalists.** Roper surveyed by telephone 1,041 print and broadcast journalists from across the nation who had one to 11 years of journalism experience as of summer 1995. The reasoning was that a journalist would need at least a year in the profession to judge the usefulness of his or her educational preparation. The 11-year cutoff ensured that contemporary journalism education was being evaluated.
- **Newsroom recruiters and supervisors.** Also by telephone, Roper surveyed 500 newsroom recruiters and supervisors at print and broadcast media organizations. This survey focused on newsroom professionals responsible for recruiting and/or supervising student interns or newly hired journalists.
- **Journalism educators.** Roper surveyed 446 university journalism educators by mail.

The scientific sample of new journalists is designed so that the sample is representative of all U.S. journalists who have been working in journalism for one to 11 years. In order to represent institutional policies, practices and attitudes of news organizations toward recruitment and journalism education, the scientific sample of recruiters/supervisors is designed to represent news organizations across the United States. The scientific sample of educators is designed to represent all faculty members who teach journalism at four-year institutions of higher education.

The project director and the Roper Center developed the questionnaires jointly. Roper provided both substantive input on questionnaire content and technical advice on question wording, question ordering and measurement-response scale.

Telephone surveys: new journalists and newsroom recruiters/supervisors

Telephone questionnaires were pretested with 15 to 20 respondents. The pretest was used to ensure that the questionnaires took 20-25 minutes to complete. The pretest also allowed for fine-tuning of the questionnaires.

The following sources were used to identify new journalists and newsroom recruiters and supervisors:

- A comprehensive list of daily newspapers from the "1995 *Editor & Publisher* International Year Book."
- The "News Media Yellow Book" published by Monitor Publishing.
- "*Broadcasting & Cable* Yearbook" (1995).

These surveys included new journalists and newsroom recruiters and supervisors from daily newspapers, weekly newspapers, television, radio, news magazines and news services. The tables at right outline the sample distributions for new journalists and newsroom recruiters and supervisors samples.

Field work

Telephone interviewing with the new journalists took place in May-June 1995, and with newsroom recruiters and supervisors in September 1995.

The interviewing took place during the work day. All interviewing was conducted at the Roper Center's telephone center. Survey staff called telephone numbers provided in the sample sources (described above) and screened each potential respondent to include only those who met the specifications (i.e., new journalists who had one to 11 years' experience and news-

■ Daily newspapers

	# of New J	# of R & S
Small	193	96
Medium	203	102
Large	154	77

■ Categories within daily newspapers

	# of New J	# of R & S
Supervisors/ managers	132	275
Copy editors	99	–
Reporters	259	–
Photographers	60	–
Total	550	275

■ Weekly newspapers

	# of New J	# of R & S
Supervisors/ managers	34	70
Copy editors	25	–
Reporters	66	–
Photographers	15	–
Total	140	70

■ News magazines

	# of New J	# of R & S
Supervisors/ managers	11	25
Copy editors	8	–
Reporters	24	–
Photographers	7	–
Total	50	25

■ News services

	# of New J	# of R & S
Supervisors/ managers	11	25
Copy editors	8	–
Reporters	24	–
Photographers	7	–
Total	50	25

■ Television

	# of New J	# of R & S
Reporters	40	–
Producers	20	30
News directors	15	30
Assistant news directors	7	–
Photographers/ cameramen	8	–
Field producers	9	–
News anchors	10	–
Tape editors	1	–
Assignment editors	10	–
Total	120	60

■ Radio

	# of New J	# of R & S
Reporters	27	–
Producers	11	20
Editors	12	–
News directors	32	20
Assistant news directors	8	5
Total	90	45

room recruiters and supervisors who were responsible for recruiting/supervising interns/ new journalists).

For those new journalists/newsroom recruiters and supervisors who could not answer survey questions on the first call, interviewers scheduled callbacks at better times. An 800 number also was offered so the journalists/ newsroom recruiters and supervisors could call back when it was convenient. Respondents preferring to be called at home at specific times were accommodated.

Mail survey: journalism educators

Mail questionnaires — about 10 pages long and including five open-ended questions — were sent to 2,000 journalism/mass communication educators across the nation. The educators were randomly selected from the 1994-95 AEJMC "Journalism & Mass Communication Directory." To ensure adequate representation from broadcast programs, Roper cross-referenced the Broadcast Education Association's "Directory of Media Programs of North American Colleges."

Each of the 2,000 educators was mailed a packet with a cover letter explaining the project, a questionnaire and a postage-paid reply envelope. Reminder cards went out a week after the packet mailing. Educators were asked to fill out the questionnaire if they were full-time teachers who taught at least some journalism courses. If they did not meet this requirement, they were asked to give the questionnaire to someone on their journalism/mass communication faculty who did. Non-responders were telephoned after two weeks and urged to participate.

Data processing and weighting

The Roper Center processed all completed questionnaires. It coded the responses to open-ended questions (i.e., questions for which answers were taken verbatim). Then the data from the telephone and mail questionnaires were entered into a machine-readable database.

Weighting (sample balancing) was done to offset different rates of non-response in the survey sample. For the new journalists, sample balancing weights were applied to six types of media organizations. The weighting factors for this sample were determined by a comparison of the relative size of each sample subgroup with the most recent journalist-population estimates (based on the 1992 Indiana

University survey on "The American Journalist in the 1990s.")

Weighting also was done for ethnic-minority journalists. Membership lists were obtained from minority journalists' organizations. After determining their portion in the overall group of new journalists, ethnic-minority journalists were over-surveyed to yield a sample sufficiently large for scientific analysis.

Work done by the Roper Center was directed by Kenneth Dautrich, associate director, assisted by Jila Salari-Beck and Jennifer Necci, project managers, and Melanie Chebro, administrative assistant.

Sampling error

Sampling error for the full sample of new journalists is ±3% at the 95% level of confidence. This means, for example, that if 50% of the sample answered "yes" to a question, there is a 95% probability that the actual figure in the full population of new journalists would be somewhere between 47% and 53%. The response rate for this survey was 76%.

Sampling error for the full samples of newsroom recruiters/supervisors and of educators is ±4.5% at the 95% level of confidence. The response rate to the survey of recruiters/ supervisors was 72%. For the survey of educators, the response rate was 22%.

Sampling error associated with percentages for subgroups of new journalists, recruiters/ supervisors and educators is higher than the sampling error for the full samples. For example, when referring to the responses of new journalists who studied journalism, sampling error is based on a subgroup sample size of 739 new journalists (and is ±3.6% in this instance), as opposed to all 1,041 new journalists in the full sample (for whom, as stated above, the sampling error is ±3%).

Other research

Researchers interviewed and corresponded with hundreds of journalists and journalism educators. Excerpts from those conversations and writings are included in the main body of the study and in the "Voices" sections of the appendix.

Research included an extensive search of historical and contemporary literature on journalism and journalism education, plus the following:

- An examination of accrediting reports of all journalism education programs that were reviewed by the Accrediting Council on Education in Journalism and Mass Communications from 1989-90 through 1995-96.
- Statistical analysis of accreditation reports included in the study cover the last six-year cycle during which all presently accredited programs were evaluated, 1990-91 through 1995 96.
- Interviews with unit heads, search committee chairs or designated spokespersons at 112 of the 117 journalism education programs that advertised for full-time journalism faculty positions for 1995-1996 in *The Chronicle of Higher Education* and *Editor & Publisher*. (Only programs that specifically advertised for faculty members to teach journalism were chosen for the survey pool. They constituted one-fourth of all positions advertised during that year under the headings of mass communications, communication, broadcasting and journalism.)
- A survey of educational backgrounds of recent recipients of Pulitzer Prizes, Alfred I. du Pont Awards, Nieman Fellowships at Harvard University and Knight Fellowships at Stanford University.
- An examination of the results of the annual William Randolph Hearst Foundation Journalism Awards Program, 1989-90 through 1994-95.

Research assistance was provided by Elizabeth Wright, oral historian, San Francisco, and by Kathleen Williams, journalism educator, Montana State University, Bozeman.

Valuable ideas for survey questions and other research were suggested by an advisory committee:

- Jo-Ann Huff Albers, head, Department of Journalism, Western Kentucky University
- Douglas A. Anderson, director, Walter Cronkite School of Journalism and Telecommunication, Arizona State University
- Don Barlett, investigative reporter, *The Philadelphia Inquirer*
- Mary Kay Blake, director, recruiting and placement, Gannett Co. Inc.
- Trevor Brown, dean, School of Journalism, Indiana University
- Jerome M. Ceppos, senior vice president and executive editor, *San Jose* (Calif.) *Mercury News*
- Lisa Chung, former executive director, Asian American Journalists Association
- Mary Dedinsky, associate dean, Medill School of Journalism, Northwestern University
- Robert H. Giles, editor and publisher, *The Detroit News*
- Linda Wright Moore, columnist and editorial writer, *Philadelphia Daily News*
- Gene Roberts, managing editor, *The New York Times*
- Jacqueline Sharkey, professor, Department of Journalism, University of Arizona
- Ray Suarez, host, "Talk of the Nation," National Public Radio

The data sets for the new journalist, educator and recruiter/supervisor surveys are available for those who would like to conduct statistical analyses of the data beyond that which is presented in this report. Anyone interested in obtaining SPSS data files and supporting documentation for any of these three surveys should contact Dr. Kenneth Dautrich at The Roper Center for Public Opinion Research. Phone: 860/486-2579. E-mail: Ken@Opinion.ISI.UCONN.EDU. Note that modest processing charges will apply.

Winds
of
Change

Challenges confronting journalism education

1 Introduction

This study has been conducted during a time when winds of change are strong in journalism education.

There is disagreement among educators and journalists about whether they are fresh winds or destructive winds. One thing is clear: They are strong winds that could profoundly change the nature of journalism education — could even eliminate journalism as a distinct area of study.

The strongest winds of change promote removing journalism education as a separate academic discipline and merging it into communication courses designed not to prepare journalists — people with a mission to stimulate public discourse and serve the public interest — but to prepare generic communicators who could be hired to serve any interests. This approach often involves increasing the number of communication courses required of students and decreasing the number of courses they take outside their major.

These strong winds enthuse, depress and

perplex journalism educators, depending on their philosophy of journalism education and their expertise. The push for these changes has been edging forward for many years, but it has gained velocity because:

- Downsizing and mergermania have become as popular on campuses as they are in corporations.
- New technologies compel faculties to learn and teach new skills, especially new research skills.
- Educators and journalists are confused about the shape of the future of journalism, even in the near future.
- It is unclear whether the future of journalism is bright and more exciting, or blurred.

Comments by some of the educators attending the 1995 convention of the Association for Education in Journalism and Mass Communication (AEJMC) reflect the push for philosophical and structural changes. They also

" I think we are getting lost. We should come back to content. We help people create content — news. That's our soul. "

Ford N. Burkhart
Department of Journalism
University of Arizona

reflect both enthusiasm and concern about what the changes would do to journalism.

At sessions on curriculum reform, a common mantra was heard: There are few differences among the communication fields — journalism, public relations, advertising and others. We will train all for all. To continue to educate for specific industries, especially journalism, would be disastrous. If we don't take responsibility for converging into communication, if we don't merge the courses as well as the programs, we are going to die. Apocalyptic reasoning was not unusual.

At one session where these ideas were presented with a sense of urgency, Ford N. Burkhart, associate professor in the Department of Journalism at the University of Arizona, listened as the philosophy and its methods were unfolded. Then, with some frustration evident in his voice, he said, "I think we are getting lost. We should come back to content. We help people create content — news. That's our soul." He was ignored. A few minutes later someone else in the audience talked about dinosaurs in the newsrooms.

A journalism educator who has led what she calls the "revolutionizing" of curriculum at the University of North Dakota, Lana R. Rakow, director of the School of Communication there, explained one of the goals of the changes: "We do not want to single out any particular field. Students will all be communicators."

Her comments were echoed by Vernon A. Keel, director of the Elliott School of Communication at Wichita State University: "There are no journalism majors, only communication majors."

After listening to this vision of what journalism/mass communications should become, Willard D. (Wick) Rowland Jr., dean of the School of Journalism and Mass Communications at the University of Colorado, pointed out the missing ingredient as he asked a question. "The word 'journalism' seems to be missing in your curriculum," he said. "Is there any chance the baby is getting thrown out with the bath water?"

"It's not the names that are important," responded Rakow. "Our students talk about information and technology, not journalism."

As that session ended, Terry Hynes, professor and dean at the College of Journalism and Communications at the University of

Florida, turned to a colleague and said, "Perhaps we have gone too far."

■ ■ ■

This study of journalism education has been a search for the "baby" Wick Rowland asked about. It's been a search for whether "we have gone too far," as Terry Hynes wondered. How is that baby, journalism, doing in the nation's colleges and universities as the year 2000 approaches? Does its condition on campus have a connection to the state of journalism in society? Is journalism education well? Is it being nourished? Is it understood? Is it respected? Is it flourishing? Or is it going down the drain?

This study explored the quality and nature of journalism education:

- By examining what journalism education programs are teaching.
- By exploring who is teaching journalism and their qualifications and expertise.
- By learning how those who studied journalism in college, entered print and broadcast journalism between 1984 and 1994, and were working as journalists in 1995 regard their education and their profession.
- By learning how new journalists with various levels of journalism education compare with each other and with new journalists who have never studied journalism.
- By examining new journalists' needs for education after they become journalists.
- By learning how newsroom recruiters and supervisors of new journalists regard journalism education today.
- By exploring the history and evolution of journalism education — as an area of study, as part of universities, and as a contributor to and critic of the profession.

■ ■ ■

This study was conducted with the premises that journalism is an intellectual activity; that journalism is of central importance in a democratic society; and that it would be valuable for professionals and educators to understand the strengths and weaknesses of journalism education today, the role it plays now and the role it should play in the future.

The term "journalism," as used throughout the study, embraces print and broadcast news media. Journalism is defined here as news and feature storygathering and storytelling in words and visual elements — on behalf of the public interest and through any means of distribution — by independent gatherers, organizers and analyzers of information and ideas (rather than by representatives of special interests, as happens in advertising and public relations).

Journalism can be found in many different types of university structures — in departments, in parts of departments, in schools, in colleges — that encompass a variety of areas of study including public relations, corporate relations, advertising and general communication. This study examines only journalism education — wherever it is found. Other areas come into play here only as their presence may affect the quality and nature of journalism education. The study assumes that the nature and mission of journalism are different from those of other fields of communication, and that in large part its skills, values and historical development also are different.

Key findings

- Journalism education is very important to news organizations. Among those who became journalists between 1984 and 1994 and were employed as journalists in 1995, 71% studied journalism at some level. They included 47% who majored in journalism at the undergraduate level and 9% who have master's degrees in journalism.
- The future of journalism education is jeopardized by college and university hiring policies and philosophies of journalism education that have led to a decline in hiring faculty with significant experience and expertise in journalism, and by not respecting or utilizing the research expertise of many current faculty members. Increasingly, the essential requirement for being hired to teach journalism is a doctoral degree, without regard for the quality or length of experience as a journalist. In fact, 17% of journalism educators never worked as journalists and an additional 47% have less than 10 years' experience as journalists.
- Journalism educators themselves, including ones who have doctoral degrees, do not strongly support the doctorate as a criterion for hiring journalism educators. Though 67% of all journalism educators — 84% of those hired in the last 10 years — have Ph.D.s, just 37% of journalism educators think journalism educators should be required to have them, including only 14% who "strongly" support such a requirement. Only 5% of journalism educators think journalism educators should be required to have a doctorate in mass communication, the major doctoral degree granted by journalism and mass communication programs and the degree held by 48% of journalism

educators.
- The accreditation process, the most powerful national force in journalism education, pressures journalism education programs to place more emphasis on doctoral degrees than on professional expertise in hiring faculty members. In the last round of campus visits that included all accredited programs, accreditation evaluators urged programs to produce traditional scholarly research rather than in-depth journalistic research. Faculty at 68% of the programs had not done enough scholarly research, the evaluators said.
- A majority of new journalists — 57% — said their best journalism teachers had extensive professional journalistic experience and no doctoral degrees. Another 31% said their best journalism teachers had extensive professional experience and doctoral degrees.
- Journalism educators are very confused about what is expected of them for promotion and tenure. Faculty at 66% of the accredited programs — including those with and without doctoral degrees — told evaluators they were confused.
- Newsroom recruiters and supervisors expressed very low regard for the expertise of journalism educators. Only 3% strongly agreed that journalism educators are on the cutting edge of journalism issues and have a strong influence on change in the profession; the same portion agreed that people in their news organizations often ask journalism professors for advice on newsroom issues.
- The future of journalism is jeopardized by low salaries that are driving out the next

generation of journalists. Among new journalists age 25 and under, 57% earn less than $20,000 a year, including 22% who earn less than $15,000 a year. This age group, which accounted for 12% of all journalists in 1982 and 1971, now makes up 4% of all journalists. An annual Michigan State University survey of recruiting trends found that this year's graduating students who take journalism jobs will have the lowest starting salaries of any college-educated workers entering the public or private work force.

- Fifty-two percent of journalism educators said the number of students who plan to become journalists has decreased over the last 10 years — 12% said decreased substantially, 40% said decreased somewhat.

- Today's new journalists, those who have been journalists one to 11 years, are the most educated in history. At least 94% of them have bachelor's degrees. This compares with 82% of all journalists, according to a study by David H. Weaver and G. Cleveland Wilhoit of Indiana University.

- New journalists who never studied journalism are doing as well as or better than the ones who studied journalism — in job satisfaction, in income, in achieving managerial positions and in winning the most prestigious awards and fellowships in journalism.

- An extraordinarily large portion of new journalists — 95% — said they like their jobs — 73% "a lot," 22% "some." Nevertheless, 43% said they might leave journalism; low pay was the chief reason given.

- Current trends in journalism education are diametrically opposed to what newsroom supervisors think is needed to improve journalism. Changes that the supervisors said would improve journalism education

"not at all" are the changes topping the agenda of those pushing for journalism to be merged into communication studies.

- The accrediting process pays little or no attention to areas that are of deepest concern to both educators and journalists. No reports commented on the quality of student writing, 74% contained no comment about the quality of writing instruction, 78% did not comment on the quality of campus newspapers or broadcast journalism, and 50% made no comment about ethics instruction.

- The programs with the largest portion of journalism students who become journalists have a much lower portion of doctoral degree-holding faculty members than does the average journalism program. At the eight programs that reported half or more of their journalism-major graduates were working as journalists three years later, the portion of doctoral-degree faculty ranged from 9% to 55%, compared with an average of 68% for all journalism programs.

- All parties involved — new journalists, newsroom supervisors and journalism educators — expressed strong interest in collaborating on the creation of local continuing-education programs for journalists, a tradition never firmly established in journalism, unlike other professions. New journalists expressed a strong interest in professional development — 88% said they think they would benefit from it, 56% even thought they should be required by their employers to take courses on an ongoing basis. Only a quarter of journalism education programs have such programs now, but 68% said they would be interested in creating them.

2 Competing visions

The intellectual skills of journalism vs. generic communication

The question, "What's the story?" remarkably concentrates the mind. It is where journalists begin. It is where the education of journalists begins.

Learning how to answer that question involves the development and the application of agile perceptions as well as continuous intellectual examination and growth. It also involves asking many questions: What happened? Who was responsible? Why did they do it? Where did they do it? What impelled them? Are my preconceptions or stereotypes guiding my questions? What else do I need to know in order to understand what I've just learned? What do I still need to learn? What does it add up to?

These are some of the questions that good journalism teachers plant in the journalistic mind. They are the habitual questions that lead to the creation of stories and guide what journalists do in words, photographs, graphs and illustrations. Be it heavy and important or light and easy, it is an intellectual process. Whether executed masterfully or superficially or shoddily, it is, nevertheless, a process of critical thinking and decision-making. The well-trained journalist's mind inquires, weaves, thinks again, unravels, asks again, corrects, goes back again, weaves again and then — either under great time pressure or the luxury of additional time for an in-depth project — decides what the story is and creates the words and images to tell it. The message to the public is: "This is what our newsroom decided was most important, most interesting, and what we thought you would most need and want. Here's the news today."

Teaching journalism involves teaching a multifaceted concentration of the mind. The journalism teacher welcomes minds that, during their prior educational experience, have meandered through literature, history, politi-

cal science and physics — sometimes memorizing, often grabbing a snippet. But seldom have they truly examined or made connections between and among the many ideas and facts passed before them.

Students enter the journalism classroom often looking for a formula. Instead, they are asked to think — carefully, critically, precisely — and to do so beyond their own interests, to think of the public's interests and needs. The teacher sends them into the world. When they return, she asks, "What happened?" They think diffusely and uncritically. They guess at what the magic formula is. They respond with a list of facts, beginning with who called the meeting to order and at what time, or with a press release. "No, what happened that matters to people, to the public?" That question, they begin to see, is not simple.

They go out again. They listen more carefully, they begin to ask questions in order to understand what they observe. They are assessing, questioning continuously as they listen and read. Some will realize that they have found the magic formula: Thinking!

They return to class. Now the answer to "What happened?" is very different: "The School Board voted last night to close the only bilingual school in the city. The action will mean. … " They have begun to discover how to find essence and meaning, an intellectual skill that requires razor-sharp concentration, patience, wise reflection, absorbing more knowledge at various depths as needed and maintaining a constant awareness of the public for whom the journalist is reporting.

Following the only formula of journalism: thinking

That can be the beginning of the most important thing the journalism teacher does: teaching students to concentrate the mind to a

To be a journalism teacher as the year 2000 nears is to live in a Tower of Babel amid opposing ideas about what journalism education should teach and what a journalism program should do and be.

higher degree than most have before; to use the mind to explore, to discover, to make decisions about what they learn; to express what they learn clearly, honestly and as fully as time and resources permit.

Learning to tell simple or complex stories to the public — on behalf of the public interest and while connected to the public but not controlled by any part of it — is a major achievement. When the lessons take root, a journalism teacher has the pleasure of seeing students develop awareness that creativity and public service are more likely to make a greater journalistic contribution and bring greater fulfillment if they are nurtured to maturity by a well-trained mind rather than if left to intuition, serendipity or luck.

It is not unusual for journalism students to report, after a few weeks in their introductory newswriting class, that they are now learning more in their other courses. With better-trained minds, they are now reading and listening in a more analytical and absorbing way, as if they were going to have to answer that question, "What's the story?"

Serving journalism and the university

Journalism teachers who understand the purpose of journalism and how its skills are developed and polished have the great satisfaction of knowing that they toil at the heart of two invaluable tasks:

- Preparing the next generation of minds that will stimulate the discourse of democracy, the main purpose of journalism.
- Teaching the skill that is critical to journalism but that is also central to the mission of any university — the concentration of the mind and the clear expression of what one discovers.

To be a fine journalism teacher is to live in the midst of the constant intellectual growth that is stimulated by the journalistic imperative: to concentrate the mind in order to find out for the public what is happening in the world, be it down the street or on the other side of the planet. The journalism teacher is engaged in the life of the mind on behalf of two of the most important public enterprises, the university and journalism.

Teachers get mixed signals

But to be a journalism teacher as the year

2000 nears is to live in a Tower of Babel amid opposing ideas about what journalism education should teach and what a journalism program should do and be. The voices are many — confusing, conflicting, creative and destructive:

- Teach how to get out of cars gracefully, how to hold the camera and how to get back to the station fast, say some who hire television journalists.
- Teach how to get to and from a fire fast so the individual can do five more stories that day, say some who hire journalists for small newspapers.
- Add five courses on Web page building, database searching and traveling the Internet, say some faculty members who have decided the sum and substance of the future is in the sum of information, not the substance of journalism. Learning to shovel information, not to find and tell stories, should be at the heart of the curriculum, they say.
- Do not give me journalism nerds, give me well-rounded people who know more than journalism, say editors of medium-size newspapers who may not even know the majors of the people hired in the last year.
- Stop teaching vocational skills courses. Just introduce students to the nature of various communications occupations and spend the rest of the time pursuing the broad, conceptual, intellectually worthy communication courses, say educators who advocate producing generic communicators.

What's a journalism educator to do?

Though there are many approaches to teaching journalism, two competing paths dominate today:

1. Hold firm to the vision embodied in the standards that are supposed to guide evaluation of schools by the Accrediting Council on Education in Journalism and Mass Communications (ACEJMC), a joint education/profession voluntary evaluation system established immediately after World War II. In other words, keep the ratio of journalism and mass communication courses at no more than 25% of the classes a student takes as an undergraduate journalism major. Make sure the courses in the major are a combination of

skills, theory and survey courses, which usually means a combination of basic and advanced skills courses, introduction to mass communication, journalism history, law and ethics, and selected electives. Make sure students take a rich mixture of liberal arts and science courses.

2. Create a new vision — the integrated curriculum, the "new professionalism." Permit or require students to take 50% or more of their university units in journalism/mass communication, reduce the number of writing courses they may take, and require them to take a very large portion of their major courses in communication theory — a blend of concepts about the mass communication professions and concepts about personal-communication theories.

Those two propositions, stated in the midst of a group of uninhibited journalism educators, can ignite an extremely heated debate.

To someone from outside university life, the issues may seem arcane, but to people inside the ivy walls they involve deep philosophical differences. The few journalists who pay close attention to journalism education have watched the debate with keen interest but seldom have joined it.

Proponents of the first approach — the model probably still in place at most schools but under strong criticism — believe that the journalism curriculum should not dominate the education of journalism majors. It should help instill the intellectual skills of writing and research needed to enter journalism. It should also provide students with survey and theory courses that will inform them about the history, ethics and laws of journalism. In this only-25%-journalism paradigm, the journalism program places as much emphasis on the units taken outside the major, primarily in the liberal arts and sciences, as it does on its own courses. Such an education, according to this approach, will open areas of knowledge and interest that will stimulate a lifetime of learning in diverse areas. It is designed to prepare the minds of journalists, but, in fact, it sharpens minds in ways that are useful in any number of professions.

Proponents of what is sometimes called the integrated curriculum model — the wind that currently is the most powerful force in discussions about change in journalism education — want communication studies to be generally accepted as a liberal-arts field. In their eyes, these courses are worthy of occupying twice as much of a student's overall university coursework as is allowed under current accrediting standards. Under the integrated curriculum model, students would be trained as generic communicators. Such a curriculum, in universities where it is now in place, gives students a little public relations, a little advertising, a little journalism and a lot of theory about communications in general. Equipped with these pieces of education, advocates say, students are prepared to move fluidly all their lives from being one kind of communication professional to being another kind.

The push: move away from 'occupational' training

Two chief proponents of the integrated form of communication studies, Professors Robert O. Blanchard and William G. Christ of Trinity University in San Antonio, spelled out the main tenets in their book, "Media Education and the Liberal Arts: A Blueprint for the New Professionalism." They include these prescriptions for change:

"Students take a few integrated conceptual core courses and engage in some experiential learning that emphasizes familiarity and experimentation with … media message-making technology (over technical competence). But they devote most of the communication and media academic work to intellectually challenging conceptual studies of mass media and communication that provide bridges to the behavioral and social sciences, arts and humanities. … Occupational training is neither mandatory nor the center of the curriculum. It does not absorb a great deal of faculty time and effort, and only a little of it, if any, is for academic credit. … Basic skills is the practitioners' (journalists') code for the functions of mass screening and socialization and indoctrination for the occupational culture they expect programs to perform, if not exclusively, above all other priorities."

This analysis of journalism as an academic discipline — or rationale for why the skills of journalism do not deserve to be part of an academic discipline — suggests a lack of understanding of the intellectual nature of the skills of journalism. Indeed, the analysis seems to reject the notion that these skills fall under the category of "intellectual," despite the fact that some of those emphasized in introductory journalism courses — research, critical thinking, organization of material and clear expression — are among the key skills the university tries, but often fails, to teach all students as essential parts of their liberal education. This analysis also suggests an ignorance of what journalism is and the connections that journalism needs to other studies in order to develop the intellectual skills of the journalist.

The term "occupational training" is intended to disgrace journalism in the university. If journalism education is mere occupational or "trade school" training, then no self-respecting university would want to support it and journalism should be submerged within communication studies. According to this reasoning, communication studies — heavily laden with theory courses and offering only superficial glimpses of occupational uses of communication — deserves, in contrast to journalism, to be a partner with other university disciplines. Eric Meyer, a journalist who recently became a journalism lecturer at Milwaukee's Marquette University, observed that professional schools cannot afford to diminish in their courses the skills that are essential to the job. "If engineering, medicine or law were to become as theoretical as journalism has," Meyer said, "I'd be afraid to cross a bridge, be treated for the injuries I receive when it collapses or sue the contractor responsible."

The apparent failure to understand the nature of journalism skills has been expressed repeatedly in histories of communication studies and in recent studies of journalism/mass communication education. One of the recent task force reports of the Association for Education in Journalism and Mass Communication (AEJMC) went so far as to advocate that journalism skills should be taught in high school rather than at the university level.

Blanchard and Christ said the integrated communication curriculum would move educational programs away from preparing students for "occupations" and toward preparing them for a "new professionalism" that would make it easier to move from one "information job" to another and would establish "the primacy of liberal over occupational values" in the communication program.

To know what to teach, Christ told a curriculum-reform session of the 1995 AEJMC convention, "We should ask ourselves, if we could not teach skills courses, what would we have to offer, and if there were no newsrooms jobs, what would we teach?"

The integrated-communication approach would mean the number of units in the communication major would increase considerably while the skills courses would decline in number and value. Because the overall units a university requires for graduation cannot be increased, this substantial expansion of communication courses taken by majors would decrease substantially their opportunity to take the current (required for accreditation) 75% or more of their courses in other areas of study.

To those who believe in limiting the journalism content of a major in order to guarantee a wide liberal-arts education, the integrated-communication approach would erase the possibility of the major graduating with a rich and diverse liberal-arts education, let alone a menu of challenging skills courses. No, say those who propose the 50/50 and similar approaches, their communication graduates would have a greater liberal-arts education. With the liberal-arts seal of approval, they reason, the added theoretical communication courses can be justified as required for the major. The liberal-arts label, they say, also would enhance a communication course's reputation on campus.

This view ignores the fact that on many campuses journalism has been considered part of liberal arts for many years. It also ignores the fact that the accrediting standard that limits the number of journalism units a major can take was created not because of the failure of journalism courses to be liberal arts but to force students to study extensively outside the major — to stretch their minds and build their knowledge.

Some of the nation's most respected journalism education programs, including the only ones that are exclusively graduate programs — Columbia University in New York City and the University of California at Berkeley — continue to be regarded within their respective institutions with great respect despite the fact (or is it because?) they emphasize and specialize in the journalism courses that a growing number of professors at other schools consider to be vocational rather than intellectual.

Pressure builds to leave profession behind

It is unclear what will happen to curriculum as these philosophical differences persist. In some recent years including the last two, large task forces of journalism educators have issued long reports that recommended radical changes in curriculum and in the relationship of journalism education to the journalism profession. In 1994, the Vision 2000 Task Force of AEJMC proposed the "separation of journalism and mass communication units from their industrial moorings." The report noted that journalism/mass communication education has seen "increasing enrollments but decreasing viability" within universities and concluded, "Maintaining some degree of visibility within the core of the university is at odds with the provision of skills."

A similar disdain was expressed in fall 1995 at a meeting of a planning committee at the University of Arizona. Responding to a question about writing courses in the proposed new information school into which the university's journalism program may be merged, a committee member reportedly said, "Writing? We won't teach writing in this new school. Writing is remedial." Such a conclusion would surely surprise the thousands of professors of creative writing, English composition, foreign languages and other fields whose lives have been dedicated to the proposition that teaching writing was one of the most important things a university did and that writing was the critical intellectual skill through which a student would demonstrate most learning.

In 1995, another AEJMC group, the Curriculum Task Force, issued a report that was even more condemnatory of journalism as a distinct curriculum. The report called for a fully integrated communication curriculum and for 50% of a major's courses to be taken in it. Also recommended were a change in accreditation policy and other changes that would, in large measure, eliminate journalism as a star in the mass communication education constellation. The previous year's task force proposed, but was unable to get a unanimous task force vote for, eliminating "journalism" as part of the name of the educators' association.

There are other issues that prompt talk of change in journalism education — the continually evolving technologies that give journalists new tools and create new media, the desire to reform and revitalize how newsrooms operate, and the substance of what journalists produce and how they relate to the public. Those issues tend to excite and challenge the journalism educators who are committed to preparing the next generation of journalists. The other issues — the ones proposed over the last decade as the integrated curriculum that creates generic communicators — tend to chill and frighten many people.

In the midst of this sometimes enlivening, sometimes despairing debate, how's the baby doing, that baby — journalism — that Colorado's Dean Rowland feared might be getting thrown out with the bath water? How is it doing in American universities?

As part of this study, The Roper Center for Public Opinion Research scientifically surveyed three groups:

- 1,041 new journalists, people who have worked in print or broadcast journalism for one to 11 years.
- 503 newsroom recruiters and supervisors from the same wide array of sizes and types of news organizations as the new journalists.
- 446 journalism educators, all of whom teach full-time in journalism/mass communication programs and teach at least some journalism courses.

Their answers, as well as the comments from many other people who participated in this study in other ways, provide insights into what journalism education has been, what it is and what it is becoming. They also provide insight into where journalism education has failed, where it has succeeded and what it needs to do to avoid forfeiting its role in educating professionals who understand and are able to perform the functions of journalists in a democratic society.

Preparing journalists less important

In the Roper Center survey, 74% of the educators said preparing students to enter journalism was very important in their programs 10 years ago; 67% said preparing students to enter journalism is very important in

In 1994, the Vision 2000 Task Force of AEJMC proposed the "separation of journalism and mass communication units from their industrial moorings.

their programs today.

Interestingly, the decrease in importance of journalism was greater in accredited programs than in non-accredited programs, although accredited programs reported higher percentages than non-accredited in both responses. In accredited programs, educators said, preparing students to enter journalism was very important in 83% of the programs in 1985 and in 75% of the programs in 1995. In non-accredited programs, the decline was from 60% in 1985 to 55% in 1995. Non-accredited programs may have moved away from journalism earlier than accredited programs because they were not guided by the mission that is supposed to be central to the accreditation process: academic preparation for the profession.

Most educators reported changes in emphasis on a number of fronts — some seemingly contradictory.

- 73% said their programs widened their focus in the last 10 years to include more communications professions.
- 48% said their programs increased the emphasis on preparing students to enter journalism.
- 35% said their programs placed more emphasis on mass communication theory courses.
- 12% said their programs de-emphasized preparing students to enter journalism.
- 11% said their programs de-emphasized preparing students for entering any profession.

These responses seem to indicate competing philosophies are being implemented simultaneously in some programs, other programs are increasing a strong focus on journalism, while still other programs are moving away from journalism.

Student interest in journalism declines

The educators also reported the following changes over the 10-year period in students' interest in becoming journalists:

- 12% said it decreased substantially.
- 40% said it decreased somewhat.
- 24% said it stayed the same.
- 14% said it increased somewhat.
- 7% said it increased substantially.

Those who said student interest had decreased substantially or somewhat were asked to indicate the importance of various factors in contributing to that decline. They rated the factors "very important" at the following levels:

- 70%, low salaries in the profession.
- 63%, students are more interested in public relations and advertising.
- 39%, less student interest in news.
- 28%, less student interest in the public-service aspect of journalism.
- 25%, less student respect for journalism.
- 20%, student interest in less-challenging curriculum.
- 12%, increase in standards in writing courses.
- 10%, shift away from journalism emphasis in program.
- 10%, decline in strong professional expertise/interest in journalism on the part of faculty.
- 9%, more instructor interest in public relations/advertising.

A substantially greater portion of faculty from non-accredited programs thought increased interest in public relations and advertising was a significant factor in the decline in student interest in journalism — 70% of them versus 53% from accredited programs.

New journalists: the major was good

The Roper Center asked new journalists whether their choice of major was a good decision, or whether they wish they had majored in another field:

- 75% of those who studied journalism said it was a good choice.
- 17% of those who studied journalism said another major would have been better preparation for being a journalist.
- 59% of those who did not study journalism said that decision was a good one.
- 22% of those who did not study journalism said majoring in journalism would have better prepared them for being a journalist.
- 12% of those who did not major in journalism and 4% of those who did said that, as preparation for being a journalist, one's major doesn't matter.

New journalists who studied journalism

rated the overall quality of their journalism instruction as:

- 38%, very good.
- 39%, good.
- 20%, average.
- 3%, poor.

Dissatisfaction varied among those who studied journalism at different levels. New journalists who rated their journalism instruction as average or poor included:

- 33% of those who minored or took a few journalism courses.
- 22% of undergraduate journalism majors.
- 11% of those who studied journalism only at the master's level.

Asked to rate their instructors, those who studied journalism said:

- 7%, all were very good.
- 53%, the majority were very good.
- 28%, half were very good.
- 12%, a minority were very good.

Regarding the academic impact of studying journalism:

- 79% of new journalists who studied journalism said the journalism courses trained their minds in ways that made them better students in all courses.
- 51% said "A" was their average grade in journalism courses.
- 29% said "A" was their average grade in non-journalism courses.

The survey found a large gap between the superior academic performance in journalism courses achieved by women, 61% of whom were "A" students, and that achieved by men, 41% of whom were "A" students. The same gap existed in non-journalism studies: 36% of women journalism students earned "A" averages, compared with 21% of men.

Contrary to newsroom lore, there may be a correlation between academic achievement and success in the profession — at least financial success. Income levels were somewhat higher as academic achievement increased: 56% of those who earned more than $40,000 annually had "A" averages in journalism courses, compared with 47% of those who earned less than $20,000.

The new journalists also indicated that the move to de-emphasize journalism in journalism/mass communication programs is well-established. Thirty-seven percent said their journalism major was not focused on preparing them for a journalism career.

If income is an indicator of progressing well in the profession, it seems to matter whether a major was strongly focused on journalism. Those working at higher income levels include a larger portion of graduates of programs that had a strong emphasis on journalism:

- 73% of those who make between $30,000 and $40,000.
- 61% of those who make between $20,000 and $30,000.
- 52% of those who make under $20,000.

One aspect of a strong emphasis on journalism is a focus on writing. The survey of journalism educators found that writing standards have changed in the following ways in their programs over the last 10 years:

- 41% said the standards stayed the same.
- 39% said they increased.
- 18% said they decreased.

The educators were asked if their programs require majors to complete the survey courses often regarded by many educators as most important ones for a journalism major:

- 88% require journalism law.
- 44% require journalism history.
- 44% require journalism ethics.

Fewer than half require ethics courses

Only 38% of new journalists who studied journalism said their journalism education prepared them very well to deal with ethical issues.

Faculty reported that a larger portion of non-accredited programs, 49%, than accredited programs, 41%, require students to take a journalism ethics course. Some programs profess no need for an ethics course, let alone require students to take one, because they include ethical discussions throughout their courses. This is one of several areas where journalism education differs from other professional education. Nearly all business, law and medical schools have required students to study professional ethics since at least the early 1980s.

When Roper asked how important it is to

Contrary to newsroom lore, there may be a correlation between academic achievement and success in the profession — at least financial success.

teach the exploration of ethical issues, a substantially higher portion of journalism educators (79%) than newsroom recruiters and supervisors (59%) said it was important.

Perhaps a stronger indication of the need for more schooling in journalism ethics is found in the responses of new journalists when asked if they were worried about the impact of sensationalized coverage on journalism's reputation. Eighty-nine percent said they were worried (64% strongly, 25% mildly). They included:

- 77% of new journalists in broadcast journalism.
- 65% at large dailies.
- 63% at weeklies and small dailies.
- 53% at medium-size dailies.

The same worry was expressed by newsroom recruiters and supervisors. Eighty-nine percent said they were concerned (61% strongly, 28% mildly) about the impact of sensationalized coverage.

Instruction in diversity expands

Fifty-five percent of the journalism educators said their programs offer instruction on the history of contemporary movements regarding inclusion and exclusion of ethnic-minority issues in journalism — 61% of those from accredited programs, 47% of those from non-accredited programs.

Instruction in communicating effectively with people from diverse racial, cultural and economic backgrounds has increased during the last 11 years. The new journalists who said their instruction included such study included:

- 59% of those who have been journalists one to 3 years.
- 41% who have been journalists 4-7 years.
- 30% who have been journalists 8-11 years.

Rating themselves, 47% of new journalists said they were very good at communicating with people from backgrounds different from their own. White and ethnic-minority new journalists assessed themselves quite differently on this issue — 41% of whites rated themselves very good, while 72% of ethnic minorities rated themselves that way. By type of news organization, the lowest self-rating was by new journalists on small dailies (38% "very good") and the highest by those on large dailies (55%) and in broadcast journalism (54%).

Learning to work effectively in an ethni-

cally diverse environment is an area that journalism educators and newsrooms recruiters and supervisors agreed is significant in journalism education. It was considered very important by 73% of the educators and by 72% of the newsroom recruiters and supervisors. Both gave lower ratings on how well educators have been preparing students in the ability to converse with sources from a wide variety of backgrounds — 45% of educators and 38% of recruiters and supervisors said educators were doing a good or very good job of it.

Technology brings many challenges

New technology has entered the journalism curriculum in various ways in the last decade. Many journalism education programs have been struggling with how they should adapt their courses and overall programs to reflect important changes in technology. For some programs, cost is a significant factor. So are philosophical differences about curriculum and about journalism itself.

For some educators, the new multimedia herald the arrival of truly converged media, not only a distribution mix of audio, video and text, but also a communication mix of journalism, public relations, advertising and entertainment, with the distinguishing characteristics of each somewhat blurred.

For other educators and for most journalists, the new media herald new ways to distribute messages but with the same need as always for the practitioners and the public to know the difference between what is journalism and what is not. For them the convergence of delivery does not herald the convergence of journalism and other forms of communicating any more than when radio and television were born, or when ads and news were first placed together on printed pages. In fact, they see it as an obligation of journalists to ensure that the types of communication do not converge while the means of distribution do converge.

These different perspectives on technology are another part of the confusion that permeates journalism education today.

Journalism educators reported that the teaching of computer research and communication skills is widespread — in 87% of journalism education programs (92% of accredited programs, 80% of non-accredited programs):

- 72% include instruction in computer

research and communication skills in reporting courses.

- 35% created a special course for such instruction.

However, only a third of the programs require journalism majors to take courses in which these skills are taught.

New journalists felt strongly about the need for journalism education to include instruction in the use of computers as research and communication tools, but they showed relatively low usage themselves:

- 86% of new journalists said such instruction was very important in journalism education.
- 70% of journalism educators said such instruction was important.
- 55% of newsroom recruiters and supervisors said such instruction was important.
- 20% of newsroom recruiters and supervisors it was very important that a recently graduated job applicant have computer research skills (55% said somewhat important, 20% said not too important, 4% said not at all important).

In assessing how well such skills were being taught, 65% of the educators said they thought they were doing a good job, and 53% of the supervisors concurred.

Forty-three percent of new journalists used computers for research and analysis of data from sources outside their news organizations' libraries. Computers were used in this way for research and data analysis by a larger portion of ethnic-minority (49%) than white (41%) new journalists and by a larger portion of men (46%) than women (39%). The survey found an even larger gap in computer usage between new journalists who were managers (56%) and those who were not (38%). This could mean a facility in using computers to collect and analyze data is now a criterion for selecting newsroom leadership.

The youngest of the new journalists, those age 25 and under, reported the lowest use of computers for research and analysis, yet they registered the highest support, 92%, for the teaching of computer use in journalism education programs.

Despite using computers less than men for research and analysis, women were more enthusiastic than men about technological

changes in journalism — 60% of women, 52% of men.

While instruction in using computers for research is taking place in a majority of journalism education programs, many programs have found it difficult to decide how and whether to teach "across platforms" — simultaneously instruct students in how to write/edit/produce stories for newspapers, magazines, television, radio, on-line and multimedia. Faculty at several major journalism education programs have been struggling with this issue for the last several years. Many schools have reached philosophical agreement that multimedia teaching should take place, but they have found it hard to agree on how it should be done. The alternative approaches: Classes would be taught by teams of faculty members, each one an expert in a different medium; or faculty would be retrained so each faculty member would become proficient in teaching how to prepare a story for all media. Foundations granted millions of dollars in 1995 to help journalism educators plan how to accomplish this change.

Surveys of new journalists and newsroom recruiters and supervisors indicate that educators perhaps are making more of this issue than need be. Only 11% of newsroom recruiters and supervisors said it was very important for a beginning journalist to be able to create stories for both broadcast and print media (24% thought it was somewhat important, 29% not too important and 34% not at all important). This was an area where print and broadcast recruiters and supervisors had somewhat different views, though neither group attached great significance to such teaching; 22% of those from electronic journalism, in contrast to 8% from print journalism, said the ability to prepare stories for both print and broadcast media was very important.

An important signal about this issue comes from the new journalists — their confidence and apparent success in being able to demonstrate versatility across media. Most of them, 95%, said they would be able to use their present skills in another form of journalism; they would be able to move from print to broadcast, and from broadcast to print, and from either to on-line. This near-unanimous agreement was expressed by all segments of the new-journalists group. It also was

Many schools have reached philosophical agreement that multimedia teaching should take place, but they have found it hard to agree on how it should be done.

" Our instruction must focus on showing students how to use the technology to make them better reporters and editors. "

Douglas A. Anderson
Walter Cronkite School of
Journalism and
Telecommunication,
Arizona State University

expressed by professionals in numerous interviews. Don't worry about the medium, worry about learning to find and tell stories, they said. Become familiar with new media, experiment with them, but don't fret about being thoroughly skilled in new technology. That's easy to learn; basic storytelling isn't. There was concern among faculty and journalists that, in a quest for equal expertise across media, educators would diminish the value of their separate and distinct expertise and would end up focusing more on expertise in technology than on expertise in story-telling.

In making their case that students be trained to work in an array of media, some educators noted that students skilled in on-line use are in high demand at news organizations' on-line services. Until this election year, on-line specialists were hired primarily to package news previously published or broadcast. Very little journalism was originated for on-line distribution until spring 1996. The new on-line publications that were gearing up at that time were hiring primarily seasoned print and broadcast journalists who had little or no prior experience with on-line journalism. Clearly, the field is wide open, exciting and uncertain in every aspect.

Fifty-seven percent of the educators thought their programs were doing a good or very good job of preparing students to tell stories in various types of media, while 32% of recruiters and supervisors thought educators were doing a good or very good job in this area.

One of the schools that has done the most to integrate new technology into its teaching, particularly the teaching of computer-assisted reporting, is the Walter Cronkite School of Journalism and Telecommunication at Arizona State University. Douglas A. Anderson, director of the school and one of the leading thinkers about the role of technology in journalism and journalism education, is both enthusiastic and cautious in his reflections about technology and journalism education.

"Technology ... has had more impact on our programs than any other variable," Anderson said. "A new breed of reporter and editor has emerged and will continue to emerge: a journalist adept at ferreting out valuable information from electronic sources. We have to prepare our students to take full advantage of the technology at their disposal.

The emphasis in our courses should not be on the hardware. ... Rather, our instruction must focus on showing students how to use the technology to make them better reporters and editors."

Most majors are campus journalists

It has long been assumed that students' experience as campus journalists played an important positive role in their development as beginning journalists.

- 56% of faculty said their programs require journalism majors to publish or broadcast stories.
- 66% of new journalists who studied journalism said they were required to publish or broadcast stories while studying journalism (69% of those who were majors, 57% of those who were minors or took a few courses, and 60% of those who studied journalism at the master's degree level).
- 78% of new journalists worked as journalists on campus newspapers, magazines, radio or television stations (88% of those who were undergraduate journalism majors, 57% of those who did not study journalism).

Ethnic minorities constituted 15% of new journalists who were campus journalists and 17% of those who were not campus journalists.

Twenty-two percent of new journalists had no experience as campus journalists.

Purpose of writing courses blurs

Newswriting and reporting, usually a journalism student's introductory practical courses, are considered to be the places where the crucial foundation is laid for the research, writing and analytical skills that will be developed throughout the study of journalism.

In the Roper survey, journalism educators agreed at the following levels that these terms accurately describe newswriting and reporting courses:

- 93%, involve teaching critical thinking.
- 91%, should be taught by instructors with substantial experience in using the skills being taught.
- 89%, courses I am qualified to teach.
- 82%, courses I like to teach.
- 82%, involve teaching research skills.
- 78%, nuts and bolts courses.

- 56%, intellectual courses.
- 38%, should be taught by professionals who teach part-time.
- 29%, writing-formula courses.
- 11%, mere skills courses.
- 3%, courses anyone who can read well can teach.
- 3%, child's play.

Those who said they were qualified to teach newswriting and reporting included 69% of those who said they never worked full-time as journalists. Those who said they liked to teach newswriting and reporting included 88% of those who have worked as journalists and 55% of those who have not. Those who agreed that these courses should be taught by people with substantial experience in using the skills being taught included 95% of those who have worked full-time as journalists and 73% of those who have not.

Despite the educators' high regard for the newswriting and reporting courses, there has been a push to reshape (and rename) them in a more generic way: "writing for the media" — print and broadcast journalism, but also public relations and advertising. Numerous textbooks now accommodate this merged approach; they often do not stress learning to concentrate the mind and serve the public's interest. This new introductory course has replaced newswriting in many journalism education programs.

New journalists who studied journalism reported that journalism has indeed been de-

Technology and the lessons of history

One of the people who has explored extensively the fate of journalism in the digital age is Katherine Fulton, a former newspaper editor in North Carolina and now a consultant with Global Business Network in Berkeley, Calif. She believes it is critically important for present and future journalists to be up-to-date on the use of new technologies and on the evolution of new digital media into a revolutionary medium that may push old media aside, or at least challenge them in important ways.

Though cautious about whether it is possible to predict the future of digital media in distributing news, Fulton wrote in the March/April 1996 *Columbia Journalism Review*, after two and one-half years of study, "Everything I've learned argues that digital technologies will continue to grow, eventually creating a new medium that will force all previous communications media to redefine themselves, just as radio had to do when television came along."

Katherine Fulton

But she fears that journalists could miss the opportunity to shape the future of news and that it could be shaped with journalism itself sacrificed as a result of journalists not being prepared to create stories for new media.

Her message is an important one for journalism educators under pressure to fold journalism into generic communication. "Of my many fears about the future of journalism, this is the one that scares me the most: that journalists and their companies will keep their eyes on the horizon of the next deadline, the next paycheck, or the next quarterly shareholder report and fail to understand the horizon of history, which could yet yield a journalistic renaissance. ... I worry that the profits that now support the great journalism a democracy needs will disappear into niche businesses run by people with little interest in journalism but more imagination or staying power. I worry that too many of the best journalists will cling to the past, which will work about as well as it did for the guilds in the Industrial Revolution. And I worry that the most successful innovators – the ones who will write the rules for the new medium – will be technophiles who don't give a damn about the difference between a news story and an ad and who think the First Amendment is a license to print money."

Her advice for journalists is good as well for teachers of journalism and their students: "The wisest strategy, I believe, is to remain committed to high-quality reporting and story-telling — and to invest seriously in understanding new media. That doesn't mean you have to take on the near-impossible task of mastering all the changing currents and cross-currents. ... But we still have to keep our eye on the big picture."

Among journalism educators there is a strong sense that their greatest value to the profession is as a source, particularly for the smallest news organizations, of fresh, cheap labor every graduation day.

emphasized in the introductory course. Their answers also indicate that the nature of the introductory course may have a significant impact on the level of success some students eventually achieve in journalism:

- 23% said their introductory journalism writing classes were not tightly focused on covering news. This included 17% who said the course was an introduction to writing for various media, including public relations and advertising.
- 90% of those who studied journalism only at the master's degree level had introductory writing courses that were tightly focused on writing news, compared with 77% of those who studied journalism as undergraduate majors.
- 85% of those who earn more than $40,000 a year had introductory writing courses that were tightly focused on news, compared with 70% of those who earn less than $20,000.

New journalists who work at large dailies (85% of them) were most likely to have had introductory writing courses with a news focus, and the least likely were those in broadcast journalism (61%).

The lesson for today: journalism is dying

As some journalism education programs decreased their journalism emphasis, many teachers took a dim view of the future of journalism.

More than half of the new journalists — 52% — said they had journalism and other mass communication instructors who expressed the opinion that journalism is a dying profession.

This opinion among journalism educators apparently increased during the last 11 years. It was reported by:

- 46% of those who have been journalists 8-11 years.
- 52% of those who have been journalists 4-7 years.
- 59% of those who have been journalists 1-3 years.

In addition, 63% of all new journalists who studied journalism said they had instructors who expressed the opinion that journalism usually panders to the lowest instincts of the public.

About one-third of new journalists who were journalism majors and minors said journalists rarely or never were guest speakers in their journalism classes (20% of those with master's degrees in journalism said so).

There has been very little close observation and constructive criticism of journalism education by professional journalists. Journalists have seldom used the skills of their profession, let alone their enlightened professional interests, to examine journalism education closely. Among journalism educators there is a strong sense that their greatest value to the profession is as a source, particularly for the smallest news organizations, of fresh, cheap labor every graduation day.

However, two important developments over the past two decades have increased the amount of conversation that takes place between journalists and journalism educators. Many schools in the 1980s created advisory committees composed, at least in part, of journalists who visit the schools perhaps once a year. And numerous news organizations have stepped up their recruitment efforts on campus.

Some newsrooms did not recruit interns or young staff members until recent years, said Dennis Stern, now associate managing editor of *The New York Times*, an organization that until very recently had no desire for student interns. Now the *Times* recruits actively and regularly. *The Washington Post* has had internships for many years but didn't actively recruit. Top editors, many of them graduates of Ivy League schools, trekked every spring to the *Harvard Crimson* and other proper breeding grounds to interview would-be interns. Interns from distant parts of the country and non-tony schools got in on their own, without any visits by editors to their campuses. Now the *Post*, like the *Times* and many other news organizations, has a staff of former reporters and editors who work full-time on recruitment of interns and new journalists.

The recruitment efforts accelerated after the late Robert C. Maynard and others convinced the American Society of Newspaper Editors in the late 1970s to set a goal to ethnically diversify newspaper newsrooms by the year 2000 to match U.S. population. News organizations — broadcast as well as print — did what seemed most logical. Like Willie Sutton, who said he robbed banks because that's where the money was, news executives decided that if they were going to diversify their newsrooms, they would have to go to where journalists were being grown — the journalism education programs. Some local news organizations had recruited at schools in their area, but national recruitment existed at very few schools.

One irony of recruitment being stimulated by the need to diversify was that many journalism programs were even less ethnically diverse than the news organizations — and still are, though both have increased. The synergy of Maynard's original dream of newsrooms that would reflect America's ethnic diversity spread to journalism education. The accrediting council adopted what became known as Standard 12, "Minority/Female Representation." It requires journalism programs to demonstrate efforts to recruit and retain ethnic minority and women students and faculty members. Of the 12 standards, this is the one in which schools are most often found not in compliance. Nevertheless, it apparently has had an impact on diversifying student populations: Ethnic minorities are 18% of the new journalists who studied journalism at accredited programs and 15% of the new journalists who studied at non-accredited programs.

Faculty remain far less diverse — 8% of current journalism faculty are ethnic minorities, compared with 17% of faculty from all disciplines, according to the National Center for Education Statistics.

Maynard's dream has led to two interesting and totally unanticipated results, one in newsrooms and the other in journalism education.

The move to ethnically diversify the nation's newsrooms meant that white students who didn't go to Harvard, Yale or Princeton now had a better shot at getting an internship at the nation's largest newspapers, where their chances were previously fairly dim. That's because when newsroom recruiters fan out every year in their search for a greater number of ethnic minorities, journalism students of all races who never would meet a recruiter otherwise now have chance of doing so and of getting an internship. The push for diversity also meant that more internships were created, opening doors for all kinds of people, not just ethnic minorities.

The other unanticipated result has been the introduction of a group of newsroom leaders, these traveling newsroom recruiters, to journalism education. They have at least annual contact with journalism educators and thereby have some direct knowledge of the most important aspects of journalism education — what the students are learning. Their critiques of journalism education would not have been available before the era of expanded national recruiting.

Faculty seen far from cutting edge

Based on their experiences recruiting on campuses and working with interns and new journalists, newsroom recruiters and supervisors expressed extremely low regard for the expertise of journalism faculty and said the quality of journalism education needs to be improved a great deal.

Minuscule portions of the recruiters/ supervisors surveyed for this study said journalism educators are leaders of change in the profession and possess up-to-date expertise that would be helpful in solving newsroom problems:

■ 3% strongly agreed that journalism professors are on the cutting edge of journalism issues and have a strong influence on change in the profession (26% mildly agreed, 38% mildly disagreed, 23% strongly disagreed).
■ 3% strongly agreed that people at their news organization often ask journalism professors for advice on newsroom issues (14% mildly agreed, 28% mildly disagreed, 54% strongly disagreed).

A small portion of the recruiters and supervisors — 11% — strongly agreed with the statement, "In recent years journalism education programs have been doing a good job of preparing students for the profession." Fifty-five percent mildly agreed, 22% mildly disagreed, and 9% strongly disagreed. The strongest disagreement was expressed by those from broadcast journalism; 19% of them strongly disagreed with the notion that educators were doing a good job of preparing students for the profession.

The recruiters and supervisors said journalism education needs to improve a great deal — 35% strongly agreed and 42% mildly agreed, while 16% mildly disagreed and 4% strongly disagreed. The need for improvement was cited by those who had majored in journalism (79%) and non-majors (75%) alike.

Asked to indicate how much they thought various proposals would improve journalism education ("a lot," "some," "a little" or "not at all"), the recruiters gave the following "a lot" and "not at all" responses:

- Higher standards in writing courses — 81% a lot, 0 not at all.
- More student interest in news — 79% a lot, 1% not at all.
- More emphasis on students becoming critical thinkers and problem-solvers — 75% a lot, 2% not at all.
- More emphasis on students having a wide general knowledge base — 70% a lot, 1% not at all.
- More full-time faculty members with extensive backgrounds as professional journalists — 70% a lot, 1% not at all.
- More ethnically diverse graduates — 44% a lot, 7% not at all.
- Greater separation of journalism from public relations and advertising — 43% a lot, 16% not at all.
- More emphasis on journalism ethics — 40% a lot, 3% not at all.
- More ethnically diverse faculty — 40% a lot, 10% not at all.
- More emphasis on visual journalism — 27% a lot, 14% not at all.
- More full-time faculty members who focus their research and writing on issues directly related to journalism — 24% a lot, 9% not at all.
- More emphasis on learning a second language — 13% a lot, 19% not at all.
- More full-time faculty members with extensive backgrounds as academic scholars in mass communication — 7% a lot, 39% not at all.
- Eliminating journalism as a major or emphasis and replacing it with a major that prepares students for communication fields in general, including public relations and advertising — 7% a lot, 66% not at all.
- More emphasis on mass communication theory — 6% a lot, 42% not at all.

It is instructive to isolate the three changes that the largest number of newsroom supervisors and recruiters said would improve

journalism education "not at all": eliminating journalism as a major or emphasis, giving more emphasis to mass communication theory and having more full-time faculty with extensive backgrounds as academic scholars of mass communication. These selections illustrate the disconnection that exists between the journalism profession and journalism education. They are the very changes that are at the top of the agenda of the dominant winds of change in journalism education today.

Undergraduate major best preparation

More than a third of the newsroom recruiters and supervisors surveyed — 38% — strongly agreed that journalism education programs were their news organization's most valuable source of future employees. An additional 36% mildly agreed. (Others: 18% mildly disagreed, 8% strongly disagreed.)

The newsroom recruiters and supervisors said an undergraduate major in journalism is the best educational preparation for a journalism career. Asked to rate the importance of various educational backgrounds as preparation for such a career, the recruiters and newsroom supervisors gave the following ratings:

- Undergraduate major in journalism: 34% very important, 49% somewhat important, 12% not too important, 4% not at all important. (Forty-five percent of those who majored in journalism thought an undergraduate degree in journalism was very important, while 21% of those who did not major in journalism thought it was very important.)
- Undergraduate degree in a field other than journalism: 12% very important, 56% somewhat important, 24% not too important, 7% not at all important.
- Graduate degree in journalism: 8% very important, 30% somewhat important, 37% not too important, 24% not at all important.
- Graduate degree in a field other than journalism: 4% very important, 30% somewhat important, 40% not too important, 25% not at all important.
- Undergraduate and graduate degree in journalism: 5% very important, 31% somewhat important, 40% not too important, 23% not at all important.

Priority for students: general knowledge, enthusiasm

Asked to indicate the importance of the following steps students could take to be well-prepared for an internship or an entry-level job in journalism, the recruiters and supervisors in the following portions rated as "very important":

- Having enthusiasm for journalism, 95%.
- Having an education that stresses wide general knowledge, 71%.
- Working on campus newspapers or broadcast outlets, 54%.
- Majoring in journalism, 27%. (Thirty-three percent of recruiters and supervisors from electronic journalism and 26% from print said it was very important.)
- Having had a previous internship, 19%.
- Obtaining a high grade-point average, 7%.

Many of the recruiters and supervisors said they selected journalism majors in the past year as interns:

- 49% indicated that 76-100% of their 1995 interns were undergraduate journalism majors.
- 3% said 76-100% of their interns were studying for master's degrees in journalism.
- 9% said 76-100% of their interns were not studying journalism at any level.

Twice as many newsroom recruiters and supervisors identified working as a campus journalist than identified majoring in journalism as very important. Their hiring patterns seem to follow this preference: Fifty-five percent said they hired 76-100% of their interns from among those who were either print or broadcast campus journalists.

The recruiters and supervisors also were asked to compare the performance of interns who studied journalism with those who had not:

- 36% said their best interns were journalism majors.
- 25% said they could see no difference between the performance of majors and non-majors.
- 25% said they could not answer the question because all interns were journalism majors.
- 4% said their best interns were non-journalism majors.

The recruiters and supervisors drew no clear distinction between those who studied journalism at the undergraduate level and those who did so at the master's degree level.

Sleazy journalism doesn't help

Many forces affect what happens to journalism education. There are the struggling philosophies within programs, some of which demean the importance and very nature of journalism. There are the political, budgetary and philosophical motivations of central administrators who may or may not understand the nature of journalism.

In recent years, journalism educators have acquired another albatross that can easily be used by those in the university who would weaken journalism: the bad behavior of the profession. Just as Watergate, for a few shining moments, brought renewed respect to journalism, the increased sensationalism of journalism in recent years has brought increasing disrespect to journalism in many quarters, but perhaps especially in the university, where journalism always has been dogged by disrespect. Journalism's bad behavior, unfairly or not, rubs off on journalism education. The clutter of journalism, such as the endless O.J. Simpson diet, often becomes a defining characteristic, while the fine specimens of journalism — such as the repeated good investigative work of certain news organizations — are seldom brought up by university administrators, public critics or even journalists themselves.

Journalists, journalism educators and journalism students are all affected today by the growth of bad journalistic performance. Many journalism educators who are dedicated to preparing students to enter journalism are stymied and saddened by what many people inside and outside the field see as an expanding sleaze factor. Concern about it is reflected in the groups surveyed for this study. Twenty-five percent of faculty members said they thought a decrease in students' respect for journalism was a very important factor in the decline over the last 10 years in the number of students interested in becoming journalists. Large portions of new journalists and newsroom recruiters and supervisors said they were very worried about the impact of sensationalized coverage on journalism's reputation.

Deborah Potter, reporter for CBS and CNN

In recent years, journalism educators have acquired another albatross that can easily be used by those in the university who would weaken journalism: the bad behavior of the profession.

for more than 20 years, talked to her colleagues in Washington, D.C., about this as she was preparing in 1995 to leave journalism and begin her new job as an instructor at The Poynter Institute for Media Studies in St. Petersburg, Fla.

"There is a sense of disenchantment with this calling among many of my colleagues," she said, "and I'm talking about all levels, and I'm talking about print and broadcast: the tilt toward the sensational, the lack of respect for the work that we do ... the poor quality of so much of the work we see and the poor quality of the leadership that we are asked to follow. ... It's a daily struggle to keep your job and keep your integrity.

"Students hear this, they see this. They say to themselves, 'Wait a minute. What am I supposed to think of this profession I thought I wanted to get into?'"

Trevor Brown, dean of the School of Journalism at Indiana University, has been especially troubled by the values he felt were reflected in the Associated Press top 10 stories of 1994, a list chosen by 357 news executives. Over the years, he has noticed as a South African and as a journalism teacher that the U.S. press has not been indifferent to South Africa. But in 1994, the year that South Africa made the historic transition from white-minority to black-majority rule, the April election did not make the AP's top-10 list. News executives did not choose it, he said, although "many editorial writers and columnists judged it among the most significant events of the decade, some said of the 20th century."

"What should journalism teachers learn from the collective judgment of the news executives at the end of 1994?" Brown asked. "What news values should we teach that will enable students to impress newspaper and broadcast recruiters? Should we seek instruction from the stories that made the top five — O.J. Simpson, Susan Smith, (Nancy) Kerrigan-(Tonya) Harding, and the baseball and hockey strikes? AP's list mainly of murder, slaughter and sports says something disturbing about journalism and American society. Perhaps news isn't vital to the conversation of self-governance. It's a commodity sold in a marketplace not of information and ideas but of sensation and titillation.

"Journalism teachers cannot in good con-

science teach those values. We can try only to understand them and to teach about them. ... Even though the events in April 1994 ... killed only hopelessness and despair, young journalists should know that such stories can grip, inform and inspire. They should know that the Nobel Prize for peace and the Pulitzer Prize for journalism occasionally reward the same values, even though those values may not make the top 10."

Dean Brown's observations help illuminate the complex dilemma that faces those journalism educators who are not confused about the mission of journalism. The dilemma has to do with what they teach, but it goes far beyond whether they should add some instruction about ethnic diversity, add some instruction on using computers, or subtract a little of this and a little of that.

The deeper dilemma comes from within journalism education and from within journalism. From within journalism education, the struggle seems to be caused by those who either never knew or those who no longer care whether journalism has a unique mission in society, a home in the academy and thoughtful experts teaching it. To these inside critics of journalism education, journalism should

Journalism education fundamental to society

For those who are uncertain of the place of journalism in the university, James W. Carey, professor at Columbia University's Graduate School of Journalism, articulates the critical importance of keeping journalism alive and well in the university.

"Journalism must be protected. That interaction between professional life and academic life is essential," said Carey. Recalling his years, as dean of the University of Illinois College of Communications, Carey said, "I privileged journalism. I thought it was the only thing we did that was indispensable. The other things done in communications programs may be worthy, but they are not indispensable. The one thing that cannot be assimilated is journalism. You can try to do it, but it can't be done. ... When someone says journalism is a mere skill, that's wrong-thinking. It's fundamental to society. It's as fundamental to the education of people as you can imagine. You can't say that about any other part of communications studies."

How well are educators preparing students for journalism?

Journalism educators and newsroom supervisors were asked:

- How well are journalism educators teaching in the following areas?
- How important is each area in preparing people to enter journalism?

	JOURNALISM EDUCATORS		NEWSROOM SUPERVISORS	
	Very well/ well	Important	Very well/ well	Important
Basic newsgathering and newswriting skills	81%	95%	71%	98%
Interviewing skills	64%	89%	45%	95%
Analyzing information and ideas	63%	96%	46%	94%
Clear writing skills	80%	95%	67%	97%
Writing on deadline	73%	78%	58%	82%
In-depth reporting research skills	55%	73%	27%	67%
Developing and covering a beat	55%	53%	27%	67%
Enthusiastic commitment to journalism	70%	70%	66%	66%
Ability to develop story ideas on their own	79%	68%	58%	76%
Well-informed about current events	46%	83%	70%	78%
Ability to converse effectively with sources from a wide variety of backgrounds	45%	73%	38%	72%
Solving ethical dilemmas	60%	79%	56%	59%
Ability to recognize holes in coverage	44%	76%	44%	77%
Well-informed about changes taking place in journalism	54%	53%	45%	31%
Ability to organize complex stories with clarity and grace	49%	78%	36%	86%
Understanding that accuracy and truthfulness are essential in journalism	85%	92%	85%	96%
Using computers as a research and communication tool	65%	70%	53%	55%
Awareness that a journalist may need to be courageous	53%	45%	42%	36%
Awareness that a journalist needs to be sensitive	62%	61%	46%	58%
Commitment to First Amendment values	81%	85%	71%	77%
Awareness of the responsibility to provide information people need to be informed citizens	73%	84%	64%	73%
Experience in various means of telling stories — for newspapers, magazines, broadcast, on-line	57%	48%	32%	21%
Knowledge of press law	78%	66%	61%	48%
Familiarity with contemporary critiques of journalism	45%	35%	31%	15%
Familiarity with how newsrooms are organized and operate	59%	44%	39%	40%
Experience in using government access laws	45%	50%	25%	49%
Introduction to use of photos, design and graphics in storytelling	58%	55%	43%	51%
Knowledge of the history and evolution of U.S. journalism	50%	36%	49%	15%
Ready to enter the profession as competent beginning journalist	77%	83%	57%	79%

become — or already has, with their approval, become — part of a world of blurred, generic communication.

From within journalism, the educators' struggle seems to be caused by people who do know what journalism's distinct values and mission are but are willing, for market and other reasons, to distort journalism's values and mission, to damage journalism's reputation, and, in doing so, to hurt journalism's relationship with the public and with its future practitioners, today's students.

It is a tough and exciting time to be a journalism teacher and to be a journalism student on the edge of a beginning career. The possibilities are startling. Journalism could be sacrificed as a discipline in many programs. There could be revolutionary times ahead in journalism itself. To be a young journalist today could mean being in on the ground floor of reshaping the way people get their news — coming up with innovative ways of helping news organizations provide more and better journalism. Or it could mean being an observer to the disappearance of journalism as the key provider of the ideas and information that serve and connect the public's interest and stimulate the public's discourse.

If teachers are honest, some of the lessons they will teach are about the quite harsh realities of journalism that coexist alongside the exciting possibilities of journalism. Will there be an explosion of opportunities or an explosion of journalism?

Many wise teachers are saying, "Class, be ready for a risky ride." It's not clear what the shape or the values of journalism will be, even in the immediate future. Sometimes the sands seem to shift steeply, then slowly or not all. It's not clear whether ABC mogul Mickey Mouse (and others like him) will learn to blow smoke in the face of the cigarette industry (and others like it) in defense of stories the public needs. It's not clear whether the heads of news corporations will return to caring as much for reporting the news, serving their communities and respecting the needs of their staffs as much as they now care for the praise of their stockholders. It's not clear whether small newspapers and broadcast stations — and a growing number of larger news organizations that have created special low-pay/no-benefit tiers of new journalists — will stop "eating their young" and realize that paying new journalists at or below the poverty line is going to cause the next generation of journalists to leave the profession in less time than it took them to get their degrees.

3 | Who are new journalists?

How they were educated and why they love journalism but may leave it

What does journalism education produce? How important is journalism education to the journalism profession? Who are the new journalists of today?

What is the difference between a journalist who has studied journalism and one who hasn't?

These questions were asked in this study to learn more about how well journalism education has been preparing people to enter print, broadcast and now on-line journalism.

The answers raise other questions about the direction and value of journalism education, as well as questions about how news organizations treat new journalists. Are the journalists now entering the profession encouraged to believe it is possible, with commitment, hard work and well-developed competence, to be valued and to advance in the profession? Or do news organizations prefer that today's youngest journalists think, as increasing numbers of them do, that even if they are committed, work hard and become quite competent, they are likely to be valued only as long as they constitute cheap labor?

Today's new journalists, those who had been journalists one to 11 years as of summer 1995, are the most educated in U.S. history — at least 94% of those under age 36 have bachelor's degrees, according to a survey conducted for this study by the Roper Center. The last three decades of this century have seen sustained, dramatic increases in the education levels of journalists.

On the edge of the millennium, the vision articulated early in this century by Joseph Pulitzer and others of an educated newsroom work force is nearly fulfilled in all types of news organizations. National studies of journalists, conducted in 1982 and 1992 by journalism professors David H. Weaver and G. Cleveland Wilhoit of Indiana University and in 1971 by John W.C. Johnstone and others at the University of Illinois at Chicago, have shown that among all journalists in the newsroom work force, the portion with bachelor's degrees surged in the last 25 years. Among all journalists, those with bachelor's degrees constituted:

- 58.2% of the newsroom work force in 1971.
- 73.7% in 1982.
- 82.1% in 1992.

56% have journalism degrees

Journalism education is very important to news organizations. Among those who became journalists between 1984 and 1994 and were employed as journalists in 1995, 71% studied journalism at some college or university level.

Forty-seven percent have bachelor's degrees in journalism. They include:

- 43%, bachelor's in journalism, no other study.
- 2%, bachelor's in journalism, some master's level journalism study but no degree.
- 1%, bachelor's in journalism, Ph.D. in another field.
- 1%, bachelor's in journalism, master's degree in another field.

Nine percent have master's degrees in journalism. They include:

- 6%, master's in journalism, no other journalism study.
- 1%, master's in journalism and bachelor's in journalism.
- 1%, master's in journalism and undergraduate minor in journalism.

Fifteen percent minored in journalism.

Twenty-seven percent studied no journalism. They include:

- 20%, bachelor's degree and no other study.
- 3%, bachelor's and master's degrees.

- 4%, no degrees.

(Two percent declined to discuss their education.)

The portion of new journalism hires who have journalism degrees has not increased significantly in recent years, contrary to the estimates of many editors and news directors — which many journalism educators hoped were true — that as many as 80% of recent new hires have journalism degrees. In their studies, professors Weaver and Wilhoit reported relatively little change in the proportion of all journalists who have undergraduate journalism degrees:

- 34% in 1971.
- 39.8% in 1982.
- 39.4% in 1992.

Among new journalists, the largest portion of undergraduate degrees in journalism is found in the under-age-25 group — 60% in the Roper survey conducted for this study and 66% in the 1992 Weaver-Wilhoit study. With each five-year increase in age, the portion of new journalists who majored in journalism decreases.

Interestingly, 43% of the new journalists who did not study journalism also never worked as campus journalists. This suggests that newsroom mentors have served as their primary teachers.

Lowest salaries of any college-educated workers

Though it is more educated than any previous group of journalists, the latest crop of new journalists faces very bad economic news. With average starting annual salaries of $20,154, this year's students who go into journalism will be the lowest paid of any college-educated people entering the public or private work force, according to the annual recruiting trends survey conducted by Michigan State University.

A portion will join the 22% of all new journalists age 25 and under whose salaries are below $15,000, as revealed in the Roper survey. An additional 35% of all new journalists age 25 and under earn between $15,000 and $20,000. This means that more than half — 57% — of all journalists age 25 and under make less than $20,000.

The low salaries of beginning journalists probably account for the sharp decline in the portion of working journalists under age 24 that Weaver-Wilhoit found in their most recent survey: Those under 24 shrank from making up 12% of all journalists in both 1982 and 1971 to constituting just 4% in 1992. As previously noted in this report, 70% of the journalism educators surveyed by Roper said low salaries in the profession were a very important factor in the decline in student interest in journalism that has taken place over the last 10 years.

The starting salaries in journalism are a source of continuing consternation and shame to journalism teachers and of profound discouragement to journalism students. It is unclear if newsroom employers understand the growing impact of the very low salaries they offer, especially in entry-level jobs. In the last five years, jobs with very low salaries and no benefits have been routinely offered not only by many of the smallest news organizations but also by an increasing number of large news organizations. Many of them now offer longer internships and part-time jobs to new graduates, often without benefits and without a realistic possibility of future employment with the news organizations — even though these new graduates often are given assignments formerly done by bought-out and now-departed mid-career journalists. It has long been popular for older journalists and some teachers to tell students that journalism, unlike many other fields, is a "calling," a special kind of work that involves dedicated service to finding and reporting the truth about many facets of public life. Regrettably, students now need to realize that this calling, like being a priest or nun, can involve, at least in the early years, a virtual vow of poverty.

Journalism educators, and even some in the profession, have taken a certain amount of pride in the fact that some new journalists leave the profession to become lawyers. Many new journalists do leave journalism, but few leave to become lawyers, as is shown later in this chapter. Anecdotal evidence suggests that many new journalists would improve their economic situation if they became waiters and waitresses.

Even as they become older and more experienced, a significant portion of new journalists continue to have low incomes:

- 25% of new journalists age 26-30 earn less

than $20,000 a year.

- 12% of new journalists age 31-40 earn less than $20,000 a year.

The lowest salaries were in broadcast journalism, at weeklies and at small dailies. The portions of new journalists of all ages earning less than $20,000 a year included:

- 48% of new journalists at weeklies.
- 38% of those at small dailies.
- 32% of those in broadcast journalism.
- 5% of those at medium-size dailies.
- None at large dailies.

The highest salaries are earned by new journalists at medium-size and large dailies. Twenty-five percent of them make more than $40,000 annually, including:

- 68% of those at large dailies.
- 22% of those at medium-size dailies.
- 12% of those in broadcast journalism.
- 6% of those at small dailies.
- 4% of those at weeklies.

Journalism education does not improve income

Income for journalists does not seem to be increased by studying journalism at the undergraduate level. In fact, a person who majored or minored in journalism is more likely to be among those earning the lowest salaries in the profession.

New journalists of all ages who make under $20,000 a year include:

- 23% of those with undergraduate journalism majors.
- 32% who had a minor or took a few courses in journalism.
- 23% who never studied journalism.
- 12% who studied journalism at the master's degree level.

The top earners among new journalists, those who earn more than $40,000 a year, include:

- 34% of those who studied journalism at the master's degree level.
- 28% who never studied journalism.
- 19% with undergraduate journalism majors.
- 16% who minored or took a few courses in journalism.

Most high achievers are not journalism graduates

To ascertain whether journalists regarded as the best in the business were more or less likely to have studied journalism, surveys were taken of journalists who in recent years have been awarded some of the news business's most prestigious awards and fellowships — print journalists who won Pulitzer Prizes, broadcast journalists who won the Alfred I. du Pont Awards, and recipients of Nieman Fellowships at Harvard University and John S. Knight Fellowships at Stanford University.

Pulitzer Prize winners from 1991-95 included 30% who had undergraduate journalism degrees, 2% who studied journalism only at the master's degree level, and 9% who had both undergraduate and master's degrees in journalism.

Winners of the **Alfred I. du Pont** Awards from 1991-94 included 10% who had undergraduate journalism degrees, 5% who studied journalism only at the master's level, and 10% who had both undergraduate and master's degrees in journalism.

Among the **Nieman fellows** from 1990-91 through 1995-96, 20% had undergraduate journalism degrees, 17% studied journalism only at the master's level, and 5% had both undergraduate and master's degrees in journalism.

The records of **Knight fellows** were reviewed for two periods — the last six years of the program (1990-91 through 1995-96), and the entire length of the program (1966-67 through 1995-96). During the more recent period, Knight fellows included 33% with undergraduate journalism degrees, 12% who studied journalism only at the master's degree level, and 4% who had both undergraduate and master's degrees in journalism. From 1966 to the present the breakdown was: 33%, undergraduate journalism degrees; 10%, studied journalism only at the master's degree level; and 3%, both undergraduate and master's degrees in journalism.

These findings indicate that one may have a better chance of achieving the highest levels of accomplishment without a journalism degree. Those who never studied journalism included:

- 59% of recent Pulitzer Prize winners.
- 75% of recent Alfred I. du Pont Award winners.
- 58% of recent Nieman fellows.
- 51% of recent Knight fellows and 54% of those from 1966 to the present.

With average starting annual salaries of $20,154, this year's students who go into journalism will be the lowest paid of any college-educated people entering the public or private work force, according to the annual recruiting trends survey conducted by Michigan State University.

Twenty-one percent of the recruiters and supervisors said "sink or swim without much assistance" accurately describes their news organizations' view of interns.

Among the Pulitzer and du Pont winners, 58% of those who did not major in journalism majored in either English (36%) or history (22%). Other majors were political science, psychology, anthropology, economics, biology, philosophy, art, religion, American studies, mathematics and elementary education.

Journalism majors not more likely to be managers

Nor does a journalism degree, undergraduate or graduate, necessarily increase a journalist's chances of becoming a newsroom manager. In fact, when viewed by educational background, the segment with the lowest portion in newsroom management is composed of master's degree recipients.

According to the Roper survey, the 29% of new journalists who became newsroom managers within their first 11 years of newsroom work included:

- 33% of those who minored or took a few journalism courses.
- 29% of those who majored in journalism as undergraduates.
- 29% of those who never studied journalism.
- 16% of those who studied journalism only at the master's level.

Experience as a campus journalist on student newspapers, magazines, television or radio also was not an indicator of whether a new journalist would become a newsroom manager. The same portion of those who were campus journalists as were not — 29% — made it into the managerial ranks of newsrooms.

Where new journalists work

The survey detailed where the new journalists are employed:

- 24% at small dailies (23% of men, 25% of women).
- 22% at medium-size dailies (22% of men, 21% of women).
- 15% at large dailies (14% of men, 15% of women).
- 14% at weeklies (13% of men, 15% of women).
- 10% in television journalism (9% of men, 10% of women).
- 8% in radio journalism (10% of men, 6% of women).
- 5% in magazine journalism (4% of men, 6% of women).
- 2% in wire-service journalism (3% of men, 1% of women).
- 1% in on-line journalism (1% of both men and women).

Most new journalists had internships

The importance of internships is reflected in the recent growth of the portion of new journalists who had them. Among all new journalists, 74% said they had internship experience. By age groups, those who studied journalism and had internships included:

- 85% of those 25 and under.
- 77% of those 26-30.

By educational background, where new journalists work

	Undergraduate journalism degrees	Minored or took a few journalism courses	Received master's degree in journalism	Did not study journalism
Small dailies	28%	25%	16%	17%
Medium-size dailies	24%	18%	36%	18%
Large dailies	15%	11%	16%	14%
Weeklies	10%	16%	10%	20%
Television	10%	16%	5%	10%
Radio	8%	12%	5%	6%
Magazines	4%	2%	11%	11%
Wire services	2%	1%	1%	2%
On-line services	1%	0%	1%	1%

- 73% of those 31-36.
- 59% of those over 36.

A larger percentage of those who studied journalism at the master's degree level, 31%, than those who have undergraduate journalism degrees, 22%, did not have internships before they became journalists.

The level of teaching that goes on during newsroom internships varies. According to the newsroom recruiters and supervisors surveyed, only 56% of news organizations that had interns assigned mentors to them. Twenty-one percent of the recruiters and supervisors said "sink or swim without much assistance" accurately describes their news organizations' view of interns; that attitude was expressed by 23% of those from print media and 14% of those from broadcast media.

The level of written feedback given to interns also varies. Thirty-three percent said written feedback is given only at the end of the internship, 31% provide it at several points, 26% give no written feedback and 10% said the amount of feedback varies from intern to intern. The portion that gives no written feedback was twice as large among print newsrooms (29%) as among broadcast newsrooms (15%).

Internships can involve financial hardships for students. The survey found that 29% of news organizations do not pay interns. In a pattern well-known to students and teachers, the portion of no-pay internships is much greater in broadcast journalism — 79% of broadcast news organizations versus 16% in print journalism. Among those who pay interns, 14% have the same salaries for interns as for beginning reporters; 86% have lower intern salaries.

Women are 46% of new journalists

Although women have constituted about 60% of journalism education enrollments at the undergraduate and graduate levels for two decades, they have not entered the profession in that proportion. Their representation within the newsroom work force has increased substantially, however. Among all new journalists, 54% are men and 46% are women. Among the new journalists who are newsroom managers, 55% are men and 45% are women. In the overall newsroom work force, according to the Weaver-Wilhoit-Johnstone surveys, women accounted for 20.3% in 1971, 33.8% in 1983 and 34% in 1992.

By educational background of new journalists, women with master's degrees reflect the makeup of journalism education enrollments: 60% women, 40% men. The gender composition of new journalists from other educational backgrounds is:

- Undergraduate major in journalism — 53% men, 47% women.
- Minored or took a few undergraduate courses in journalism — 51% men, 49% women.
- Never studied journalism — 61% men, 39% women.

The newsroom population is almost evenly divided among those who entered journalism one to three years ago: 48% men, 52% women. That's a reversal of the gender composition of new journalists who entered the profession eight to 11 years ago — 56% men, 44% women.

The most equal representation of men and women new journalists in news organizations is at weeklies, where the ratio is 51% men, 49% women; the biggest gap is in broadcast journalism — 58% men, 42% women. Elsewhere:

- Small dailies — 52% men, 48% women.
- Medium-size dailies — 55% men, 45% women.
- Large dailies — 52% men, 48% women.

In income, new journalists who are women generally trail men at highest income levels:

- 34% of men and 33% of women earn $20,000-$30,000.
- 20% of men and 16% of women earn $30,000-$40,000.
- 11% of men and 12% of women earn $40,000-$50,000.
- 3% of men and 2% of women earn over $50,000.

But:

- 5% of men and 8% of women earn less than $15,000 a year.
- 17% of men and 19% of women earn $15,000-$20,000.

A smaller portion of women, 46%, than men, 54%, is considering leaving journalism.

Ethnic minorities are 17% of new journalists

Seventeen percent of the new journalists are ethnic minorities, Roper found. This is a

The accrediting standard that requires programs to demonstrate that their enrollments match the ethnic-minority populations of the geographic areas from which students are drawn seems to have inspired more recruitment of minority students.

considerably larger proportion than in the overall newsroom population. The ethnic-minority population of daily newspaper newsroom staffs was 11.02% in the 1996 survey conducted by the American Society of Newspaper Editors; and at 19% of television newsroom staffs and 12% of radio newsroom staffs in the 1996 study conducted by Radio-Television News Directors Association and Ball State University.

Consistent with the findings of the ASNE and RTNDA annual surveys, Roper found that very few ethnic-minority new journalists are employed at the traditional beginning points of the journalism employment pipeline, small news organizations. (According to the latest ASNE survey, 46% of all U.S. daily newspapers have no ethnic-minority journalists on their staffs.) The 17% of new journalists who are minorities and the 83% who are white make up the newsroom work forces, as follows:

- 29% of all ethnic-minority new journalists and 10% of all white new journalists are at large dailies (37% of all new journalists at large dailies are ethnic minorities).
- 24% of all ethnic-minority new journalists and 18% of all white new journalists are at medium-size dailies (22% of all new journalists at medium-size dailies are ethnic minorities).
- 19% of all ethnic-minority new journalists and 11% of all white new journalists are in television journalism (25% of all new journalists in television journalism are ethnic minorities).
- 7% of all ethnic-minority new journalists and 9% of all white new journalists are in radio journalism (14% of all new journalists in radio journalism are ethnic minorities).
- 7% of all ethnic-minority new journalists and 26% of all white new journalists are at small dailies (5% of all new journalists at small dailies are ethnic minorities).
- 7% of all ethnic-minority new journalists and 6% of all white new journalists are at magazines (20% of all new journalists at magazines are ethnic minorities).
- 2% of all ethnic-minority new journalists and 16% of all white new journalists are at weeklies (3% of all new journalists at weeklies are ethnic minorities).
- 1% of all ethnic-minority new journalists

and 2% of all white new journalists are at wire services (4% of all new journalists at wire services are ethnic minorities).
- 1% of all ethnic-minority new journalists and 1% of all white new journalists are in on-line journalism (20% of all new journalists in on-line journalism are ethnic minorities).

Because ethnic minorities either were not welcome at the smaller news organizations or did not want to live in the less ethnically diverse communities where many such news organizations are located, larger news organizations created special training programs to make up for the lack of other entry points for ethnic-minority journalists. That explains the salary differential between ethnic-minority and white new journalists:

- 7% of whites and 1% of ethnic minorities make less than $15,000 a year.
- 20% of whites and 6% of ethnic minorities make $15,000-$20,000.
- 35% of whites and 29% of ethnic minorities make $20,000-$30,000.
- 17% of whites and 25% of ethnic minorities make $30,000-$40,000.
- 11% whites and 15% ethnic minorities make $40,000-$50,000.
- 9% whites and 21% ethnic minorities make more than $50,000.

While ethnic minorities account for 17% of all new journalists, they make up 14% of new-journalist managers. By age, ethnic minorities are 16% of new journalists 25 and under, 16% of those 26-20, 18% of those 31-36 and 10% of those over 36.

The accrediting standard that requires programs to demonstrate that their enrollments match the ethnic-minority populations of the geographic areas from which students are drawn seems to have inspired more recruitment of minority students. Among all new journalists, 83% of those who majored in journalism graduated from accredited programs. But the percentage is higher for ethnic-minority new journalists. Among those who have undergraduate journalism degrees, 88% of whites graduated from accredited programs and 94% of ethnic minorities did so. At the master's degree level, 73% of whites came from accredited programs, as did 95% of ethnic minorities.

Nearly equal portions of whites and minorities had worked as campus journalists, but a larger portion of ethnic minorities, 86%, than whites, 72%, had worked as interns.

A slightly higher portion of ethnic-minority new journalists, 48%, than white new journalists, 42%, are considering leaving journalism.

New journalists rate their job performance

Thirty-seven percent of new journalists from all backgrounds said that during their first year on the job, they felt very well-prepared. Fifty percent said they felt somewhat well-prepared, 10% felt not well-prepared and 3% felt not at all prepared.

But reflecting on their first year on the job, a slightly higher portion, 41%, said they now think they were very well-prepared. The greatest change in perception was among those who never studied journalism: 31% of them reported that during the first year on the job they felt very well-prepared, but, looking back, 46% think they were. Upon reflection, the portion of undergraduate majors who thought they were well-prepared declined from 46% to 43%, the portion of minors increased from 25% to 32% and the portion of those with journalism master's degrees stayed the same, 43%.

Asked to rate their current job performance, 31% of new journalists gave themselves a very good rating. By educational background, those who never studied journalism had the highest level of confidence:

- 37% of those who never studied journalism rated themselves as very good.
- 36% of those who studied journalism at the master's degree level rated themselves as very good.
- 32% of those who minored or took a few undergraduate courses in journalism rated themselves as very good.
- 29% of those with undergraduate journalism majors rated themselves as very good.

Self-confidence increased with experience. Giving themselves very good ratings were: 20% of those with 1-3 years' experience, 34% with 4-7 years' experience and 36% of those with 8-11 years' experience.

New journalists in each educational category thought their supervisors would rate their performance higher than they rated themselves:

- 48% of those who never studied journalism.
- 60% of those who studied journalism only at the master's degree level.
- 38% of those who minored or took a few undergraduate courses in journalism.
- 41% of those who were undergraduate journalism majors.

Levels of self-confidence were nearly the same among whites and ethnic minorities.

Expectations about supervisors' ratings of new journalists varied significantly from one type of news organization to another. Very good ratings from supervisors were expected by 34% of new journalists at small dailies, 38% at weeklies, 41% in broadcast journalism, 47% at medium dailies and 59% at large dailies.

New journalists rate their supervisors

New journalists did not rate their supervisors' performance nearly as highly as they rated themselves — or as highly as they speculated they would be rated by their supervisors. Only 13% of new journalists rated their newsroom management as very good. The portions who gave very good ratings to newsroom managers varied considerably when viewed by respondents' educational backgrounds:

- 1% of those who studied journalism at the master's degree level.
- 11% of those who were undergraduate journalism majors.
- 15% of those who minored or took a few courses in journalism.
- 21% of those who never studied journalism.

Ethnic minorities and whites saw management through nearly the same lens. Managers got very good *and* poor ratings from the same portions of whites and ethnic minorities — 15% of ethnic minorities, 13% of whites. Even new-journalist managers didn't give overall management overwhelmingly high ratings: 17% of them said the quality of newsroom management was very good, while 12% of non-managers concurred. The quality of management was considered poor by 16% of non-managers and 9% of managers.

Asked to evaluate specific tasks and news-

Despite receiving relatively low pay and working in newsrooms many regard as cynical, 95% of new journalists said they like their present job — 73% "a lot," 22% "some."

room attitudes that could be considered to be the responsibility of management, new journalists gave the following combination of strongly-agree and mildly-agree responses:

- 83%, innovation and creativity are encouraged in their job.
- 82%, most journalists are paid less than they deserve.
- 79%, idealism does not dominate newsroom decisions too much.
- 74%, their career takes them away from their personal life.
- 72%, the financial bottom line dominates newsroom decisions too much.
- 65%, they are encouraged to set goals for career advancement.
- 54%, they get enough feedback on the quality of their work.

In other evaluations of overall performance of their news organizations:

- 11% of new journalists said newsrooms were preparing staffs very well for the future needs of journalism (45% said somewhat well, 29% not too well and 13% not well at all).
- 41% of new journalists said they think their news organizations are doing very well at providing people with information they need to be informed citizens (49% said somewhat well, 8% not too well and 1% not well at all).

Newsrooms are cynical, fair, honest

New journalists and newsroom recruiters and supervisors were asked how well various terms describe the atmosphere in their newsrooms.

- **Cynical** — New journalists: 24% very well, 44% somewhat well, 18% not too well, 13% not well at all. Recruiters and supervisors: 14% very well, 40% somewhat well, 28% not too well, 18% not well at all.

New journalists who said "cynical" described their newsrooms very well or somewhat well included 61% of those at weeklies, 63% in broadcast journalism, 69% at small dailies, 78% at large dailies and 81% at medium-size dailies.

By educational background, those who registered the lowest level of belief their newsrooms were cynical were those who never

studied journalism, 63%. Others: journalism majors, 70%; journalism minors, 71%; journalism master's degree holders, 72%.

Among new journalists who are newsroom managers, 62% thought cynical described their newsrooms; 70% of non-managers held that belief.

- **Fair** — New journalists: 33% very well, 49% somewhat well, 8% not too well, 4% not well at all. Recruiters and supervisors: 68% very well, 29% somewhat well, 2% not too well, 1% not well at all.

Ethnic-minority and white new journalists differed widely on whether their newsrooms were fair: 24% of ethnic minorities said it described their newsrooms very well, in contrast to 41% of whites who said so. Among other groupings, 42% of men said it described their newsrooms very well, as did 34% of women; and 46% of new-journalist managers, versus 34.4% of non-managers.

- **Honest** — New journalists: 52% very well, 39% somewhat well, 6% not too well, 2% not well at all. Recruiters and supervisors: 83% very well, 16% somewhat well, 1% not too well.
- **Open communication between managers and staff** — New journalists: 26% very well, 42% somewhat well, 19% not too well, 12% not well at all. Recruiters and supervisors: 49% very well, 42% somewhat well, 7% not too well, 2% not well at all.

The greatest contrast in reactions among new journalists from different educational backgrounds was between those who never studied journalism and those with journalism master's degrees. Twenty-one percent of those who never studied journalism thought the term described their newsrooms not too well or not well at all, but 48% of those with master's degrees thought it did. That opinion was also expressed by 36% of journalism majors and 32% of journalism minors.

Thirty-three percent of new-journalist newsroom managers said "open communication between managers and staff" characterized their newsrooms very well. Twenty-three percent of non-managers held that opinion.

New journalists like their jobs a lot

New journalists are very enthusiastic about their jobs. Despite receiving relatively low pay and working in newsrooms many regard as cynical, 95% of new journalists said they like their present job — 73% "a lot," 22% "some," 4% "a little" and 1% "not at all."

This intense liking for the profession by new journalists is much higher than the level of satisfaction registered by all journalists in the 1992 Weaver-Wilhoit survey. In that survey, 27.3% said they were very satisfied, 50.3% said fairly satisfied, 19.7% said somewhat dissatisfied and 2.7% said very dissatisfied.

The highest level of enthusiasm for jobs was expressed by ethnic-minority new journalists: 80% of them, compared with 71% of whites, reported liking their jobs "a lot." A slightly higher portion of women, 74%, than men, 71%, liked their jobs "a lot."

The enthusiasm of new journalists for their jobs was most pronounced among the oldest of them: 85% of those over age 40 said they like their jobs "a lot," compared with 71% of those age 36-40, 72% of those 31-36, 69% of those 26-30 and 71% of those age 25 and under. The older new journalists are predominantly people who have changed occupations to become journalists, a factor that might be responsible for their highest level of enthusiasm.

New journalists' enthusiasm for their newsroom jobs increased as income increased, but it was relatively high even among those who make the lowest salaries. Those who said they like their jobs "a lot" included 65% of those who make less than $20,000, 71% of those who make $20,000-$30,000 and 83% of those who make more than $40,000.

Though the level of enthusiasm varied among types of news organizations, it was fairly high in every case. Those who like their jobs "a lot" included:

- 61% of new journalists at medium-size dailies.
- 67% at small dailies.
- 68% at weeklies.
- 82% in broadcast journalism.
- 86% at large dailies.

Studying journalism at either undergraduate or graduate levels was not necessarily the key to greater job satisfaction. A significantly larger portion of new journalists who never studied journalism, 81%, like their jobs "a lot." Other groupings by educational backgrounds:

- 71% of those who minored or took a few

undergraduate courses in journalism.
- 69% of those who studied journalism at the master's degree level.
- 68% of those with undergraduate journalism degrees.

Journalism as a career exceeded the expectations of 36% of new journalists; that portion said it was more satisfying and challenging than they expected. Fifty-six percent said it was about as satisfying and challenging as they expected, and only 6% said it was less satisfying and challenging than expected.

By educational background, those who said journalism was more satisfying and challenging than expected included:

- 41% who minored or took a few undergraduate courses in journalism.
- 39% who never studied journalism.
- 32% who were undergraduate journalism majors.
- 26% who studied journalism at the master's degree level.

When asked what they liked most about their jobs, most new journalists' responses were related to the interesting nature of journalism (responses were spontaneous, without options suggested):

- 34%, variety of assignments.
- 20%, the people with whom they work.
- 14%, challenging work.
- 12%, interesting assignments.
- 7%, learn a lot.
- 7%, like the subject matter.

Asked what they dislike most about their jobs, new journalists listed the following, also spontaneously:

- 24%, long hours.
- 20%, pay.
- 7%, tedious work.
- 6%, problems with supervisor.
- 5%, problems with co-worker.
- 5%, emphasis on bottom line.

Whites were more dissatisfied with pay than ethnic minorities — 17% of whites said it was what they dislike most, compared with 8% of minorities. Men registered greater dissatisfaction than women about pay as well as schedule — 18% of the men, 12% of the women most dislike pay; 24% of the men, 18% of the women most dislike schedule.

Predictably, those who specified pay as the

This responsibility to meet the educational needs of journalists after they enter the profession has not been a strong tradition in journalism education.

aspect of their jobs they dislike most were those who are paid the least: 33% of those who make less than $20,000 annually, compared with 9% of those who make $20,000-$30,000, 4% of those who make $30,000-$40,000 and 3% of those who make more than $40,000.

New journalists beg for continuing education

Despite the fact that the quest for additional knowledge is central to the work of journalism, the journalism profession has not developed a culture that supports or endorses continuing education as a fundamental aspect of being a journalist. That seems peculiar, given the fact that most journalists are engaged daily in work that involves remembering or searching for information that will help them do their jobs better — conduct more-informed interviews, find better sources, take better photos, write better stories, edit stories better and manage staffs better.

Lawyers, public school teachers, even hairdressers are under pressure to stay current with changes in their professions — required to do so in some instances. For the journalist, staying current means not only keeping up with changes in the profession — which have exploded in the past decade — but also learning more about the subject areas one is covering.

In short, a journalist needs to learn a lot continuously. The Freedom Forum's 1992 study of 650 journalists at 123 daily and weekly newspapers, "No Train, No Gain," found that "nearly all of America's journalists want professional training, but most do not get it." This yearning for more education has not subsided. Roper's 1995 survey for this report showed that if new journalists had their say, professional-development courses would become a regular part of their work, a part of newsroom cultures everywhere. They felt so strongly about their need for education that 56% said they should be required to take ongoing professional development courses — 60% of those working for print media and 52% of those in broadcast journalism said so. Given journalists' usual strong propensity for independence, the fact that more than half of new journalists feel this way is an indication of how committed journalists are to performing their jobs better (and, perhaps, an indication of a sense of inad-

equacy). Only 5% percent of the new journalists said their employers require staff members to take professional-development courses.

Support for requiring professional development increased with age. Among the older segments of new journalists, 62% supported it; among the youngest, 54% did. A majority in every age segment supported the idea.

Asked how much they thought they would benefit from professional-development courses either in advanced journalism skills or in subjects other than journalism, 57% of new journalists said "a lot". Thirty-one percent thought they would benefit some, 8% a little and 4% not at all.

A larger portion of women, 62%, than men, 53%, thought they would benefit a lot from such courses. Among ethnic minorities, 64% felt this way, compared with 56% of whites.

By educational background, the group with the largest portion who have taken courses since they graduated are those who never studied journalism — 33%. That compares with 21% of those with master's degrees in journalism and 18% of those with undergraduate degrees in journalism.

Five percent of new journalists have taken one course, 12% have taken two to four courses, 4% have taken five to seven courses, and 4% have taken eight or more.

Newsroom recruiters and supervisors expressed strong support for professional-development education. Eighty-eight percent said they thought journalists should take such courses, and only 10% said such education was unnecessary. There was considerable difference between print and broadcast supervisors and recruiters about whether continuing education would help eliminate newsroom burnout: 48% in print journalism thought it would, 28% in broadcast journalism thought so.

Only 9% of the supervisors and recruiters said their news organizations require journalists to take courses, but 68% (77% print, 64% broadcast) reported they encourage staff members to do so — and 75% said their companies have paid tuition for staff members to take courses.

In other professions, schools of law, business, architecture, education and others play a major leadership role in shaping and providing continuing education for professionals.

Professors are presumed to be up-to-date on the needs of members of the profession and either teach or hire outside experts to teach the continuing-education courses.

This responsibility to meet the educational needs of journalists after they enter the profession has not been a strong tradition in journalism education. Only 27% of educators (35% of those at accredited programs and 14% at non-accredited programs) said their journalism programs provide professional-development sessions for journalists.

Many of those who do not provide continuing-education programs for journalists expressed strong interest in doing so: 43% said they would be extremely interested, 25% very interested, 22% somewhat interested, 5% not too interested, 3% not at all interested.

Nearly the same level of interest in such collaboration was expressed by newsroom recruiters and supervisors. Sixty-six percent said they would be interested in working with journalism educators and other news executives in their geographic area to create continuing-education courses for journalists. While the positive interest in such collaboration was nearly equal in the profession and in education, the negative interest was much stronger among the recruiters and supervisors — 23% of those from print media and 37% from broadcast media said they would have no interest in pursuing such an arrangement.

Nurturing the next generation of journalists

The Roper survey results show that among new journalists and their newsroom supervisors there is a vast, untapped source of talent willing to nurture the next generation of journalists. Schools that need mentors and coaches should note journalists' enthusiasm for working with students.

As individuals, many new journalists already are involved in coaching and mentoring students and have a high interest in providing future assistance. Only 8% of new journalists said they were not interested in working as a mentor or writing coach with journalism students at a local high school or college. Fifty-eight percent said they were very interested in working with students, and another 34% said they were somewhat interested.

Forty-eight percent of new journalists said they have been writing coaches or mentors to student journalists.

The highest interest was expressed by the youngest group — 71% of those 25 and under. Ethnic minorities expressed a deeper interest than whites and are involved more deeply in such activities. Those who are very willing to do such work include 65% of minority and 56% of white new journalists, and those already involved include 60% of ethnic minorities and 46% of whites.

Among all segments of new journalists, those who have worked with students the most are employed by large dailies, have master's degrees in journalism, make more than $40,000 a year and have been in journalism 8-11 years.

The survey also found that few news organizations hold summer journalism workshops for high school students, although there is plenty of interest in doing so. Only 24% of newsroom supervisors reported that their companies sponsor or cosponsor such workshops — 38% of medium-size and large newspapers, 10% of broadcast media. But 55% of supervisors whose news organizations do not sponsor this kind of student training said they would be interested in doing so.

New journalists love their jobs, but ...

With their extraordinary 95% level of liking their jobs, new journalists may be more content than most groups of workers. That makes all the more striking the fact that nearly half of them say they might leave journalism.

Asked if they plan to stay in journalism, 57% said yes, but 43% said they might leave. Those who said they might leave listed numerous factors; three were mentioned most frequently (responses were spontaneous, with no suggestions made by interviewers):

- 31%, low pay.
- 8%, the long hours.
- 7%, feel burned out.

Forty-seven percent of those who make less than $20,000 a year said low pay might make them leave journalism. The portions from each type of news organization who said low pay was a factor in their consideration of leaving journalism:

- 19% at large dailies.
- 21% at medium-size dailies.
- 36% at weeklies.
- 41% in broadcast journalism.
- 51% at small dailies.

By educational backgrounds, 27% to 30% of new journalists except those who studied journalism at the master's degree level (10%) said low pay was a factor in their considering leaving.

Thirty-four percent of whites, in contrast to 11% of ethnic minorities, said low pay was a factor in their considering leaving. On the other hand, burnout was a more significant factor for ethnic minorities (14%) than for whites (6%). The significance of low pay as a factor can be seen by comparing responses of segments with the highest and lowest indications that they may leave journalism within a year:

- 27% of those who make less than $20,000.
- 0% of those who make $30,000-$40,000.
- 4% of those who make more than $40,000.
- 22% of those who work at weeklies.
- None of those who work on large dailies.

The 43% who said they were considering leaving journalism were asked if there were specific changes that would keep them in journalism, and 73% of them said yes. That portion added to the 57% who said they plan to stay means 88% of new journalists either plan to stay or would stay if specific changes were made.

The change that would make the difference? Fifty-two percent said an increase in income would keep them in journalism. It was the only potential change that was stated by more than 8%. Again, money was much more important to whites than to ethnic minorities: 57% of whites said more money could keep them from leaving journalism, compared with 27% of ethnic minorities who said so.

Asked to indicate how important a number of items were in causing people to leave journalism, the newsroom recruiters and supervisors indicated:

- Low pay — 72% thought it a major reason, 23% a minor reason.
- Burnout — 70% major, 25% minor.
- Long hours — 55% major, 38% minor.
- Strong emphasis on bottom line — 40% major, 47% minor.
- Dislike current job — 31% major, 57% minor.
- Boring assignments — 9% major, 63% minor.

There was close agreement among all age groups of recruiters and supervisors on the importance of these issues in causing people to leave journalism, with the exception of long hours. That factor was given much higher priority by the youngest recruiters and supervisors: 65% of recruiters and supervisors 35 and under said it was a major issue, 55% of those 35-49, and 46% of those 50 and older.

After journalism, what?

Asked what type of work they would want to do if they left journalism, those who said they might leave listed a wide variety of possibilities. Cited most often were public relations (23%), teaching (19%), other writing (13%) and law (3%).

Those who specified public relations the most have the lowest incomes — 33% of those who make less than $20,000. Others: 28% of those who make $20,000-$30,000, 15% of those who make $30,000-$40,000 and 8% of those who make more than $40,000. Public relations was the first choice as a next career for 36% of those from small dailies, 26% of those from broadcast journalism, and 11% of those from medium-size and large dailies.

By far, the highest level of interest in public relations was expressed by those who were journalism minors, 41%. It also was the first choice of undergraduate journalism majors. The lowest interest in public relations came from those who never studied journalism, 11%.

Public relations was the most popular next-career choice of white new journalists (25%), while teaching was the most popular choice of ethnic-minority new journalists (22%).

Summary

When today's new journalists — those people who ordinarily would be expected to be on their way to becoming the experienced and leading journalists of tomorrow — are looked at closely, three things stand out:

- **Journalism education may not make much difference. The more than 27% of new journalists who never took a journalism course fare as well — and many fare better — in newsrooms than their colleagues who studied journalism. A** larger portion of the new journalists who never studied journalism make higher salaries, earn the highest honors in the field and have greater job satisfaction than those who studied journalism at some level. The same portion of those who never studied journalism advance to leadership roles as do those who have undergraduate degrees in journalism, and a much larger portion of those who never studied journalism than those with master's degrees become newsroom managers.

■ **An extraordinarily large portion of new journalists, especially ethnic minorities, like their jobs and want to help prepare the next generation of journalists.** Ninety-five percent of all new journalists like their jobs. Those who like their jobs "a lot" include 80% of ethnic minorities and 71% of whites. Impressive portions of new journalists already are serving as mentors and coaches to students: 60% of ethnic

minorities and 46% of whites. Even larger portions want to do so in the future: 65% of ethnic minorities and 56% of whites.

■ **The next generation of new journalists — those who most recently entered journalism and those who plan to enter it soon — is being discouraged by news organizations' low beginning salaries from making a full commitment to a future in journalism.** The precipitous decline of new journalists at the youngest level — from 12% of the total newsroom work force in 1982 to 4% in 1992 — may point to a crisis ahead. A profession that has believed it would always have an endless supply of young people at the door, begging to get in, may soon find itself without an ample next generation. Young journalists are being driven out by low salaries and by a management attitude that doesn't build for the future, even as older journalists are being forced and encouraged to retire early.

Young journalists are being driven out by low salaries and by a management attitude that doesn't build for the future, even as older journalists are being forced and encouraged to retire early.

4 Doctoral degree essential

Journalism educators' expertise, confusion and desire for change

To be or not to be a Ph.D.? That is "the" question for journalists and others who consider becoming journalism teachers at the college or university level. It is too bad that has become the question, for there are highly qualified journalism teachers with and without doctoral degrees. But the question about degree is having a great impact on who teaches journalism — and probably on quality and basic content of journalism education.

The question of who should teach journalism is more complex and more controversial than ever — among those already on journalism faculties as well as those who would like to be.

If journalism education faculties were chosen according to logical and wise standards based on the needs of students and the profession, they would be populated by people with various types of journalistic and scholarly expertise. The key criteria, ideally, would be proven expertise in journalism and issues related to journalism, proven competence as an effective teacher, and proven ability to publish research — journalistic or traditional scholarly — that would create new knowledge and fulfill the mission of the university while also serving the needs of the profession. Each faculty would have a substantial core of master journalists — people who have developed expertise through considerable experience and under the tutelage of peer and public review. They would have proven abilities as journalists and teachers, and as explorers and analysts of journalism. They would be people who have done terrific work as journalists and who want to share their expertise, continue their intellectual growth and prepare the next generation of journalists by teaching.

Some journalism education programs — those with wider and/or specialty missions — also would hire people who have scholarly expertise in areas other than journalism in which the program wants its students to acquire considerable knowledge. Some of these scholars might have doctoral degrees in mass communication, the high-level degree frequently held today by journalism educators. Other scholars, with shared appointments from other academic disciplines on campus, would have doctorates in areas that would help students prepare to be journalists in specialized fields. For example, scholars from history, political science, urban studies, geography, health sciences, the arts, or any number of other scholarly areas would contribute to the particular emphasis or mix of intellectual expertise and excitement a journalism education program might want for its undergraduate, graduate and continuing-education programs.

Expertise runs second to degrees

As the first century of journalism education draws to a close, those are not the criteria used to build most journalism faculties. Very different criteria exist: Doctoral degrees are the top priority, not experience as journalists. The hiring requirements have created a population of teachers — journalists and scholars alike — who are filled with bewilderment, if not outright frustration, about the puzzle that journalism education has become.

Some parts of the puzzle:

- Teachers with doctoral degrees who wish primarily to pursue scholarly research in communication-studies issues but who instead must teach journalism skills courses and introductory mass communication survey courses, neither of which sufficiently utilizes their scholarly expertise and research interests.
- Teachers with doctoral degrees and expe-

> But the tension and confusion among [journalism educators] about mission and teaching qualifications may be unique in the academic world.

rience as journalists who earned a Ph.D. only because it was required for teaching. They found that getting the degree did not increase their expertise and, perhaps, did not use or even respect their experience as journalists. Now that they are teaching, they find they are required, for tenure and promotion, to conduct a type of research that they believe will neither take advantage of their expertise nor make them better teachers.

- Teachers without doctoral degrees who have substantial experience as journalists but whose in-depth journalistic research is considered unacceptable for tenure and promotion purposes. They have been given a professional-track position, which at some universities means they will have a greater teaching load and be relieved of both the obligation to do research and the possibility of being promoted to full professor.
- Teachers without doctoral degrees who want to do traditional scholarly research but are told only people with doctorates may do it. Without a Ph.D., they will serve as short-term, non-tenure-track instructors — or, at best, fill professional-track positions that will not permit advancement to full professor.
- Teachers with or without doctoral degrees who have professional experience but who lack the time or inclination to conduct research. This could result from an excessive teaching load or from not enjoying the kind of scholarly research they are required to do. In the end, they could be laid off or forced to accept non-tenure-track positions without possibility of promotion.

Tension and confusion may be unique among educators

There are satisfied journalism educators among the few thousand in the United States, but the tension and confusion among them about mission and teaching qualifications may be unique in the academic world. While a school of architecture would not consider doing without a substantial portion of master architects on its faculty, and a school of engineering would not consider doing without a substantial portion of master engineers on its

faculty, a growing number of journalism and mass communication programs don't mind — indeed, by the nature of their qualifications, nearly guarantee — an absence of master journalists. The programs diminish or demean the expertise of the journalists on faculties by assigning them roles that connote second-class citizenship.

Strangely, in journalism and mass communication education programs today, the prospective teacher's expertise — either as teacher or as holder of the journalism skills to be taught — often is not among the requirements for the job. Instead, a doctoral degree — often without regard for the quality or substance of the scholarly work done to earn it — has become the most important requirement at many universities, to the exclusion of experience.

During this study of journalism education, information was gathered about hiring prerequisites and about the academic degrees and professional backgrounds of journalism education faculty members. Opinions about prerequisites for teaching journalism were sought from current journalism educators, former journalism students who now work as journalists, and newsroom supervisors and recruiters. The portrait that emerged is of journalism teaching requirements that have changed to reflect trends that started many years ago and have accelerated in the last 10 years — trends that are the opposite of what the teachers, former students, and newsroom supervisors and recruiters think should be happening.

The Roper survey of journalism faculty members conducted for this study found that:

- 67% of journalism faculty members have doctoral degrees (66% of faculty in accredited programs compared with 71% in non-accredited programs, 70% of men compared with 61% of women).
- The portion of journalism faculty members with doctoral degrees has doubled among those who began teaching in the last decade — 42% of those who have taught more than 10 years have doctorates, but 84% of those who have taught 10 or fewer years them.
- 48% of journalism educators have doctoral degrees in mass communication (40% of women, 51% of men), 4% have doctoral degrees in law, and 15% have doctoral

degrees in other areas of study.

- 17% of journalism faculty members have not worked as journalists. They include 13% of those 60 and older, 15% of those 45 to 59, and 23% of those 44 and younger.
- An additional 47% of journalism faculty worked 10 or fewer years as journalists.

The same trends were evident in the records provided by the 105 journalism and mass communication programs evaluated during the last six-year cycle of accreditation, 1990-91 through 1995-96. An average of 68% of the tenured and tenure-track faculty members in these programs have doctoral degrees.

Want ads show preference for degrees

Recent hiring trends were identified through a phone survey of the 117 journalism and mass communication programs that advertised during the 1994-95 academic year in *The Chronicle of Higher Education* and *Editor & Publisher* for full-time journalism teachers to begin teaching in 1995-96. If the word "journalism" did not appear in the advertisement, that university was not included in the survey. This was done to isolate the programs most likely to emphasize journalism. Nearly all of the schools — 112 — participated in the confidential survey. Among the teachers hired, 71% had doctoral degrees. Several who did not have doctorates were hired with an agreement that while teaching they would earn a Ph.D. and that they would not be placed on a tenure track until achieving it.

In 61% of the ads, the doctoral degree was described as either preferred or required. But faculty members at some programs where the advertisements indicated "preferred" said they actually required it.

The confidential comments made by spokespeople for journalism education search committees shed light on the current issues in hiring faculty to teach journalism:

"This is a very warm issue with me. The speech people in our department are always pushing scholarly types. I'm pushing for professional involvement to count. I'm always telling them to look at the turnover rate of Ph.Ds. versus journalists. The Ph.Ds. with no experience are unhappy on the job. The journalists are happy on the job, and the students love them. We've been most successful with those, by far."
— *Search committee chair.*

"The pool consisted of all the way from goofy to three serious candidates ... lots of ABDs (all but dissertation). This institution worships Ph.Ds. next to God. There is no tenure without a Ph.D."
— *Search committee member.*

"The critical words I keep hearing are 'high standards.' People try to get journalistic practice advocates to say they think a lower standard is important for some faculty, meaning those who teach journalism. I almost bit but am now wary. The high standards are for all faculty. ... Achieving those high standards in a variety of ways is the real issue."
— *Assistant professor.*

"Although the vast majority of our faculty have doctorates, we have at times found professionals who are smart. We are about to lose our professional. He's retiring next year. The university administration might not let us replace him with a professional."
— *Professor.*

"Journalism is being merged with communication at this institution. We're fighting over the name. They think even the word 'journalism' corrupts their academic integrity. ... you have to have a good sense of the absurd to play this game with the university. What they want here is a Ph.D. with 30 years of experience on *The New York Times*. That journalist might be acceptable."
— *Search committee chair.*

"We hired three professionals in the past who had to start over if they wanted tenure. That's the way they looked at it, like they were being expected to go back to college. ... There is a strong feeling in our faculty that we need to be more academic. I discuss often with them the need to serve undergraduates by having professionals in the classroom. I'm not sure they are listening."
— *Search committee chair.*

"In our search, we saw a lot of ABDs who were looking for a place to land. Forty percent were totally inexperienced, 20-30 percent had unrelated/indirect experience. Only 10-15 percent had experience we could consider as valuable to the classroom and the program. We hired an M.A. who is working on a Ph.D. in communication."
— *Search committee chair.*

> Although two of every three journalism educators have doctoral degrees, only one in seven strongly agreed that journalism educators should have doctorates.

"The ad was a mirage. … Those of us who are journalists are not sure that what we came to the university to do is still here. I'm not sure the horse I am riding is still alive. Deans have no idea what journalism means. They want respectability and quality, but they don't know what this is and, honestly, they don't care to find out."
— *Search committee chair.*

"We've had a hard time hiring for a variety of reasons. The university froze the advertising and public relations positions on us. We were unable to fill a mass comm. position because the person turned us down — get this — because they didn't want to teach a writing course. That's what you get with a brand new Ph.D."
— *Search committee chair.*

Several people in charge of searches were near cynicism, clearly disappointed. They seemed to feel the requirements forced them to hire people with qualifications that matched altogether different positions and to reject people who would have been right for the jobs. The process was dysfunctional, but they felt they could not do anything about it — that the hiring process was shaped and controlled by factors other than standards based on the needs of students and the profession.

Educators question need for doctorates

Journalism educators themselves do not believe in those requirements that increasingly govern hiring, tenure and promotion, the Roper survey also found.

Although two of every three journalism educators have doctoral degrees, only one in seven (14%) strongly agreed that journalism educators should have doctorates (23% mildly agreed, 22% neither agreed nor disagreed, 18% mildly disagreed, and 22% strongly disagreed).

Of those with doctoral degrees, just 22% strongly believe journalism educators should be required to have them. Among those who worked 10 or fewer years as journalists, 21% strongly agreed, compared with 5% of those who worked as journalists more than 10 years.

Perhaps more significant is the very small portion of journalism educators, 5% overall and 9% of Ph.D.s, who strongly agreed that journalism educators should have a doctoral degree in mass communication — the area in which the largest portion of journalism educators, 48%, have doctorates. It is also the one granted by the doctoral degree-granting journalism and mass communication programs. Such low enthusiasm for the mass communication doctorate raises questions about its value. Other responses on whether journalism educators should have doctoral degrees in mass communication: 19% mildly agreed they should, 26% neither agreed nor disagreed, 20% mildly disagreed and 29% strongly disagreed.

The Roper survey found that faculty members from non-accredited programs were more likely than their counterparts from accredited programs to report that university administrators were requiring journalism and mass communication programs to hire people with doctoral degrees for faculty openings. Thirty-three percent said their universities had such a requirement — 21% of those from accredited programs and 54% from non-accredited programs.

The numbers suggest that journalism professionals are generally more welcome at accredited schools than at non-accredited ones. Yet accreditation reports for the last six years show that visiting committees have consistently urged journalism programs to hire more faculty members with doctoral degrees.

Research is essential for promotion

The shift toward doctoral-degree-only faculty policies at many journalism and mass communication programs reflects the key role of research today in the American university.

To be tenured and promoted at most universities, a faculty member must also engage in research that yields new knowledge and new insights that add to the basic tenets or understanding of the discipline. In other words, teaching is only part of a faculty member's obligation.

Accordingly, the journalism education "establishment," in various forms but most powerfully in its accreditation-review process, regards research as essential. Unfortunately, many leaders in journalism education do not appreciate the research potential of the master journalist and regard doctoral degree-holding educators as the only people suitably equipped to fulfill research obligations. Thus, the repeated advice in accreditation report is: Hire young Ph.Ds. to increase the program's research output.

The requirement for tenure-track and tenured educators to engage in research is an issue that has been confusing — and defeating — to many journalism educators. It is at the heart of why the place of the experienced journalist in journalism education has diminished over the last few decades.

Many prestigious universities have no problem accepting non-traditional research on a par with traditional scholarly research. For instance, the University of California, Berkeley, embraces with equal respect many types of research. This policy makes it possible for people in the performing arts, journalism and other disciplines to conduct research that is more closely related to the nature and needs of the professions in which they have their expertise.

Other universities, including some "trying to make it big," are less secure. As such, they are more likely to establish only-Ph.D. hiring rules and only-scholarly-research rules.

The widespread requirement that professors be researchers as well as teachers, while firmly established in higher education, also has come under much criticism from diverse corners, including undergraduate students at some large universities. They have complained about minimal contact with tenure-track and tenured professors, who are fully occupied with research and with teaching graduate students, while graduate students and part-time lecturers teach undergraduates. That trend in journalism education was evident in some universities in the most recent cycle of journalism education accreditation reports. Journalism students made such complaints at the University of Minnesota last year.

The emphasis on research is greater today than ever, but it is not a new phenomenon. As communication studies professors took over journalism education after the middle of this century, in-depth journalistic research — the type in which most master journalists have expertise — was no longer recognized by many schools as acceptable. These professors had used their promised scholarly research about communications as a way of taking over journalism education programs (a subject that will be explored in the next chapter) and convincing university administrators that journalists were not serious academics.

On top of that, some journalism educators who had been journalists were stubbornly resistant, for various reasons, about doing research.

Lee Stinnett, executive director of the American Society of Newspaper Editors, echoed the sentiments of those who think research has hurt teaching. "Journalism education, I hope, will lead the way in returning universities to teaching, which they have abandoned in favor of academic research," Stinnett said. "If they led universities in this way, journalism schools would achieve a very high degree of respect within the university. This would be earthshaking. J-schools could save universities from the pending public wrath that is about to descend with a fury as more and more demands are made for more emphasis on teaching as university budgets get pinched."

Research *is* important

While it is true that an excessive emphasis on research can hurt the teaching mission of a university, there are good reasons for requiring research. Thomas C. Leonard, associate dean in the Graduate School of Journalism at the University of California, Berkeley, outlined some of the strengths and weaknesses in the research requirement.

"The Ph.D. octopus, as William James called it, has been around for a very long time and is clearly related to the mania for credentials that has spanned this century. All professional schools have this problem to some degree. I would not write this off," Leonard said, "as simply the protective behavior of an entrenched educational bureaucracy, though it is partly that.

"The research model has triumphed in higher education since World War II. It has seemed far more important to expand knowledge than to polish students' skills or to nurture them. Even the small, traditional liberal-arts colleges have gone this route. It was inevitable, then, that journalism programs would churn out research. One problem has been that little of this research has impressed folks in other fields. When this goes on long enough, it is a green light for cutbacks. It doesn't help if practitioners are ready to testify that they ignore the research."

Not only professionals are ready to offer such testimony. So are some educators. Janet Hill Keefer, dean of the School of Journalism

I fear our 'research' very often asks questions that are no more relevant than the 'How-many-angels-can-dance-on-the-head-of-a-pin?' question was in an earlier time, or is as obvious as 'Roof leaks can be detected in the rain.'

"

Janet Hill Keefer
School of Journalism
and Mass Communication
Drake University

and Mass Communication at Drake University in Des Moines, Iowa, said, "I fear our 'research' very often asks questions that are no more relevant than the 'How-many-angels-can-dance-on-the-head-of-a-pin?' question was in an earlier time, or is as obvious as 'Roof leaks can be detected in the rain.' ... No wonder our scholarship has such a hard time being taken seriously. ... I think we are guilty of doing and publishing research simply for the sake of fulfilling the expectations of promotion and tenure committees, rather than to advance knowledge in our field."

[Cal-Berkeley's] Leonard makes the case for meaningful research as a way to improve the professor.

"I've seen instances of hunkering down and defensiveness (by journalists who become academics). I'd understand this if the challenge was to fill *Journalism Quarterly*. But at the universities that will count distinguished reporting as tenure-worthy, the failure to produce does journalism education real harm. Modern universities and colleges just aren't set up to reward the dedicated teaching of fundamentals. ... There is a powerful argument behind this: A professional's skills and experience may be superb now, but in time they will grow stale. The best guarantee for distinguished teaching over time is continual production that is reviewed and judged by the best people in the field and compared with work in other academic departments."

Ironically, journalists are probably better prepared to conduct research and write the results than teachers in any other discipline. They have developed their expertise as gatherers and analysts of information of all levels of complexity. Experienced in examining issues and concepts that are new to them, they are in an ideal position to establish areas of research to pursue during their careers as teachers. Some journalism educators, such as Erna Smith, chair of the Department of Journalism at San Francisco State University, have proven themselves capable of conducting traditional scholarly research. They have an ability that not all scholars possess — to write in clear and interesting ways that make the information useful and that help gain the respect of academics in other disciplines, journalism educator colleagues and professional journalists. Students also benefit,

acquiring insights from the results and also helping to conduct the research.

Journalistic research has wide support

In the Roper survey, journalism educators were asked their opinions on the type of research journalism educators should be required to engage in — the rigorous discipline of traditional academic research and writing and/or the rigorous discipline of journalistic research and writing. They were then asked what type of research and writing journalism educators should be required to produce to obtain tenure and be promoted.

On whether journalism educators should be required to experience traditional academic research and writing:

- 48% thought they should (21% strongly agreed, 27% mildly agreed. The highest level of very strong agreement was among those who have never worked as journalists, 34%, and those who have doctoral degrees, 31%.)
- 18% neither agreed nor disagreed.
- 33% thought they should not be so required (18% mildly disagreed, 15% strongly disagreed).

On whether journalism educators should be required to experience in-depth journalistic research and writing:

- 77% thought they should (41% strongly agreed, 36% mildly agreed. The highest level of agreement was among those who had been journalists more than 10 years, 81%. The lowest level of agreement was among those who never worked as journalists, 68%.)
- More than 75% of educators in all but one category — the exception being those who never worked as journalists — agreed it was important for journalism educators to experience in-depth journalistic research and writing. Forty-one percent in all categories strongly agreed it was important.
- There was very close agreement between those who have and those who do not have doctoral degrees. Seventy-eight percent of those who have doctorates and 75% of those who do not agreed it was important for journalism educators

to experience in-depth journalistic research and writing.

- 15% neither agreed nor disagreed.
- 8% thought they should not be so required (4% mildly disagreed, 4% strongly disagreed).

On whether journalism educators should be required to experience either the rigorous discipline of traditional academic or in-depth journalistic research and writing:

- 64% thought they should (39% strongly agreed, 25% mildly agreed).
- 17% neither agreed nor disagreed.
- 18% thought they should not be so required (10 percent mildly disagreed, 8% strongly disagreed).
- A majority of those who have the doctoral degree and of those who do not have it support the "either" requirement: 58% of those who do not have doctoral degrees and 69% of those who have them.

Educators want research options

In addition to playing a major role in faculty hiring decisions, the type of research and writing done by educators is crucial in the evaluations that determine who will be tenured and promoted from assistant professor to associate professor to professor. Research materials are evaluated not only by

Degrees of support

In summary fashion, here are the degrees of support journalism educators gave to three options for meeting research and writing requirements:

- 48%, requiring traditional academic research and writing (21% strongly support).
- 77%, requiring in-depth journalistic research and writing (41% strongly support).
- 64%, requiring either traditional academic or in-depth journalistic research and writing (39% strongly support).

Journalism educators opposed each of the three research policies as follows:

- 33%, requiring academic research and writing.
- 18%, permitting either type of research.
- 8%, requiring in-depth journalistic research and writing.

peers in the journalism education program but also by teachers in other academic disciplines and by central administrators. The strong trend in recent years has been for journalism programs to require tenure-track faculty members to engage only in traditional academic research and to hire only people viewed as most likely to be able to do such work successfully — those with doctoral degrees.

But the Roper survey showed that journalism educators, including those with doctoral degrees, do not agree with either the requirement that journalism educators have doctorates or with the requirement that journalism educators — with or without that degree — be limited to traditional academic research as a requirement for tenure or promotion.

Asked to indicate what type of research options should be acceptable for evaluation in hiring, tenure and promotion, faculty members expressed opinions that do not match current policy and practice trends. This is how they responded when asked if either traditional academic or in-depth journalistic research and writing should be accepted:

- 79% thought either should be accepted (54% strongly agreed, 25% mildly agreed).
- 6% neither agreed nor disagreed.
- 14% thought there should not be a choice (9% mildly disagreed, 5 percent strongly disagreed).

There was close and high agreement between people from different backgrounds on supporting either type of research for hiring, tenure and promotion:

- 75% of those who have taught 10 or fewer years and 78% of those who have taught 11 or more years agreed.
- 79% of those who had worked as journalists and 78% of those who had never worked as journalists agreed.
- 79% of those who had worked 10 or fewer years as a journalist and 80% of those who had worked more than 10 years as a journalist agreed.
- 80% of those without doctoral degrees and 78% of those with doctoral degrees agreed.

The widest disagreements — only a 10-point spread — were between tenured and tenure-track faculty and between educators from accredited and non-accredited units:

- 77% of tenured faculty supported either form of research, and 87% of tenure-track faculty — the group with the highest portion of doctoral degrees and the people who would be affected most immediately by such a policy — supported it.
- 83% of educators from accredited programs and 73% of educators from non-accredited programs supported both types of research.

When asked why they thought there had been a decline in the number of people hired as journalism educators whose research and writing credentials were based on professional experience, journalism educators selected the following explanations:

- 68% — In a quest for respectability, some universities have established the doctoral-degree requirement without considering the unique needs of some disciplines to evaluate scholarly qualifications and potential through accomplishments other than doctoral research and writing.
- 58% — Many university administrators do not understand what may be the best credentials for teaching journalism.
- 42% — Journalism educators believe that hiring only people with doctoral degrees will enhance their program's prestige on campus.
- 35% — Journalism administrators have not done an adequate job of informing central administrators about the variety of qualifications needed for teaching journalism.

Educators value professional experience

Extensive professional experience, though diminished in importance by current practices, is highly regarded by journalism educators. In contrast to the lack of regard for professional experience shown in 1994-95 advertisements for journalism teachers and in recent hiring decisions, journalism educators overwhelmingly agreed that journalism faculties should include people who have extensive professional experience as journalists:

- 94% agreed (80% strongly, 14% mildly).
- 4% neither agreed nor disagreed.
- 2% disagreed.

These findings parallel those from a 1990 survey of members of the Association for Education in Journalism and Mass Communication conducted by Ted Pease at The Freedom Forum Media Studies Center in New York City. From the responses of 652 journalism educators, Pease, now head of the Department of Communication at Utah State University, concluded:

"Although professional-turned-teachers agree that real-world experience increases their classroom effectiveness and informs their research activities, many ... said the commodities that made them attractive to journalism schools in the first place — their professional experience and industry contacts — sometimes work against them once on campus." Pease said respondents' comments demonstrated the "depth of resentment among some faculty" and documented "that the two-tier system of professionally oriented faculty and scholarly researchers creates tensions that translate into a sense of second-class citizenship among some faculty."

Under current practices, faculty members with the longest experience are less likely to succeed in the areas that mark financial success and advancement in the university environment, as evidenced by the following Roper survey findings:

- Full professors include 25% of those with more than 10 years' experience as journalists and 42% of those with 10 or fewer years' experience.
- Associate professors include 27% of those with more than 10 years' experience as journalists and 30% of those with 10 or fewer years' experience.
- Assistant professors, those at the lowest rung on the tenure-track ladder, include 29% of those with more than 10 years' experience as journalists and 21% of those with 10 or fewer years' experience.
- Journalism educators who teach full-time but are neither tenured nor on a tenure track include 29% of those with more than 10 years' experience and 9% of those with 10 or fewer years' experience.
- Full professors include 42% of those with

doctoral degrees and 19% of those without them.

- Non-tenured and non tenure-track positions include 30% of those who do not have doctoral degrees and 2% of those who have them.
- Journalism educators who are tenured include 74% of those with 10 or fewer years' experience as journalists and 50% of those with more than 10 years' experience.
- Journalism educators who are tenured include 74% of those with doctoral degrees and 47% of those without them.

Journalism educators rank low on academic totem pole

Compared with teachers in other disciplines, journalism educators tend to have lower status. This may be because journalism education programs have not established clear research criteria that use the expertise of faculty with or without doctoral degrees — a problem repeatedly noted in accreditation reviews.

The lower status of journalism and mass communication faculty overall, not just journalism educators, was documented by Alexis S. Tan, director of the Edward R. Murrow School of Communication at Washington State University, in his 1990 study, "Journalism and Mass Communication Programs in the University." Tan concluded, "This study confirms our worst fears: We do not have a good image in the university."

The prevalence of the doctoral-degree requirement — and even the offering of the doctoral degree — did not immunize journalism programs from having their existence threatened between 1985 and 1995. Twenty-nine percent of the faculty surveyed by Roper indicated their programs' existence had been threatened during that time — 33% of those from institutions that grant doctoral degrees in journalism, 16% of those from institutions that do not grant such degrees. Twenty-two percent overall reported their programs had merged with other campus departments or schools over that 10-year period.

Journalism educators were asked to indicate the reason or reasons cited by administrators for the challenges to their programs:

- 55%, too costly.
- 53%, not central to the university's mission.

- 50%, faculty not doing sufficient or appropriate research. (Sixty percent of educators 44 and younger said administrators gave this reason.)
- 37%, negative stories about the university or its administrators published or broadcast by journalism students.
- 24%, hostility of the campus community to the program.
- 21%, lack of focus.
- 15%, hostility of the profession to the program.

Students favor faculty with professional experience

When former journalism students who have been working as journalists one to 11 years were asked what type of professional/ educational backgrounds their best teachers had, their choices reflect the belief of teachers themselves and the opposite of recent trends in hiring requirements:

- 56% said their best journalism teachers had extensive professional experience as journalists and did not have doctoral degrees.
- 31% said their best journalism teachers had extensive professional experience as journalists and had doctoral degrees.
- 6% said their best journalism teachers had doctoral degrees and little or no experience as journalists.

When former journalism students who now work as journalists were asked, based on their experience as journalism students and as professional journalists, how important they thought it was for journalism educators to have professional experience:

- 95% said it was very important.
- 4% said it was somewhat important.
- 1% said it was not too important.

Asked how important it was for journalism educators to study mass communication theory at the doctoral level:

- 7% of the journalists who once studied journalism said it was very important.
- 29% said it was somewhat important.
- 39% said it was not too important.
- 21% said it was not at all important.

The strongest opposition to journalism educators studying mass communication theo-

> The prevalence of the doctoral-degree requirement … did not immunize journalism programs from having their existence threatened between 1985 and 1995. Twenty-nine percent of the faculty surveyed by Roper indicated their programs' existence had been threatened during that time.

The question of the expertise faculty members bring to teaching, in journalism or in scholarly research, is conspicuously missing from places where its mention and evaluation might be most expected — in teacher-wanted advertisements and accreditation reviews.

ry at the doctoral level came from those over age 36 (27% said it was not at all important), those who work for large dailies (27%) and recipients of master's degrees (36%).

Opinions of recruiters and supervisors mirror those of most teachers and former students — and are the opposite of trends regarding backgrounds of journalism educators. Given a series of potential recommendations and asked to indicate how much they thought each would improve journalism education, 70% of the recruiters and supervisors said hiring more full-time faculty with extensive backgrounds as professional journalists would improve it "a lot," while just 1% of them said "not at all." In contrast, 7% said hiring more full-time faculty with extensive backgrounds as academic scholars in mass communication would help "a lot" and 39% said it would help "not at all."

The question of the expertise faculty members bring to teaching, in journalism or in scholarly research, is conspicuously missing from places where its mention and evaluation might be most expected — in teacher-wanted advertisements and accreditation reviews. In the advertisements less than half the journalism education programs — 45% — said experience was required, 35% said it was preferred and 20% did not mention experience.

A review of the last six years of visiting committee accreditation reports — 105 in all — also shows minimal attention paid to faculty expertise.

- Two programs were described as having faculty members who were distinguished, seasoned journalists.
- Two programs were described as having national reputations for their expertise as researchers in scholarly and journalistic work.
- Three programs were noted for expertise in specific areas of research and teaching.
- Nine programs were described as having national reputations for impressive scholarly work in general.

Where are journalists grown?

How important is journalism within the journalism and mass communication program at colleges and universities?

Some clues were found by analyzing data provided at the time of the 105 programs' most recent accreditation reviews.

- There were about 53,000 students in accredited undergraduate and master's degree journalism and mass communication programs. Of them, about 24,000 were print or broadcast journalism majors.
- The number of print or broadcast journalism graduates three years prior to the accreditation reviews was about 6,000. Three years after graduation, only 2,000 of them — one in every three — were reported to be working as journalists.
- 15 programs offered only journalism — that is, no advertising, public relations, communication studies or other major — and therefore 100% of their students were journalism majors.
- For the remaining programs, the portion of students who majored in print or broadcast journalism ranged from 89% to 12%. (Two schools reported having integrated programs, with no majors in specific areas of mass communication; a few others reported they were considering this format.)
- The median was 44% — half of the schools had more than 44% of their majors in journalism, half had less than 44% in journalism.
- Including the two schools without specialized majors, only nine programs had fewer than 25% of their majors in journalism.

This study also determined the educational backgrounds of faculty members at schools that were highly successful in three visible ways — winning the monthly William Randolph Hearst Journalism Awards, and having the largest number and portion of journalism majors who were working as journalists three years after graduation. These measures are available only for the 105 accredited programs, but given the fact that 89% of all new journalists who studied journalism came from those programs, these programs well worth examining. (Only programs that graduated at least 20 journalism majors were considered in the following analyses.)

- Eight programs — 7.6% of all accredited

programs — reported that 50% or more of their graduates who majored in journalism (print or broadcast) were working as journalists three years after they graduated.

- Among these eight programs, the portion of their tenured and tenure-track faculties with doctoral degrees ranged from 9% to 55% — well-below the 68% average for all accredited programs.
- Twenty programs — 19% of all accredited programs — had 20 or more journalism majors working as journalists three years after graduation.
- Among these 20 programs, the portion of their tenured and tenure-track faculty with doctoral degrees ranged from 9% to 95%. Sixty-five percent of these faculties had a lesser percentage of doctoral degree-holders than the average of 68% for all accredited programs.

Among all 105 accredited programs, 49% said 10 or fewer journalism graduates were working as journalists three years after they graduated. Two had none.

The analysis of winners of the Hearst competitions during a six-year period (1989-90 to 1994-95) found that:

- Eleven journalism programs had 20 or more students place among the top-10 winners in the writing, photojournalism or broadcast journalism competitions.
- Eight of these 11 schools also were among the accredited schools that had the largest number or portion of graduates working as journalists.
- Among the 11, 73% had below the 68% average of doctoral degree-holders on accredited programs' faculties.

In all, there were 25 schools that demonstrated strong student accomplishment in journalism — that is, with a large portion (50% or more) and/or large number (20 or more) of journalism majors working as journalists three years after graduation, and/or a large number of Hearst winners. Of these 25 schools, 72% had below, and most of them well below, the average 68% portion of doctoral degree-holders on accredited programs' faculties.

There may be numerous other factors that

Where journalists come from: programs that produce quantity and quality

P = Programs (8 programs or 7.6% of all accredited programs) that graduated at least 20 journalism majors in a recent year and 50% or more of them were working as journalists three years afterward. (Based on data provided by programs during their last accreditation review.)

N = Programs (22 programs or 21% of all accredited programs) that had 20 or more journalism majors from a recent graduating class working as journalists three years after graduation, but did not reach the 50% working-journalist level. (Also based on data provided during the last accreditation review.)

H = Programs (11 programs or 10% of all accredited programs) that had 20 or more students place among the top 10 in all categories in the William Randolph Hearst Foundation Journalism Awards Program between 1989-90 and 1994-95. (Data from Hearst Foundation records.)

School	P	N	H
University of Arizona		N	
Arizona State University		N	H
University of California, Berkeley*	P	N	
California State University, Northridge		N	
University of Colorado		N	
Columbia University*	P	N	
University of Florida			H
University of Illinois, Champaign-Urbana		N	
Indiana University		N	H
University of Kansas		N	H
Kent State University			H
University of Maryland		N	
University of Mississippi	P	N	
University of Missouri-Columbia		N	H
University of Nebraska		N	H
University of North Carolina	P	N	H
Northwestern University	P	N	H
Ohio University		N	
Ohio State University		N	
Oklahoma State University	P	N	
San Francisco State University	P	N	H
University of Southern California		N	
Syracuse University		N	
University of Texas		N	
Western Kentucky University	P		H

Graduate programs may not enter the Hearst competition.

foster strong student interest and accomplishment in journalism. In view of these findings, however, it seems likely that having been taught by faculty members whose primary qualifications were their accomplishments as journalists is a significant factor in the successful professional performance of journalism majors. These educators' journalistic expertise is what makes them not just valuable but essential to the effective teaching of journalism — but it will be available to students only if people with such qualifications continue to be hired for journalism faculties.

Takeover of journalism education

How journalism education has been submerged during the last half of the 20th century

To be or not to be a Ph.D.? Why is that the question? The question arises from the way journalism education has evolved during the first century of its existence. For 50 years it was shaped primarily by two goals: to improve the minds of journalism and to improve the image of journalism. In the second half of the century, journalism education has been shaped by goals that often have had less to do with journalism and more to do with academic image.

Here is A. Ross Hill, president of the University of Missouri, upon the opening in 1908 of the university's School of Journalism, the first of its kind:

"I believe it is possible for this school to give dignity to the profession of journalism, to anticipate to some extent the difficulties that journalists must meet and to prepare its graduates to overcome them, to give prospective journalists a professional spirit and high ideals of service, to discover those with real talent for the work and discourage those who are likely to prove failures in the profession, and to give the state better newspapers and newspapermen and a better citizenship."

Here is Willard G. Bleyer, founder of journalism education at the University of Wisconsin, creator of the first doctoral research program in journalism and early proponent of accreditation of journalism education programs, speaking in 1905:

The graduates of journalism schools are "necessary to protect society and government against immature, half-educated, unscrupulous journalists."

Here is William Preston Johnston, a professor at Washington College (now Washington and Lee University) in Lexington, Va., which in 1869 became the first college to invite people interested in becoming journalists to earn a college degree. Answering a question by a reporter from the *New York Sun*, "Just what do you propose to do with these Press Scholarships?" Johnston replied:

"Printing is one of the arts which diffuse education and we should therefore seek to qualify printers for this task of educating as far as possible. We do not hope to make men fit for the editorial chair at once, but we do hope to give them as good an education as possible that they may make better and more cultivated editors."

John Plaxton of the Nashville Typographical Union, in an 1869 letter to Professor Johnston, said, "We look upon this action of Washington College as a very important step toward raising American journalism from the slough of venality, corruption and party subserviency into which it has too notoriously fallen to the high position it should occupy."

Journalism education was going to transform the reputation of the profession. The image of rough drunks of the newsroom would be replaced by an image of a thoughtful, educated journalist. Journalism schools would be, in part, the finishing schools of journalism.

Professor James W. Carey of the Columbia Graduate School of Journalism discussed the founders' motives in a 1992 address to the Columbia faculty and the staff and fellows of The Freedom Forum Media Studies Center. "Reporters were not educated men and most assuredly thereby were not men of letters," Carey said. "They were an unlikely collection of itinerant scribblers, aspiring or, more often, failed novelists, ne'er-do-well sons of established families and, most importantly, the upwardly mobile children of immigrants with an inherited rather than an educated gift of language, without much education and certainly without much refinement."

> "
> If news instinct as born were turned loose in any newspaper office in New York without the control of sound judgment bred by considerable experience and training, the results would be much more pleasing to the lawyers than to the editor.
> "
>
> **Joseph Pulitzer**
> *New York World*

Pulitzer wanted to improve minds

Some newspaper publishers and editors, Joseph Pulitzer among them, believed that education would "improve" reporters. The leaders of journalism, Carey said, were not alone at that time in "believing that university education might domesticate this unruly class, turn them into disciplined workers and end their flirtation with socialism and trade unions." To varying degrees, the universities themselves welcomed the opportunity to make "the quest for knowledge and professional standards" available to those preparing to enter journalism and other professions, he said.

Pulitzer of the *New York World* and *St. Louis Post-Dispatch* focused more sharply on the need to improve the minds of journalists. When Pulitzer first proposed endowing a school of journalism, first at Harvard and later at Columbia, he had to sell the idea. Finally, Columbia accepted. But a public debate took place over several years, with many influential journalists and educators participating in it. Responding to those critics who said a journalism education was ridiculous because news instinct must be born, not taught, Pulitzer wrote a 1904 article in *North American Review* magazine that expanded his vision of journalism education:

"If news instinct as born were turned loose in any newspaper office in New York without the control of sound judgment bred by considerable experience and training, the results would be much more pleasing to the lawyers than to the editor. One of the chief difficulties in journalism now is to keep the news instinct from running rampant over the restraints of accuracy and conscience. And if a 'nose for news' is born in the cradle, does not the instinct, like other great qualities, need development by teaching, by training, by practical object-lessons illustrating the good and the bad, the Right and the Wrong, the popular and the unpopular, the things that succeed and the things that fail, and above all the things that deserve to succeed, and the things that do not — not the things only that make circulation for today, but the things that make character and influence and public confidence?"

In short, journalism education would help future journalists develop minds that would be filled with knowledge and curious about everything.

Each of the principal visionaries of journalism education — Bleyer at the University of Wisconsin, founder Walter Williams at the University of Missouri School of Journalism, and Pulitzer — looked beyond the immediate goal of educating journalists and improving newspapers. The larger goal to which they aspired was to produce a more-informed citizenry through better journalism.

Pulitzer was especially eloquent in expressing that goal: "While it is a great pleasure to feel that a large number of young men will be helped to a better start in life by means of this college, this is not my primary object. Neither is the elevation of the profession which I love so much and regard so highly. In all my planning the chief end I had in view was the welfare of the Republic. It will be the object of the college to make better journalists, who will make better newspapers, which will better serve the public."

At Wisconsin, after establishing undergraduate courses in journalism, Bleyer pioneered graduate-school journalism education. He stressed that research about journalism should be as important a part of journalism education as preparing students to enter the profession. The two scholarly functions would coexist side by side and enrich each other, as Bleyer saw it: teaching the skills of journalism and, additionally, studying journalism as an institution — its history, how it is practiced, its impact. Many of the people who earned doctoral degrees in his program later became the heads of journalism programs elsewhere.

The birth of accreditation

A former journalist with a doctoral degree in English, Bleyer kept close ties with journalists and, as his many papers at the University of Wisconsin Library show, he was a frequent critic of journalism, monitor of how it was changing and a perpetual advocate for the profession's support of journalism education. He was instrumental in the creation of two pillars of the journalism education establishment: the association of journalism education administrators (now known as the Association of Schools of Journalism and Mass Communication) and the accrediting body for journalism programs (now known as the Accrediting Council on Education in Journalism and Mass Communications).

The plan for accrediting journalism programs was developed by a Joint Committee of Editors and Educators, created at Bleyer's instigation by the American Society of Newspaper Editors. Although Bleyer did not live to see it (he died in 1935), the accrediting organization was up and running in 1947. At the ASNE convention that year, the society's president, Nathaniel R. Howard, made what he described as a "historic" announcement: the joint committee had "crossed the Rubicon" and determined the procedures to "classify American schools of journalism as to their effectiveness." He said editors' campus visits, which had just started, represented "an assertion of our influence in American education" and "may serve as a turning point for the country's schools of journalism."

The editors who revered Bleyer and supported his goals in those early days did want journalism to be improved through better minds. Bleyer helped them understand that journalism had intellectual needs, not just image needs, and that the mission of the university melded perfectly with the intellectual task of journalism itself and with the expansive knowledge and methods of inquiry that the university would provide future journalists.

By the 1940s, as Everette E. Dennis, a senior vice president at The Freedom Forum and former journalism dean, wrote in his 1989 book, "Reshaping the Media: Mass Communication in an Information Age," "the field seemed to have achieved some maturity."

That was about to change.

Communication studies moves in

By the mid-1950s, a new force was taking root in some journalism education programs. Eventually, it would permeate most programs. This new force — communication studies — would radically rewrite the rules governing who should teach journalism, and it would lead to changes and confusion that dog journalism education even today.

The uniting of communication studies and journalism grew, in substantial part, out of a mix of bureaucratic expediency and a lack of understanding of journalism. The union did not result from an altruistic desire for new philosophical understandings about journalism and/or a new commitment to academic or professional excellence.

Communication studies had existed for many years in the United States and in other countries, but the scholars who studied various communication problems did so from their bases in other disciplines, such as psychology, sociology, history, political science or anthropology. At mid-century communication studies became a distinct discipline, with its teachers bearing the title communication professors. It established a home in journalism education.

There is wide agreement with the claim made by Everett M. Rogers in his 1994 book, "A History of Communication Study," that Wilbur Schramm, head of journalism education at Iowa shortly after World War II and later the founder of institutes of communication research at the University of Illinois and Stanford University, was "the founder of the field, the first individual to identify himself as a communication scholar." Schramm created "the first academic degree-granting programs with communication in their name; and he trained the first generation of communication scholars. ... Schramm set in motion the patterns of scholarly work in communication study that continue to this day," wrote Rogers, chairman of the Department of Communication and Journalism at the University of New Mexico.

The development of communication studies in the 20th century was inevitable. As technologies expanded the size of the audience for various kinds of communication, it was natural that some scholars of human behavior would feel compelled to study what a mass audience was and how it behaved, how mass media behaved, and what impact they had on demographic groups as well as the overall population. There were political and commercial interests eager to understand and use whatever could be learned about — or could be done to or for — the masses. Scholars served commercial and political as well as scholarly interests in their research on communication issues.

Schramm began to shape his vision of communication during a year of working in Washington, D.C., in the federal government's Office of Facts and Figures. He was influenced by social scientists there who were studying and designing projects to sell the war effort to the American public.

When Schramm, a founder of the much-respected Iowa Writers Workshop, returned to the University of Iowa in 1943, he turned his vision into a "Blueprint for a School of Journalism," written for the administrators at the university. He wrote: "I should like to see the kind of School of Journalism that would be not as weak as itself, but as strong as the university. Not a group of teachers and students sitting on the periphery of the university, playing with their toys, putting together the picture of who, what, where, and when in the first paragraph — not that, but a School that would be in the very heart of the university, which would begin with the assumption that the students it wants to produce will be the students in the whole university best equipped to understand and talk about the world."

Creating a new academic discipline is a difficult bureaucratic task, given the reluctance of universities to adopt new structures. Schramm cleverly avoided that hassle by looking for an existing structure on which to graft communication studies. He chose journalism at Iowa, as he would later at Illinois and Stanford.

That was the beginning of the vision Schramm and his scholarly descendants would build and the beginning of his own volu-minous body of writing on communication study. "Most media scholars are heavy users of Wilbur Schramm's great organizing principles, his scholarly output and his instincts for institution building," wrote The Freedom Forum's Dennis. "He gave our field what Tom Wolfe would call 'a rocket boost of energy' and a good deal more."

Journalism education is cast in inferior role

That also was the beginning of the institutional marriage that was replicated repeatedly and exists today in most journalism education programs. Schramm and the graduate students he and other communication studies scholars sent into the field made their home in journalism education. It was a home they eventually rebuilt, with journalism in a considerably diminished position and no longer in charge.

For his part, Schramm came to believe that the attachment to journalism had a significant disadvantage. As Rogers wrote in his 1994 book, people from other disciplines "would be less likely to participate in communication study if such research were headquartered in a school of journalism, which other disciplines were likely to perceive as irrelevant to their research interests." Schramm addressed that problem by establishing his "institutes" of communication studies — within the journalism programs but with enough autonomy to appeal to academics from other fields.

In exchange for providing the home for such institutes, journalism education programs were offered a chance to enhance their dignity. "A communication research institute could serve as a source of prestige for a school of journalism that may have been looked down upon by professors in other fields because of the perceived trade school nature of journalism training," Rogers noted.

When Schramm established his Ph.D.-granting programs in the late 1940s and '50s, Rogers added, he "went one big step beyond Bleyer: He established a doctoral program in mass communication, not in journalism as at Wisconsin." Many of the newly minted Ph.D.s in mass communication were hired by Bleyer's former students. And within a decade, Ph.D.s educated in the Schramm tradition fanned out

---

Partnership with history

Gene Roberts, managing editor of *The New York Times*, who is on leave from teaching journalism at the University of Maryland, believes a university partnership between journalism and history would have been far preferable to the prevailing one between journalism and communication. Roberts noted that history searches, as journalism does, for the people, information and ideas that tell the stories of communities, countries, movements, issues, problems, and celebrations of events great and small, ugly and beautiful.

"I think journalism education took some sort of wrong turn and went into communications esoterica instead of taking a turn into history," he said. "I think history would have been a much better partnership for journalism. I think if it had broken that way … we would be exploring other paths and looking for (other) answers to the future."

to faculties around the country. The stage was set for an elevation of Ph.D in mass communication as the standard for journalism teachers.

There was a significant difference between the Bleyer stream and Schramm stream of scholars. Those who studied under Bleyer had been journalists, and their primary interest remained journalism. Those who studied under Schramm had found the infrastructure of journalism education crucial to their existence, and their interest in journalism was secondary.

Rogers and Stanford University communication Professor Steven H. Chaffee wrote in 1994 in "Communication and Journalism from 'Daddy' Bleyer to Wilbur Schramm: A Palimpsest," in *Journalism Monographs*: "Schramm's goal was to study what mass media institutions do and how they affect people. … If journalism, or journalism education, got upgraded in the process, so much the better, but that was not Schramm's primary concern." For Schramm, according to Rogers and Chaffee, work on issues directly related to journalism was "an episode, not a career."

Through Schramm and his academic descendants, the "takeover of existing university units" continued — first and with great success the takeovers of journalism education programs, and later, but with much less success, "communication study also began to invade departments of speech," Rogers wrote in his book.

Originally, doctoral students in communication studies were required, as a condition of admission to the communication doctoral programs, to have "several years of experience in the mass media, ideally in newspaper journalism. An unstated reason for this requirement," Rogers wrote, "was so that when these students completed their Ph.D. degrees, they would be considered for employment in schools of journalism. Eventually, by the mid-1960s, the media experience requirement was changed officially in graduate school catalogs to 'or equivalent,' and finally it was dropped." Despite eliminating professional experience as a qualification for teaching in journalism programs, Rogers noted that communication professors "must teach their students, especially undergraduates, the practical skills of communication: effective public speaking, newswriting, film-making, how to design and pretest advertising messages."

According to surveys conducted for this study, the notion that expertise is not needed to teach journalism skills is now commonplace in journalism education.

'Green-Eyeshades' and 'Chi-Squares' square off

Not all journalism educators sat passively as the infrastructures of their programs were taken over by communication studies scholars, even as they sheltered this new discipline. Nor did all journalism educators easily accept the idea that professors with doctoral degrees and no professional experience could teach the basic and advanced intellectual skills of journalism.

There was a fight. It usually was framed as being between the "Green-Eyeshades" and "Chi-Squares," the demeaning nicknames each side gave the other. Journalism educators with backgrounds as journalists referred to their communication studies colleagues as "Chi-Squares" because of their considerable reliance on statistical research. The Green-Eyeshades got their label from the celluloid visor "once worn by newspaper copy editors to cut down on glare" from newsroom overhead lights, Rogers wrote, adding that the Green-Eyeshades "scoffed at the young communication scholars, whom they felt were irrelevant to the training of future journalists." The Chi-Squares, for their part, "had little respect" for the Green-Eyeshades and "opposed the older generation of journalism professors."

The scholarly approach of the young scholars with Ph.D. degrees "won the intellectual revolution in the schools bit by bit," as university administrators "were previously somewhat puzzled by their vocationally oriented schools of journalism," according to Rogers. He quoted Wayne Danielson, an academic descendant of Schramm and now professor and former dean of the College of Communication at the University of Texas, as saying journalism schools were regarded by university administrators as "something equivalent to a school of trailer park management."

Unfortunately, the intellectual nature and expertise of the two approaches apparently were not a significant part of the debate, even during the national fight between the two groups of educators. The power started to shift

> Not all journalism educators sat passively as the infrastructures of their programs were taken over by communication studies scholars, even as they sheltered this new discipline. Nor did all journalism educators easily accept the idea that professors with doctoral degrees and no professional experience could teach the basic and advanced intellectual skills of journalism.

Except in those few places where journalism feels that its intellectual underpinnings, dignity and strength are securely rooted and protected, the discipline needs to look carefully at the tangle it has become and make decisions about its future.

toward the Chi-Squares very quickly. A dramatic turn took place in 1955, when for the first time the Chi-Squares gained control of the Association for Education in Journalism, predecessor of the Association for Education in Journalism and Mass Communication. They have never relinquished it.

"Eventually, the younger generation of Chi-Squares outlived the Green-Eyeshades," Rogers wrote, "which settled their dispute on an actuarial basis at most schools of journalism in the United States."

Schramm's dream was not only that journalism education faculties would be populated primarily or exclusively by communication studies scholars and would exclude journalists. It also included the hope that these programs would change their names from "journalism" to "communication." It is disappointing, Rogers noted, that "journalism" was largely retained while "communication" was added to the name, as in "School of Journalism and Mass Communication." An AEJMC task force recommended deletion of the word "journalism" in 1994.

Thus, the push continues to complete the change started at mid-century.

But Lyle Nelson, a close friend of Wilbur Schramm for 25 years before Schramm's death in 1987, thinks Schramm probably would not approve of the changes that have evolved from his original vision. "It's dreadful what (the field of) communication studies has done to journalism education," said Nelson, former vice president of Stanford University and former chair of Stanford's Department of Communication.

Nelson was responsible for raising much of the considerable private money that supported Schramm's research at Stanford. "Wilbur was a brilliant man," said Nelson. "He invented the discipline of communication studies. It is important to understand that he had precious little interest in journalism (as a profession), but I am sure he did not want to destroy journalism (education), which is what has been happening in recent years."

Accreditation exacerbates the problem

Where does all of this leave journalism education today?

Except in those few places where journal-

ism feels that its intellectual underpinnings, dignity and strength are securely rooted and protected, the discipline needs to look carefully at the tangle it has become and make decisions about its future. In many programs it is a dysfunctional arrangement that seems to have grown like Topsy. Policies now fixed in concrete were adopted without a rational base. Many people have been left to perpetuate a journalism education system they did not create, may not even endorse but accept as inevitable.

That seems to be the case for the most powerful force in journalism education — the Accrediting Council on Education in Journalism and Mass Communications. A combination of representatives of educators and professionals, this group has enormous impact on the programs it evaluates and decides whether to accredit. The greatest impact comes from the reports written by the small evaluation teams (usually composed of one professional and two or three educators) that visit the journalism programs. The most recent evaluations of the 105 programs reviewed during the last six-year accreditation cycle revealed criticisms that later became the substance of policy changes, a road map for the future.

These evaluations are read not only by a program's administrators and faculty members, they also are presented to university central administrators. The philosophies endorsed and promoted in the evaluations cause actions to be taken by administrators both for and against journalism/mass communication programs.

The last six years of accreditation reports have three overarching messages:

- Faculty must do scholarly research.
- Journalism education programs should hire more faculty members with doctoral degrees.
- Faculty members are confused.

Indeed, the visiting committee reports indicated that the road to accreditation or reaccreditation is paved with doctoral degrees and shelves of refereed articles, often with more regard for quantity than quality. The reports also included comments by journalism educators, including new ones with doctoral degrees, suggesting widespread confusion about research and other requirements for tenure and promotion. That confusion was documented by two-thirds of the visiting committees. Stronger words were used in some cases: anxiety, even paralysis.

The visiting committee reports may have helped to reduce some of the confusion, so emphatic were they about the need for more scholarly research. Sixty-eight percent of the programs were told they had done too little of it. These specific suggestions were offered for remedying this perceived deficiency:

- Programs should hire more faculty members with doctoral degrees.
- Programs should establish clearer rewards for scholarly research.
- Faculty should spend less time with students.
- Faculty should spend less time critiquing student writing.
- Faculty should write more refereed articles.
- Faculty should write in more mainstream, less esoteric, scholarly journals.

Some other key findings from the analysis of the accreditation reports regarding faculty research:

- 17% of the reports said scholarly research had increased since the previous review of the program, though not enough in some of those cases.
- 32% of the programs were told they were producing a sufficient quantity of scholarly research.
- 66% of the evaluations included no comment on the quality of research being done. Comments that were made were a mix of positive and negative observations and often were general rather than specific, such as noting that a faculty has a national reputation for impressive research.

Though most visiting committees recommended hiring faculty with doctoral degrees as a way of increasing research production, whether a faculty had a large portion of doctoral degree holders did not seem to be an indicator of research volume. And while programs regarded as producing an inadequate quantity of research often were advised to hire young faculty members with doctoral degrees, some programs' young faculty members with

doctorates were criticized for not meeting research expectations. The expertise of faculty in the skills they teach is seldom mentioned in the evaluations.

Some of the highest praise for research was made about two of the very few programs that accept either scholarly or in-depth journalistic research — the practice that was strongly supported by faculty members in the Roper survey conducted for this study:

- The most superlative comments about the quality of research — either scholarly or journalistic — were made about the University of California, Berkeley, where only 18% of faculty members have doctoral degrees and where faculty members without doctoral degrees do both scholarly and journalistic research.
- Some of the highest praise for journalistic research was bestowed on the University of West Florida, where 91% of faculty members have doctoral degrees but most of them do journalistic research.

Accrediting teams try to influence program missions

Visiting teams are directed to place great emphasis on the mission that journalism programs have established and to conduct accreditation evaluations with strong respect for those missions. However, many team reports appear to be more an endorsement of team members' view of whether the program is what they think it should be, not whether is it living up to its mission. This is particularly evident in the evaluation of faculty qualifications and research. For instance:

- In 26% of the reports, visiting committees urged programs to accept only scholarly research, not journalistic research, as appropriate faculty research.
- 4% of the committees, in reporting on lack of policies on research, recommended programs establish policies that would accept either kind of research for tenure and promotion evaluations.

At New York University, faculty members received high praise from the accrediting team for several things, including their research. They were complimented for "rigorous teaching, critical inquiry" and were char-

Even at Missouri, ACEJMC emphasizes Ph.D.s and research

The venerable University of Missouri School of Journalism has long been considered one of the programs most strongly rooted in the teaching and understanding of journalism. But the last two evaluation teams to visit the school on behalf of the Accrediting Council for Education in Journalism and Mass Communications placed an emphasis on doctoral degrees and scholarly research that has become increasingly typical of accreditation reviews nationwide.

In the most recent reaccrediting report, the evaluators noted in October 1992 that the previous visiting team had expressed concern about faculty in-breeding and the number of faculty members without doctorates. The evaluators then applauded the school's response to that earlier criticism: "All tenure track hirings but one since 1989 have terminal degrees from other universities; hirings of additional faculty with doctorates have been made." Elsewhere in the report, the evaluators noted that "about half of the faculty with the rank of assistant professor or

above hold doctorates or a law degree. The most recent hires have tended to be individuals with doctorate(s), so this percentage has been increasing." The professional practitioners hired recently, the report noted, are not on a tenure track but work under contract, and "most spend from two to five years on the instructional staff."

The 1992 team also approvingly reported, "Following the 1986 re-accreditation visit, the School placed research productivity high on its priority list for improvements, and it is well on its way to establishing a reputation for significant contributions to the field — both scholarly and applied."

Two elements of the 1992 report are somewhat unusual compared with other evaluations. First, it spoke of scholarly research and "creative works" — an academic term for research other than traditional scholarly research — though the emphasis was clearly on scholarly research. Accrediting reviews more typically emphasize

only scholarly research.

Even more uncharacteristic was the team's expression of caution regarding the rush to increase the number of doctoral degree-holding faculty members and the quantity of scholarly research. The evaluators wrote that because "it will take some time before this new culture (of research) is firmly established [at Missouri], care must be taken to maintain the School's traditional role in journalism education." In accrediting reports elsewhere, concern about maintaining a focus on journalism is seldom noted.

But as at many other schools, new faculty at Missouri said they were confused about what was expected of them. They also expressed confusion about a proposed "professional employment track" designated for people hired primarily because of the strength of their professional backgrounds. "Some of the newer faculty were unclear and unsure of what would be expected of them" if they chose that track, the evaluators noted.

acterized as being "prolific in publishing ... books of current and enduring interest." They also were congratulated for involving students in their research and writing. This faculty is composed primarily of experienced journalists, and their research consists largely of in-depth journalism and sophisticated historical and critical analysis of journalism.

The program, despite its attributes, received a report that demonstrates how ingrained the push for the doctoral degree and scholarly research has become in the accreditation-review process — and how the review process itself could become an instrument to force a program with a well-conceived mission to turn that mission on its head. The committee wrote that it was concerned at the outset of the visit about whether the faculty's nontraditional research would meet the expectations of the university. However, as the visit unfolded, the team's conversations with uni-

versity administrators revealed that the university strongly supported diverse types of research and was particularly pleased with that being done by the journalism professors. Still, the team was not satisfied. It concluded that the program should assume that future administrators of the university might not have such a lenient view and instead might require traditional scholarly research.

There are indications in other accreditation reports that visiting review committees also feel free to recommend radical shifts in program mission. A program with a strong journalism emphasis was told it should add advertising and public relations emphases. Several programs were told they should consider convergence into one general curriculum. Strangely, one program was advised both that its faculty was spread too thinly and that it should consider adding three more areas of emphasis.

Writing gets little attention

While a visiting team's task is large, given what it must accomplish during a short stay on campus, most teams pay little or no attention to what most journalism educators and journalists would consider critical matters: whether teachers teach writing well, whether students are writing well and whether ethics is being taught.

- 74% of the accrediting reports for the last six years included no comment about the quality of writing instruction in the journalism program. (Seven percent included positive comments about writing instruction; 19% included negative comments.)
- No reports included comments about the quality of student writing.
- 78% of the reports included no comments about the quality of campus print or broadcast journalism.
- 50% of the reports included no comment about ethics instruction.

The emphasis of recent visiting teams on whether faculty members have doctoral degrees and are producing sufficient scholarly research is not supported in the official purpose and stated standards of the Accrediting Council. The standards are much more flexible and allow much more diversity of philosophies than the teams themselves tend to support. The teams' emphases, endorsed by the Accrediting Council's adoption of the reports each year, seem to have emerged spontaneously from the educators who have majority membership on the teams, and from the increasingly dominant culture of journalism/mass communication programs. That culture pays decreasing regard for expertise when hiring faculty and evaluating programs; it likewise pays decreasing regard for whether the intellectual skills and related historical and ethical groundings of journalism are being taught well.

There's also a culture of friendly fear in journalism programs, particularly among administrators and others involved in the accrediting process. It's a culture that inhibits philosophical discussions of some of the most important issues in journalism education.

One administrator, Joan Konner, dean of the Graduate School of Journalism at Columbia University, discussed this culture of fear associated with the accreditation process. "The tendency is to be more generous and silent than we think we ought to be because representatives of other institutions will sit in judgment on our institution," she noted. "Because of this — it's really a conflict of interest — we don't have the philosophical discussions that need to happen in order to protect journalism from what's happening in a lot of schools."

Some other administrators expressed similar views during interviews for this study, but they declined to go on the record with their comments.

Journalism education was stunted at mid-century

What has the tangle journalism education has become done to journalism programs and to journalism?

The takeover of journalism education by communication studies probably means that both journalism and journalism education lost substantial progress that likely would have grown from the journalism education seeds sown during the first half of this century.

Those first deep thinkers about journalism education — Bleyer, Pulitzer and others — planted and nourished a view of journalism that was focused on improving journalists by going beyond mere training. They wanted to educate and encourage minds to become curious and searching. They wanted to use the "best traditions of the university," as Columbia University's Carey put it, to help build a more mature, more enlightened form of journalism.

One of the most visible results of the stunting of journalism education is the diffusion of master's degree programs. In the last six-year accreditation cycle, which included all schools now accredited, 56% of the master's programs were described in visiting committee reports as unfocused and in need of restructuring or elimination.

Students enroll in these programs to gain preparation for becoming journalists or for going on to doctoral work, but in many schools they find neither need fulfilled. From the accreditation records, it appears that the master's degree programs are where the sometimes schizophrenic nature of today's journalism education is most evident. Many of these programs consist of a few journalism skills

> "
> We don't have the philosophical discussions that need to happen in order to protect journalism from what's happening in a lot of schools.
> "
>
> **Joan Konner**
> Dean of the Graduate School
> of Journalism
> Columbia University

courses but not enough to prepare someone adequately as beginning journalist, and, on the other hand, a few communication studies theory courses but not enough to prepare someone for advanced scholarly work. The programs try to be all things to all students, but they end up, regrettably, being not enough for anyone.

The changes in journalism education over the last half of the 20th century may have affected journalism as deeply as they affected journalism education. Just as journalism education was limited in its progress at mid-century, so was its contribution to the profession.

At their best, journalism education programs seldom get beyond producing graduates with only beginning skills, not the kind of graduates that schools of business and architecture are expected to produce. Business and architecture students learn from people whose expertise helps prepare students to be "so far ahead of the curve on technical advancement that mid-career professionals in their fields shudder to see them coming," as Philip Meyer, University of North Carolina journalism professor, put it. "They know that the kids have useful information that hadn't even been discovered when they were in school," Meyer said. They expect graduates to arrive ready to challenge and stretch the profession.

Journalism and journalism education disconnect

This stunting of journalism education at mid-century probably also contributed to journalism education's increasing disconnection from journalism, a disconnection that has diminished both institutions. It undoubtedly led to the failure of journalism education to initiate or at least collaborate in continuing-education programs for journalists. If journalism education programs were no longer interested in developing expertise in journalism and did not require faculty members to be expert journalists, many of the programs eventually found themselves with inadequate expertise — not to mention lack of interest — to offer the kind of continuing education enjoyed by other professions.

This growing disconnection also probably left the profession adrift and alienated from journalism education in ways that would have been less likely without the takeover by communication studies. Once journalism education was diminished within the university, journalism, unlike some other professions, was on its own to find ways to manage rapid change, deal with ethical quandaries and address other major issues. Journalists since mid-century have not been confident that great minds in journalism education are contemplating ways to improve journalism or developing expertise in issues that affect news coverage.

In that vacuum of continuing education for the profession and general lack of leadership, inspiration and criticism from the journalism education/communication studies programs, journalists themselves have been the chief instigators of progress in the profession. That has been true during years of great pressures and changes in which a collaboration of minds might have been mutually beneficial. For all the justifiable criticism of journalism — and newsrooms did stumble through many major changes — it should be acknowledged that with minimal collaboration with its natural partner, journalism education, the profession solved thorny problems arising from introduction of new technology, developed new research methods, became more diverse in hiring and news coverage, cultivated new writing forms, found innovative uses of the visual arts, and recognized its obligation to serve communities better.

The archives of the Pulitzer Prizes, the du Pont and Peabody broadcast awards, the Investigative Reporters and Editors awards, and other respected journalism competitions contain a treasure trove of creativity and expertise that illustrate how the profession has matured. Quite a few of the editors, news directors, reporters and photographers who produced such sterling examples of journalism might be interested in becoming teachers of the intellectual skills they have developed so well. Unfortunately, despite their much-valued expertise in the profession, they would be unwelcome as tenure-track teachers in most journalism education programs today because they lack doctoral degrees.

Is the synergy working?

Journalism educators might consider assessing the "synergy" between journalism and the other elements of journalism/mass communication programs. Does the synergy support education that prepares people to become journalists?

For some striking parallels, the educators might want to ponder what is happening in the corporate world as communications companies gobble up one another. *New Yorker* news media critic Ken Auletta wrote in November 1995 that synergy, "a cant word of the 1990s," was a mantra of the heads of large corporations as they announced the purchase of media conglomerates that include news organizations. For example, Michael H. Jordan, chief executive officer of Westinghouse, said his company's 1995 purchase of CBS would save hundreds of millions of dollars a year by combining the two companies' broadcasting assets and bring about "tremendous marketing synergies."

As Auletta pondered the mega-purchases, including Disney buying Capital Cities/ABC, he said they were "no friend of journalism. ... If these trends represent 'synergy,' it's a bit too much like the synergy between cigarette smoke and lung tissue. As 'communications' companies get bigger, the role of the journalists within them is diminished and diluted. Inside a behemoth like Disney or Time Warner, news rarely matches the profit margins of other divisions, such as entertainment or computer software or cable, and thus loses internal clout. To the top executives of these giants, the news operation looks more and more like a box somewhere out on the edge of the organizational chart."

Perhaps the grafting of communication studies onto journalism education has produced a synergy similar to the one in the news business — one that submerges rather than improves and protects journalism.

Questions to ponder

This study of journalism education was conducted at a time when the decisions of some news corporation executives were causing journalists to wonder if stockholders' dividends had become more important than the quality and ideals of journalism. Perhaps without knowing it, these journalists were experiencing what journalism educators have been experiencing for years. "What's wrong with this picture?" is asked today not only in photo-

journalism classes. It is being asked by journalists and journalism educators, many of whom wonder if the main keepers of journalism are letting journalism wither.

In both institutions — the university and the news organization — many people are asking that question, often silently, for they seem to be paralyzed by what New York University journalism Professor Jay Rosen has aptly described as journalists' "devastating illusion of themselves as bystanders." It is a powerless posture journalists often assume, or feel pushed into, in newsrooms — and for a minority of them, later as journalism educators. They act as though they can have no voice in shaping the institutions in which they work, in asking basic questions about mission. Instead of assuming their role as participants in decision-making, for instance, many journalists wait while others decide what technology will do to journalism, and journalism educators wait while communication theorists and university administrators decide what to do to journalism education.

Journalism education would be well-served if faculty members would examine what has happened to their programs. Was journalism taken over, was it tangled or was it improved? Does journalism education have its integrity intact? Is it recognized as a distinct discipline that prepares the minds of a profession that has a responsibility to stimulate the discourse of democracy? Are journalism educators chosen primarily for their expertise as journalists and as expert analysts of journalism? Or does the doctoral degree, without significant regard for expertise in the intellectual skills of journalism, radiate primacy? Are journalism educators treated as full citizens of the university with equal responsibilities to teach well and to create new knowledge through research? And if the educators meet these obligations and thereby serve both the needs of journalism and the central mission of the university, do they have the same opportunities for tenure and promotion that other scholars enjoy?

If the answers to these questions indicate journalism education is not healthy, will journalism educators take steps to heal it? If journalism is dying, as many communication educators have said, will journalism educators conclude that journalism education also

"What's wrong with this picture?" is asked today not only in photo-journalism classes. It is being asked by journalists and journalism educators, many of whom wonder if the main keepers of journalism are letting journalism wither.

should die? Or will they recognize that the practice of journalism is essential to a democratic society and that if it is in fact endangered, they should help renew and save it — not be part of the deathwatch or, even worse, unwitting accomplices in the death. Journalism can fall and rise again in new places and in new media, but that can happen only if the ideals of journalism are alive.

It would help if journalists and journalism educators would give more dignity to journalism, beginning with how they describe it.

Without shame, embarrassment, false modesty or false macho, they should recognize it as an intellectual profession, not just a craft. This self-acknowledgment might help the university to better understand the true nature of journalism and the importance of the university in being the proper greenhouse for future journalists. As it moves into the 21st century, journalism will need all the brainpower it can harness to enable society to see itself reflected sensitively, honestly and fully.

6 Conclusions

How's that "baby," journalism education, doing? Is it being thrown out with the bath water, as Dean Rowland asked at the AEJMC convention in 1995?

Though its roots in American universities are more than a century old, journalism education has the characteristics of an experiment — not a dynamic, evolving experiment, but a fragile, unsure, endangered experiment. Journalism is being de-emphasized, submerged or threatened with elimination on many campuses.

The baby has had a very hard time. In some places it has been respected and encouraged to flourish. In an overwhelming majority of programs, though, it has been and continues to be vulnerable.

- Vulnerable to the communication studies forces that came into journalism education in the 1950s and announced, "Move over, we're taking over."
- Vulnerable to new forces, which are a natural evolution of the mid-century communication studies movement, that now say, "Educate generic communicators, not journalists."
- Vulnerable to some of the same budget-cutting pressures that have threatened other university disciplines in the last decade.
- Vulnerable to its own failure to explain and defend itself well.
- Vulnerable at times to its own failure to recognize the "other half" of university life: in addition to teaching, research that helps the university fulfill its responsibilities to create new knowledge. Journalists are peculiarly well-qualified to fulfill this task but often have resisted or been discouraged from doing it.
- Vulnerable to its historic inferiority complex, which made it easy prey for colleagues who did not recognize — may not have understood — the depth and sophistication of the intellectual skills possessed by master journalists.
- Vulnerable to university administrators and colleagues who too often assumed that institutional respect must be built on quantity of doctoral degrees rather than on quality of minds and expertise.
- Vulnerable to an accrediting system that increasingly has emphasized faculty degrees and traditional scholarly research instead of in-depth journalistic research and essential intellectual skills and issues of journalism.
- Vulnerable to news organizations that have not paid attention to journalism education, either as monitor of quality or as financial supporter.

Many journalism educators have made it clear during the course of this study that they would like to see journalism education recover and renew its mission. Moreover, there seems to be a vast reservoir of interest among many journalists in increasing the quality and the depth of journalism education. Some of these journalists already are on faculties (with and without doctoral degrees) but have found themselves in second-class citizenship positions there. Others would like to join faculties in the future and still others simply care deeply about journalism and about education.

Given the importance of journalism in a democratic society, it is crucial not to let the baby go down the drain. But the declining regard for journalism expertise in many journalism programs, as well as the creation of generic communication education and the low starting salaries offered by the profession, are pushing the baby toward the drain. A crucial

> Many journalism educators have made it clear that they would like to see journalism education recover and renew its mission. Moreover, there seems to be a vast reservoir of interest among many journalists in increasing the quality and the depth of journalism education.

As the 21st century nears, it seems an appropriate time for journalism education to take stock of both the right and wrong turns that took place during journalism education's first century — and choose what path to take in the new century.

finding in the Weaver-Wilhoit-Johnstone studies — that journalists age 25 and younger were 12% of all journalists in 1971 and 1982 but now only 4% — is striking evidence of what's happening to the baby.

As the 21st century nears, it seems an appropriate time for journalism education as a whole and in individual programs to take stock of both the right and wrong turns that took place during journalism education's first century — and choose what path to take in the new century.

Journalism education faculty members need to decide what they believe is the essence of journalism — as distinct from communication studies or preparation for other communications professions — and whether they want excellent teaching of journalism to be a least part of their mission. They need to recognize what journalism expertise they already have and what expertise they need to teach journalism at beginning and advanced levels. Only in doing so will they fulfill their responsibilities to students, to their universities, to the journalism profession, and to the democratic society that needs highly skilled and wise journalists.

The baby has been going through a profound identity crisis. Journalism educators and journalists who care about the future of journalism should make its rescue a priority.

Recommendations
for the improvement of journalism education

RECOMMENDATIONS FOR JOURNALISM EDUCATION PROGRAMS

Develop a journalism culture.

Wherever journalism is based on campuses — under an umbrella of mass communications or within English, business or any another area of study — it needs to be nurtured, protected and respected as a distinct area of study and not submerged into general communication courses.

The unique public-service mission of journalism should be an integral part of all aspects of journalism education, central to the culture of journalism created in the academy. Journalism education should be filled with continuous discussion of journalism and its relationship to society — including the best and worst of past and present journalism; new journalism jobs; distinguished achievements; unsavory practices; and evolving standards, technologies and ethics. Journalists and seasoned critics from various backgrounds should be active participants in these discussions.

Promote the planet as the palette of journalism and journalism education.

The study and practice of journalism are interdisciplinary. Journalism is a search for knowledge, truth and understanding through various means of inquiry across all university disciplines and all parts of the communities journalists serve. This interdisciplinary nature of journalism should be implicit and explicit in journalism education.

The student of journalism must be exposed to a wide range of academic subjects and not concentrate excessively on communication studies or journalism studies. An education as a journalism student — studying widely while also learning the skills, laws, ethics and history of journalism — should be the beginning of lifelong study.

Understand and use new and diverse technologies, but focus on the main objective: learning to find and write stories.

It is important for teachers and students to update continuously their knowledge and use of various technologies and means of distributing news and feature stories — newspapers, magazines, broadcasting and on-line. But teachers and students should not lose sight of the main point of journalism — how to find and tell word and visual stories.

Recognize journalism as an intellectual activity and journalists as educators.

Journalism educators should be recognized as equal partners with their colleagues in other academic disciplines. Journalism educators' intellectual acumen and expert knowledge place them at the heart of the central mission of any self-respecting university: engagement in intellectual search and discovery and clear description of resulting discoveries.

Even while being intellectuals, sometimes in ways that merit as much respect as the best of traditional scholarly accomplishments, journalism professionals and journalism educators often have demurred from acknowledging or recognizing the intellectual nature of their work: "Just a trade" … "Just nuts-and-bolts courses."

The language used to describe journalism needs to go beyond the language of craft and trade and embrace some of the best language of the university. Not to do so may perpetuate a false modesty that has been harmful to journalism within the university.

Recognize the master journalist as a full and needed citizen of the academic community.

A journalism education program needs to include on its faculty journalists who have developed the expertise of journalism in the creative cauldron of professional work. The master journalist needed in the classroom is a master not only of the intellectual and technical skills of written and/or visual aspects of journalism, but she or he also should be capable of analyzing, with both a close-up and a wide-angle intellectual lens, the problems and challenges of journalism.

Faculties should establish criteria for evaluating the work of journalists to determine if they are master journalists. These criteria should be determined in consultation with outstanding off-campus professionals and journalism educators and with colleagues within the university — a joint professional/academic peer review — who are part of the evaluation of applicants for teaching positions but who may not be familiar with the intellectual nature of journalism and how journalists should be evaluated.

Require all tenure and tenure-track faculty — journalists and traditional scholars — to conduct sustained research, writing and publication related to journalism.

To be fully accepted as a citizen of the university, the master journalist who aspires to teach must recognize that most universities require both teaching and research. An overemphasis on research can diminish the importance and quality of teaching. But in their most enlightened forms, research and teaching nourish each other. Student involvement — for instance, with educators in either traditional academic research or in-depth journalistic projects — is likely to expand teaching and learning significantly.

Journalism educators with and without doctoral degrees have expressed a strong interest in having the option, not now available in many universities, of conducting research and writing that is substantial journalistic works, traditional scholarly work or a combination of both. Such flexibility would encourage faculty members to develop their expertise as advanced journalists and as scholars of journalism. This open approach to required research and publication could also stimulate experimentation, advancement of skills and analysis of a wide spectrum of journalism issues.

Develop schools of thought and practice.

Journalism education units should consider creating one or more areas of emphasis in which faculty members become known for well-developed expertise in a particular school of thought and practice. This expertise would be a valuable resource to journalists, students and other journalism educators.

Examples of schools of thought and practice are the expertise in public affairs that the College of Journalism at the University of Maryland is building, the expertise in computer-assisted reporting that the Walter Cronkite School of Journalism and Telecommunication at Arizona State University is building, and the expertise in ethnic-diversity journalism issues that the Department of Journalism at San Francisco State University is building.

Develop graduate programs focused on journalism.

Develop master's degree programs that are clearly focused, either on preparing students to become journalists or on preparing them for doctoral programs. Doctoral programs should include a strong emphasis on issues affecting journalism.

Develop graduate programs that permit

students to take advantage of links between journalism and the wide range of subjects in the university and general community that are the palette of journalism. Get beyond a focus on the process of communication and develop expertise on the substance of journalism.

Educate students to think critically and adventurously.

Teach in ways that infuse students with the skills, mission and intellectual challenges posed by old and new issues in journalism. Teach in ways that help students develop as problem-spotters of the issues of both the society they will cover and the profession they will enter. Teach them to be constant explorers beyond the world of their own experience, knowledge, interest and comfort. Such an approach should help future journalists work effectively in a multicultural newsroom and in the multicultural world they will cover.

Educate students to be cutting-edge journalists.

Prepare students to think creatively in words and visual elements, to know the old methods of research and writing, and to anticipate and experiment with new methods. Prepare them to be innovative thinkers and planners about the larger issues that affect journalism.

Journalism students should graduate with more than just basic skills and a generally well-rounded education. Newsrooms should look forward to their arrival, not as people who will need remedial assistance to get to the starting line, but as people full of awareness of the world and of journalism and ready to help meet new challenges. Like the best business, law and architecture students, graduating

journalism students should be ready to infuse new energy and new ideas into newsrooms.

Expand the mission of journalism education to include professional development/continuing education for journalists.

Develop programs that serve the continuing needs of journalists for sustained education, a need expressed strongly by journalists and endorsed in this study by journalism educators. This responsibility to continue the education of graduates has long been recognized by schools of business, law, medicine, education, architecture and others.

Reform the accreditation-review process in ways that would improve journalism education.

Change the journalism accreditation process to include more evaluation of quality by outside evaluators: quality of mission statements, quality of faculty qualifications and teaching, quality of student learning as evidenced in the journalism they produce and the issues they articulate, quality of teaching skills, and quality of faculty research — both traditional scholarly research and journalistic research.

Comments in accreditation evaluations regarding the small number of doctoral degrees within a faculty and about the low number of scholarly papers published by faculty often lead to major changes in policy and practice.

The area of journalism education that is regarded as most important by both print and broadcast journalists, writing skills, also should be part of the accreditation-evaluation process.

RECOMMENDATIONS FOR NEWS ORGANIZATIONS

Share responsibility for creating the next generation of journalists.

The student boom is over. The supply of new labor no longer can be taken for granted. If news organizations want a solid future, they should help build it, not only by adopting new technologies but also by nurturing the next generation of journalists. Create internships that are designed to be learning experiences and to give a realistic introduction to what journalism is like. Assign newsroom colleagues

to be mentors to student interns throughout their internships. Set high performance standards and provide helpful feedback continuously.

Pay salaries that encourage young journalists to build a future in journalism and that remove the industry stigma of low salaries.

Inasmuch as young journalists are the future of journalism, they need to be treated as an important resource. Low-paying news organizations should compensate new hires better. Currently at many news organizations, starting salaries are so low that new journalists, despite their enthusiasm and commitment to the profession, must, out of self-respect and economic necessity, consider leaving it. Journalism students, while similarly motivated, may never enter the profession.

Larger news organizations should reverse the current trend of hiring young journalists as temporary or part-time employees with few or no benefits. Broadcasters and smaller publications should replace unpaid internships with paid internships, so students with limited resources can gain journalism experience.

Protect and support journalism as an area of study.

News organizations should carefully monitor journalism education to determine if programs teach journalism as a distinct discipline and if journalism educators have expertise in journalism and are engaged in research related to it. In a vacuum of inattention from the profession, journalism education could easily become disconnected from the mission and needs of journalism.

Build partnerships with journalism education programs.

Although the independence of academic institutions is imperative, more partnerships between journalism education and news organizations could enrich each side. News organizations could:

- Encourage news staffers to be mentors and coaches. Experiments at the San Francisco State University Department of Journalism that linked writing coaches with students demonstrated that sustained coaching by professionals significantly increased the retention of students and also significantly increased student interest in journalism.
- Ask news staffers to serve on journalism education advisory committees and peer-review committees.
- Provide money for scholarships, internships, research by students and faculty, and various small and large needs of programs for which university funds may not be available.
- Collaborate on substantial journalism projects in which journalism professors and students could produce work for publication or broadcast by news organizations.
- Collaborate with journalism education programs to introduce high school students to journalism.
- Make newsrooms available as laboratories for journalism educators' research projects on issues in journalism.

RECOMMENDATIONS FOR JOURNALISM EDUCATION PROGRAMS, NEWS ORGANIZATIONS AND FOUNDATIONS

Assist journalists in preparing to become journalism educators.

Assistance is needed in how to translate professional skills and accomplishment into academic vita, how to translate professional skills into lessons that go beyond war stories, and how to develop a plan for sustained research and writing that builds on current expertise.

Assist journalism education programs in hiring master journalists.

Some journalism education programs that want to hire master journalists need assistance in establishing hiring, tenure and promotion standards for such faculty members.

They also need assistance in convincing colleagues in other disciplines and university administrators of the intellectual merit and necessity of such expertise on faculties.

Fund independent research focused on journalism.

Research and publication should be seen as a way for faculty, working with students, to discover new ideas and methods that could help renew both journalism and journalism education.

Help create a vision of a renewed journalism education:

- That is rooted in the mission of journalism as a stimulator of informed public discourse.

- That respects the separate but shared central missions of journalism and universities to find new knowledge and to convey both old and new knowledge.
- That relies on expert journalists and other expert analysts of journalism.
- That helps create a journalism profession that vigorously protects the First Amendment rights of journalists and other citizens in order to serve the public's interests more honestly and fully.

Appendix

Survey of Journalism Educators

Profile   73
Changes in journalism education   76
Changes in student interest in journalism   78
Student requirements   80
Educators' links with profession   81
Educators' experience as journalists   82
Educators' description of selves and introductory skills   85
Qualifications/requirements for teaching journalism   87
Philosophy of journalism education   90
Links with professional development for journalists   91

Survey of Newsroom Recruiters and Supervisors

Evaluation of journalism education   92
Newsroom links with journalism education   94
Assessment of recent interns   96
Hiring practices/policies for interns   98
Hiring practices/policies for new journalists   100
Assessment of newsrooms   103
Characteristics and trends in interns/newsroom staffing   106
News organizations' involvement in education   108

Survey of New Journalists

Profile   111
Journalism vs. other majors as best preparation   115
Journalism experience as part of journalism education   116
Nature and impact of the journalism curriculum   117
Attitudes of journalism professors toward journalism   122
Quality of instruction, qualifications of instructors   123
How well journalism education prepares for profession   125
Job satisfaction   126
Performance of self and news organization   130
Technology in journalism education and in journalism   133
Atmosphere of newsroom, concern about profession   134
Education needs, interests of new journalists   136

Voices
Journalism Educators   140
News Professionals   155

University Policies
University of California, Berkeley   168
University of Colorado, Boulder   170
Kansas State University   173
Ohio University   175
University of Oregon   176

Survey of Journalism Educators

Profile

What is your sex? (Q.61)

- 79% of tenured faculty are men and 21% are women.
- 61% of faculty on tenure track are men and 39% are women.
- The proportion of women among those who have been teaching 10 years or less (30%) is twice what it is for those who have been teaching 11 years or more (15%).
- The portion of women on journalism faculties is highest in the Midwest (29%) and lowest in the West (20%).

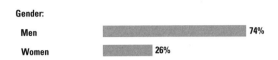

Gender:

- The gender composition when viewed by age groups: 60 and older, 85% men and 15% women; age 45-59, 76% men and 24% women; 44 and younger, 64% men and 36% women.

What is your race? (Q.62)

- The number of ethnic-minority journalism faculty members is so small that the potentially large margin of error in responses makes it impossible to analyze the data by race.

Race:

What is your age? (Q.60)

- 43% of women and 28% of men on journalism faculties are age 44 or younger.
- 48% of women and 55% of men are age 45-59.
- 9% of women and 18% of men are 60 or older.

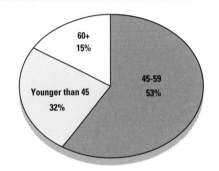

Is your unit accredited by the Accrediting Council on Education in Journalism and Mass Communications? (Q.45)

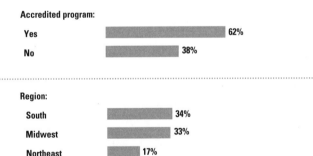

Accredited program:

Educators are from (region):

Region:

Region	%
South	34%
Midwest	33%
Northeast	17%
West	16%

Does your unit offer degrees in journalism education at the following levels? (Q.1)

- 88% of accredited programs and 28% of non-accredited programs offer degrees at the master's level.
- 35% of accredited programs and 4% of non-accredited programs offer degrees at the doctoral level.

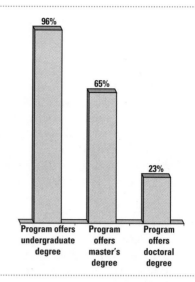

Have you ever worked full-time as a journalist? (Q.21)

- 21% of those with doctoral degrees never worked full-time as journalists, as compared with 11% of those without doctoral degrees.
- The portion of faculty, by age, who never worked full-time as journalists: 23% of those 44 and younger; 15% of those age 45-59; 13% of those 60 or older.

When viewed as portions of all journalism educators: 36% worked more than 10 years as a full-time journalist, 47% worked 10 years or less, 17% had no experience as journalists.

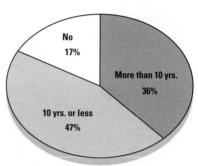

How long did you work as a full-time journalist? (Q.22)

- Portions within age groups that had more than 10 years' experience: 38% of those 44 or younger; 41% of those 45-59; 67% of those 60 or older.
- By region, the lowest portion of journalism educators who worked more than 10 years as journalists was in the South, 36%, and the highest was in the Northeast, 57%.

- 66% of those who did not have a doctoral degree and 28% of those who had a doctoral degree worked more than 10 years as journalists.
- There were significant differences in the length of full-time experience among faculty when viewed by tenure status: 33% of tenured faculty had more than 10 years' experience as journalists, in contrast with 54% of faculty on tenure track.

Which of the following degrees do you hold? (Q.50)

- (Q.50b) The same portion, 4%, of journalism educators as new journalists do not have a bachelor's degree.
- 70% of men and 61% of women on journalism faculty have doctoral degrees.
- 78% of those who are tenured and 72% of those who are on tenure track have doctoral degrees.
- Faculty in the South have the lowest portion (36%) with more than 10 years' experience, and faculty in the Northeast have the highest portion (57%) with more than 10 years' experience.
- 40% of women on journalism faculties have a doctorate in mass communication, as compared with 51% of men.
- By region, the highest concentration of mass communication doctorates is in the South, 54%, and the lowest concentration is in the Northeast, 38%.

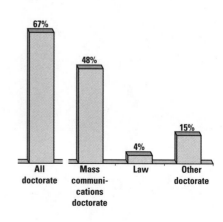

What is your current academic position or rank? (Q.53)

- With increased experience as journalists, journalism faculty rank decreases:
  - 25% of those with more than 10 years' experience as journalists are full professors, and 42% of those with less than 10 years' experience are full professors.
  - 27% of those with more than 10 years' experience are associate professors, and 30% of those with 10 years or less experience are associate professors.
  - 29% of those with more than 10 years' experience are assistant professors, the lowest rank for tenured or tenure-track faculty, and 21% of those with less than 10 years' experience are assistant professors.
  - Among adjunct and other ranks that are neither tenured nor on tenure track were 21% of the faculty who have more than 10 years' experience and 9% of the faculty who have less than 10 years' experience.
  - 38% of men and 18% of women on journalism faculties are full professors.
  - 35% of women and 20% of men are assistant professors.
  - 19% of those without doctoral degrees and 42% of those who

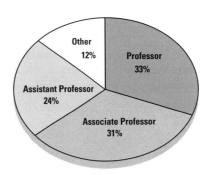

have doctoral degrees are full professors.
  - 30% of those who do not have doctoral degrees and 2% of those who have doctorates are in non-tenured and non-tenure-track positions.
  - 31% of faculty at accredited programs and 20% at non-accredited programs are assistant professors.
  - Age of full professors: 9% of those who are 44 and under; 41% of those who are 45-59; 57% of those who are 60 or older.

Are you currently tenured, on tenure track or full-time non-tenure track? (Q.56)

- 68% of men and 51% of women on journalism education faculties are tenured.
- 19% of the men and 34% of the women are in tenure-track positions.
- 12% of the men and 15% of the women are in non-tenured, non-tenure-track positions.
- 50% of those with more than 10 years' experience as journalists and 74% of those with 10 or fewer years' experience are tenured.
- 74% of those with doctoral degrees and 47% of those without doctoral degrees are tenured.
- Full-time non-tenured and non-tenure-track faculty include 31% of those who do not have doctoral degrees and 3% of those who have doctoral degrees.

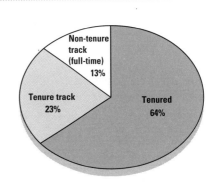

How long have you been teaching full-time? (Q.49)

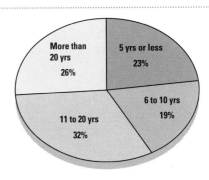

Changes in journalism education

Please indicate whether your journalism education program has experienced any of the following changes in the past 10 years. (Q.2)

- (Q.2a) 65% of educators without doctoral degrees say their programs have increased emphasis on journalism; 38% of those with doctoral degrees say their programs have increased emphasis on journalism.

- (Q.2b) 19% of faculty from non-accredited programs and 7% from accredited programs reported their programs have de-emphasized student preparation for entering journalism in the last 10 years.

- (Q.2e) 14% of faculty from non-accredited programs, in contrast to 8% from accredited programs, reported their programs have de-emphasized skills courses in the last 10 years.

- (Q.2f) 42% of faculty from non-accredited programs, in contrast with 31% from accredited programs, reported their programs have placed more emphasis on mass communication theory courses in the last 10 years.

- By age, the largest increase in emphasis on mass communication theory courses was reported by the youngest

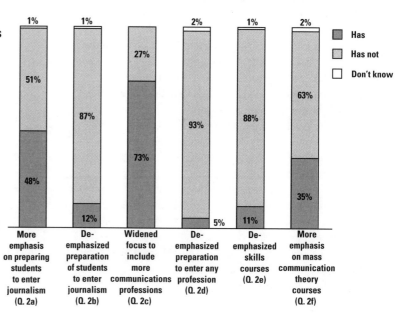

age group, faculty 44 or younger — 42% reported an increase in emphasis on mass communication theory courses in their journalism education programs.

How important was preparing students to enter journalism in your program 10 years ago? (Q.5)

- 83% of faculty from accredited programs, in contrast to 60% from non-accredited programs, reported that preparing students to enter journalism was very important 10 years ago.

How important is preparing students to enter journalism in your program now? (Q.6)

- Preparing students to enter journalism became less important from 10 years ago to the present in both accredited and non-accredited programs, but the greater decrease was reported by faculty from accredited programs:
  - The portion from accredited programs went from 83% who said it was very important 10 years ago to 75% who said it was very important today.
  - The portion from non-accredited programs went from 60% who said it was very important in their programs 10 years ago to 55% percent who said it was very important today.
  - The same portion of faculty without doctorates — 77% regarding 10 years ago, 78% regarding now — said preparing students to enter journalism was very important in their programs. The portion of those with doctoral degrees

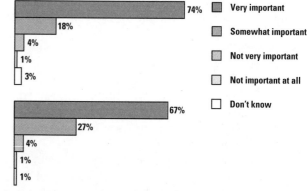

declined from 72% who said it was very important 10 years ago to 61% who said it was very important now.

- The importance of preparing students to enter journalism declined in all regions except the Northeast, where 71% reported it was very important in their programs 10 years ago and now.

- The decline, by region, was largest in the West (from 72% 10 years ago to 64% now) and Midwest (from 75% 10 years ago to 63% now).

- Among those 60 or older, 82% said preparing students to enter journalism was very important in their programs 10 years ago, and 64% of them said it was very important in their programs today.

Over the past 10 years, would you say that the writing standards for students in your program have decreased, increased, remained about the same? (Q.7)

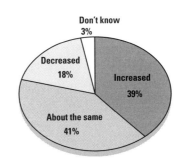

In the past 10 years, has your journalism education unit's future existence been threatened by university administrators? (Q.39)

- Units with doctoral-degree programs have been more than twice as vulnerable to being eliminated as units without doctoral-degree programs: 33% of faculty from units with doctoral-degree programs reported that their units' future existence had been threatened by university administrators in the past 10 years, while 16% of faculty from units without doctoral-degree programs reported being threatened.
- The largest portion of units being threatened was in the Midwest, 33%, and the smallest in the South, 22%.

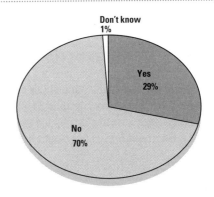

If "yes" to Q.39, which of the following were given as reasons for the challenge to your journalism education unit? (Q.40)

- (Q.40d) 60% of the youngest group surveyed, age 44 and younger, reported that faculty members not doing sufficient or appropriate research was given as a reason to threaten the existence of their units.
- (Q.40g) In all questions in this Q.40 series about threats to existence of units, a much higher than usual "don't know" response was registered, going as high as 22% in the Northeast in response to whether the explanation for the threat against the unit was reportedly related to faculty members not doing sufficient or appropriate research.
- In order of importance, the following reasons were given for threatening the existence of journalism education units, with multiple reasons indicated by some respondents:
  - 55%, program is too costly.
  - 53%, program is not central to university's mission.

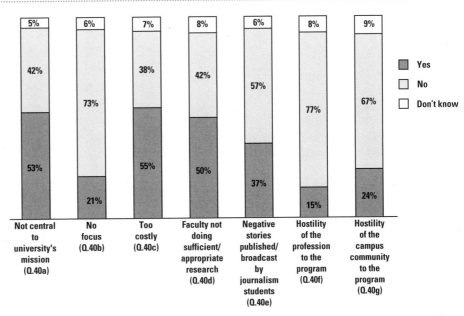

- 50%, faculty not doing sufficient or appropriate research.
- 37%, negative stories about the university or its administrators published or broadcast by journalism students.
- 24%, hostility of the campus community to the program.
- 21%, program has no focus.
- 15%, hostility of the profession to the program.

In the past 10 years, has your journalism education unit merged with other campus unit(s)? (Q.41)

- A larger portion of non-accredited units (28%) than accredited units (17%) have merged with other campus units.
- By region, the smallest portion of mergers was reported by faculty in the South, 15%.

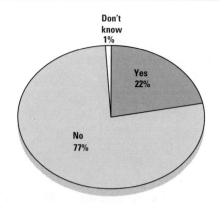

Changes in student interest in journalism

Over the past 10 years, do you think the number of students in your program who plan to become journalists has increased substantially, increased somewhat, stayed the same, decreased somewhat or decreased substantially? (Q.13)

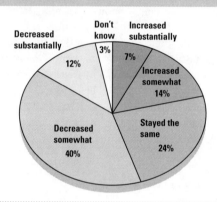

If you answered "decreased" to Q.13, for each of the following items, please indicate how important you believe each factor has been in contributing to this decrease. (Q.14)

	Very important	Somewhat important	Not too important	Not at all important	Don't know
Decline in students' interest in news (Q.14a)	39%	44%	10%	5%	3%
Shift away from journalism emphasis in program (Q.14b)	10%	17%	25%	45%	3%
Shift toward greater emphasis on journalism in program (Q.14c)	1%	4%	28%	59%	7%
Decline in strong professional expertise/interest in journalism on part of faculty (Q.14d)	10%	14%	20%	53%	3%
Increase in strong professional expertise/interest in journalism on part of faculty (Q.14e)	1%	9%	21%	61%	8%
Decline in students' respect for journalism (Q.14f)	25%	44%	17%	11%	3%
Faculty discourage students from entering journalism (Q.14g)	4%	14%	22%	57%	3%
Students are interested in less-challenging curriculum (Q.14h)	20%	30%	17%	29%	4%
Students are interested in more-challenging curriculum (Q.14i)	3%	10%	27%	56%	3%
Decline in students' interest in public-service aspect of journalism (Q.14j)	28%	41%	13%	15%	3%
Low entry salaries in the profession (Q.14k)	70%	21%	4%	3%	2%
Increase in standards in writing courses (Q.14l)	12%	26%	27%	32%	3%
Students are more interested in public relations/advertising (Q.14m)	63%	24%	6%	5%	3%
Instructors are more interested in public relations/advertising (Q.14n)	9%	18%	20%	50%	4%

- (Q.14b) 17% of women faculty members said a shift away from a journalism emphasis in their programs was a very important factor in contributing to the decrease in student interest in journalism.
- (Q.14j) 36% of women, in contrast to 24% of men, said they thought a decline in student interest in the public-service aspect of journalism contributed to the decrease in student interest in journalism.
- The same opinion was expressed by 37% of those from non-accredited programs, in contrast to 25% from accredited programs.
- (Q.14l) 17% of women said they thought an increase in standards in writing courses was a very important factor in the decrease in student interest in becoming journalists.
- (Q.14m) 71% of women, in contrast to 58% of men, said increased student interest in public relations and advertising was a very important factor in the decrease in student interest in becoming journalists.
- The same opinion was expressed by 70% of the faculty from non-accredited programs, in contrast to 53% of faculty from accredited programs.
- While 23% of the overall group thought instructors being more interested in public relations and advertising had been an important (combined very and somewhat) factor in the decrease in student interest in journalism, 38% of those on tenure track believed it was important.
- That opinion was held by 35% of faculty from non-accredited programs (in contrast to 15% from accredited programs) and 31% of faculty who were journalists for more than 10 years.

- In summary, and in ranked order, faculty chose the following as the leading factors (same order either as very important selections or as combined very and somewhat important selections) contributing to the decline in student interest in journalism:
  - 91%, low entry salaries in the profession
  - 87%, students are more interested in public relations and advertising
  - 83%, decline in students' interest in news
  - 69%, decline in students' interest in public-service aspect of journalism
  - 67%, decline in students' respect for journalism
  - 50%, students are interested in less challenging curriculum

Student requirements

Which of the following courses are required of majors in your journalism education program: journalism law, journalism ethics, journalism history? (Q.8)

- (Q.8a) 49% of non-accredited programs and 41% of accredited programs require a course in journalism ethics.
- 54% of educators without a doctoral degree and 38% of educators with a doctoral degree taught in units that required journalism ethics.
- The lowest portion, by region, of required journalism ethics courses was in the Midwest, 38%.
- The highest portion, by region, of required journalism ethics courses was in the Northeast, 54%.
- (Q.8b) 92% of accredited units and 83% of non-accredited units required a course in journalism law.

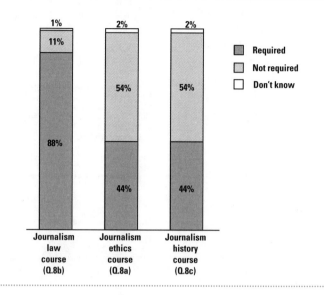

Does your journalism education program require majors to publish or broadcast stories? (Q.9)

- The highest portion of programs that do not require publication or broadcast of stories by students was 51%, those in the Midwest.

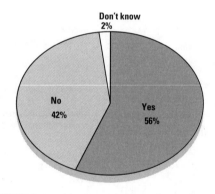

Does your journalism education program include instruction in the use of computers as a research and communication tool? (Q.10)

- 92% of faculty from accredited units and 80% from non-accredited units reported their units included instruction in using computers as research and communication tools.

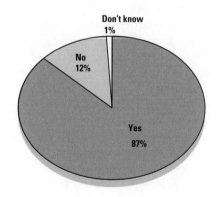

If yes to Q.10: (Q.11)

- (Q.11a) 77% of faculty from accredited units and 86% from non-accredited reported their units provided instruction in computers as research and communication tools as part of reporting courses.

- (Q.11b) 47% of faculty from accredited units and 23% from non-accredited units reported a special course was created in their units for instruction in using computers as research and communication tools.

- (Q.11c) The lowest level of required computer instruction is in the South, in 25% of units.

- The highest level of required computer instruction is in the Northeast, 40% of units.

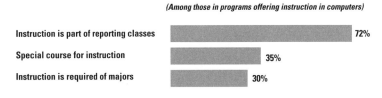

Instruction is part of reporting classes — 72%
Special course for instruction — 35%
Instruction is required of majors — 30%

Does your program offer instruction on the history of contemporary movements regarding inclusion and exclusion of ethnic minorities in journalism? (Q.12)

- 61% of faculty from accredited units and 47% from non-accredited units reported that their units offered courses in the history of contemporary movements regarding inclusion/exclusion of ethnic minorities in journalism.

- In all other questions regarding what curriculum is offered or required, answers were 100% decisive, yes or no. In this question on inclusion and exclusion of ethnic minorities, there was a "don't know" portion of responses in every category. The highest level of "don't know" was 10%, from units that have doctoral programs.

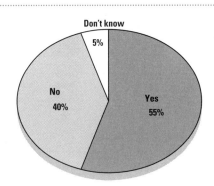

Don't know 5%
No 40%
Yes 55%

Educators' links with profession

When was the last time you talked with a journalist? (Q.15)

When was the last time you were in a newsroom (other than a campus newsroom)? (Q.16)

When was the last time you researched, published or broadcast a story? (Q.17)

When was the last time you wrote or broadcast a critical analysis of an issue in journalism? (Q.18)

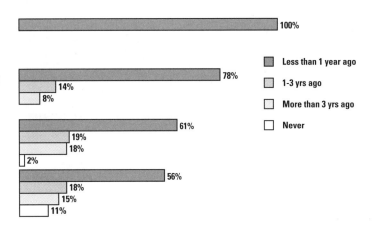

100%

78%
14%
8%

61%
19%
18%
2%

56%
18%
15%
11%

Less than 1 year ago
1-3 yrs ago
More than 3 yrs ago
Never

Educators' experience as journalists

Which of the following journalism organizations did you work for? (Q.23)

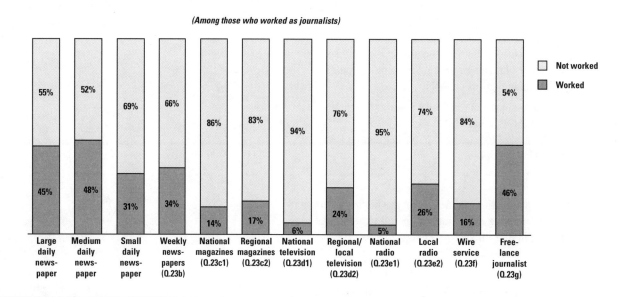

(Among those who worked as journalists)

Legend: Not worked / Worked

	Large daily newspaper	Medium daily newspaper	Small daily newspaper	Weekly newspapers (Q.23b)	National magazines (Q.23c1)	Regional magazines (Q.23c2)	National television (Q.23d1)	Regional/local television (Q.23d2)	National radio (Q.23e1)	Local radio (Q.23e2)	Wire service (Q.23f)	Free-lance journalist (Q.23g)
Not worked	55%	52%	69%	66%	86%	83%	94%	76%	95%	74%	84%	54%
Worked	45%	48%	31%	34%	14%	17%	6%	24%	5%	26%	16%	46%

Indicate whether these statements describe your attitude toward the profession at the time you left. (Q.26)

- (Q.26a) 26% of those with more than 10 years' experience and 35% of those with 10 or fewer years' experience thought at the time they left journalism there was no or little encouragement to improve.

- 19% of those 60 or older, 31% of those 45-59 and 36% of those 44 or younger had that opinion.

- (Q.26c) By age, those who thought at the time they left journalism that it required too many hours: 60 or older, 24%; 45-59, 45%; 44 or younger, 52%.

- (Q.26h) 94% of those who worked more than 10 years as journalists and 85% of those who worked 10 years or less said that at the time they left journalism they felt they had been prepared well to enter the profession.

- (Q.26i) By age, those who at the time they left journalism thought it was too stressful and demanding: 12%, 60 or older; 16%, 45-59; 30% 44 or younger.

- (Q.26j) 57% of women and 49% of men

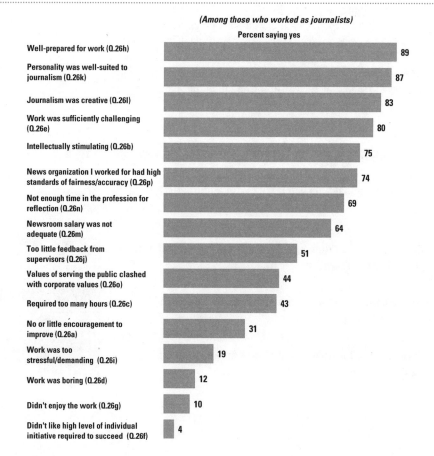

(Among those who worked as journalists)
Percent saying yes

Statement	%
Well-prepared for work (Q.26h)	89
Personality was well-suited to journalism (Q.26k)	87
Journalism was creative (Q.26l)	83
Work was sufficiently challenging (Q.26e)	80
Intellectually stimulating (Q.26b)	75
News organization I worked for had high standards of fairness/accuracy (Q.26p)	74
Not enough time in the profession for reflection (Q.26n)	69
Newsroom salary was not adequate (Q.26m)	64
Too little feedback from supervisors (Q.26j)	51
Values of serving the public clashed with corporate values (Q.26o)	44
Required too many hours (Q.26c)	43
No or little encouragement to improve (Q.26a)	31
Work was too stressful/demanding (Q.26i)	19
Work was boring (Q.26d)	12
Didn't enjoy the work (Q.26g)	10
Didn't like high level of individual initiative required to succeed (Q.26f)	4

Winds *of* Change

said at the time they left journalism they thought there was too little feedback from supervisors.

- The same opinion was expressed by 54% of those who worked 10 or fewer years and 48% of those who worked more than 10 years.

- (Q.26m) 52% of educators who were full-time journalists more than 10 years, in contrast to 76% of educators who were full-time journalists 10 or fewer years, said at the time they left journalism the newsroom salary was not adequate.

- 56% of those without doctoral degrees, in contrast to 70% of those with doctoral degrees, thought the newsroom salary was not adequate.

- By region, educators in the South had the highest level of opinion (72%) that at the time they left journalism the newsroom salary was not adequate.

- (Q.26n) 77% of educators from non-accredited programs and 65% from accredited programs thought at the time they left journalism that there was not enough time in the profession for reflection.

- By age, the portion who felt at the time they left journalism there was not enough time in the profession for reflection: 48% of those 60 or older, 76% of those 45-59, and 70% of those 44

and under.

- (Q.26o) 52% of women and 41% of men educators said at the time they left journalism they thought the values of serving the public clashed with the corporate values of the news organization.

- That perception also was higher among those who worked more than 10 years as journalists (48%) than among those who worked 10 years or less (41%).

- The belief, at the time they left journalism, that the values of serving the public clashed with the corporate values of the news organization was expressed by 46% of those who have taught 10 years or less and by 36% of those who have taught more than 10 years.

- (Q.26p) 80% of those who worked more than 10 years as journalists, in contrast with 69% of those who worked 10 years or less, said the news organization they worked for at the time they left journalism had high standards of fairness and accuracy.

- By age, those who thought the last news organization they worked for had high standards of accuracy and fairness: 83%, 60 and older; 76%, 45-59; 68%, 44 and under.

Were any of the following reasons why you became a teacher? (Q.27)

- (Q.27b) 66% of those who were journalists more than 10 years, in contrast with 41% of those who were journalists 10 or fewer years, said one of the reasons they became teachers was the fact that they liked journalism and were ready to pass it on to the next generation.
- That opinion was expressed by 45% of those with doctoral degrees and 62% of those without doctoral degrees, 46% of those age 44 and under, 53% of those 45-59, and 59% of those 60 and older.
- (Q.27c) 59% of the men, in contrast to 50% of the women, who worked full-time as journalists said one of the reasons they became teachers was their belief they would like teaching more than being a journalist.
- That opinion was expressed by 53% of those who were in journalism more than 10 years and 61% of those who were in journalism 10 or fewer years, by 63% of those with doctoral degrees and 48% of those without doctoral degrees.
- (Q.27d) 69% of those who were journalists more than 10 years and 53% of those who were journalists 10 or fewer years said one of the reasons they became teachers was they needed a change of pace.
- That opinion was expressed by 67% of those who had been teaching 10 or fewer years, in contrast to 39% of those who had been teaching 11 or more years.
- That opinion increased as age decreased: 55%, 60 or older; 57%, 45-59; 68%, 44 and under.
- (Q.27e) 70% of the men, in contrast to 61% of the women, who worked full-time as journalists said one of the reasons they became teachers was they wanted more time for reflection and discussion about the profession.
- That opinion was expressed by 71% of those with doctoral degrees and 63% of those without doctoral degrees, by 61% of those who have been teaching 11 or more years and 71% of those who have been teaching 10 or fewer years, by 59% of those 60 or older, 69% of those 45-59, 72%, 44 and under.

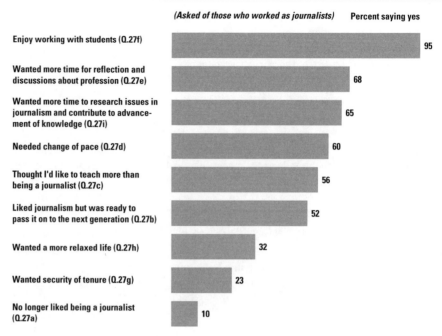

(Asked of those who worked as journalists) **Percent saying yes**

Reason	%
Enjoy working with students (Q.27f)	95
Wanted more time for reflection and discussions about profession (Q.27e)	68
Wanted more time to research issues in journalism and contribute to advancement of knowledge (Q.27i)	65
Needed change of pace (Q.27d)	60
Thought I'd like to teach more than being a journalist (Q.27c)	56
Liked journalism but was ready to pass it on to the next generation (Q.27b)	52
Wanted a more relaxed life (Q.27h)	32
Wanted security of tenure (Q.27g)	23
No longer liked being a journalist (Q.27a)	10

- (Q.27g) 25% of the men, in contrast to 18% of the women, said one of the reasons they became teachers was their desire for the security of tenure.
- This opinion was expressed by 28% of those who worked 10 years or less as a journalist and 17% of those who worked more than 10 years as a journalist; by 15% of those without doctoral degrees and 29% of those with doctoral degrees.
- (Q.27h) Among those who worked full-time as journalists, the desire for a more relaxed life as a reason for becoming teachers increased considerably as age decreased: 17% among those 60 or older, 30% among those 45-59, 46% among those 44 and under.
- That desire was stated as a reason for becoming a teacher by 22% of those who have been teaching 11 or more years and 35% of those who have taught 10 or fewer years.
- (Q.27i) 68% of men and 59% of women who worked full-time as journalists said one of the reasons they became teachers was wanting more time to research issues in journalism and contribute to advancement of knowledge.
- That opinion was expressed by 70% of those who worked 10 years or less, 60% of those with 10 or more years' experience, 52% of those without doctoral degrees and 75% of those with doctoral degrees.

Looking back at your full-time work as a journalist, at the time you left do you think your supervisors and colleagues rated your work as a journalist as excellent, good, fair or poor? (Q.28)

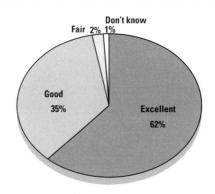

- A higher portion of women (66%) than men (59%) who worked full-time as journalists thought that at the time they left journalism their supervisors rated their work as excellent.

- That opinion was expressed by 76% of those who worked more than 10 years as journalists, in contrast to 49% of those who worked 10 or fewer years; by 72% of those without doctoral degrees and 53% of those with doctoral degrees.

Educators' description of selves and introductory skills

Which of these statements, if any, describe you? (Q.42)

Percent saying yes

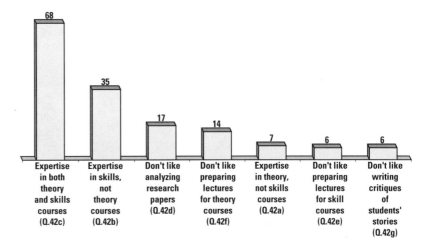

- (Q.42b) 50% of those who worked full-time as journalists more than 10 years, in contrast to 27% of those who worked 10 years or fewer, said their expertise was in teaching skills courses, not theory courses.

- That opinion was expressed by 64% of those without doctoral degrees and 16% of those with doctoral degrees. This is a much larger differential than the differential between those (Q.42a) without doctoral degrees (2%) and those with doctoral degrees (10%) who said their expertise was in teaching theory courses, not skills courses.

- Expertise in teaching skills and not theory courses decreased with age: 49%, 60 or older; 34%, 45-59; 30% 44 and under.

- (Q.42c) 70% of men and 62% of women said their expertise was in teaching both skills and theory courses.

- 62% of those who worked more than 10 years as a journalist and 75% of those who worked 10 or fewer years as a journalist said their expertise was in teaching both skills and theory courses.

- Those who said they had no experience as full-time journalists might reasonably be expected to be expert in teaching theory rather than journalism skills courses. Their responses to the three questions about types of courses they had expertise to teach:

  - Expertise was in theory and not in skills courses: 21% said yes, 73% said no, 6% did not know.

  - Expertise was in skills and not theory courses: 18% said yes, 77% said no, 5% did not know.

  - Expertise was in both theory and skills courses: 64% said yes, 30% said no, 6% did not know.

- (Q.42d) 26% of those who worked more than 10 years as journalists, in contrast to 13% of those who worked 10 or fewer years, said they did not like analyzing research papers.

- This dislike was higher among those without doctoral degrees (36%) than among those with doctoral degrees (6%).

- It was higher among those who had been teaching 10 years or less (20%) than among those who had been teaching more than 10 years (10%).

Which of the following would you use to describe newswriting and reporting courses? (Q.43)

- (Q.43a) 81% of those who taught 10 or fewer years and 70% of those who have taught 11 or more years said they would use "nuts and bolts" to describe newswriting and reporting courses.

- (Q.43b) 31% of those who taught 10 or fewer years and 24% of those who taught 11 or more years said they would use "writing formula courses" to describe newswriting and reporting courses.

- (Q.43d) 58% of those who worked full-time as journalists and 48% of those who have not worked full-time as journalists said they would use "intellectual courses" to describe newswriting and reporting courses.

- That opinion was expressed by 62% of people who worked more than 10 years as journalists and 55% of those worked 10 years or fewer.

- There was precise agreement on this term by those who have and those who do not have doctoral degrees: 56% of them would use "intellectual courses" to describe newswriting and reporting courses.

- (Q.43g) Those who said they like to teach newswriting and reporting included 88% of those who have worked as journalists, in contrast to 55% of those who have not worked as journalists; 84% of those who worked as journalists 10 years or less, 93% of those who worked as journalists more than 10 years; 75% of those age 44 and under, 85% of those age 45-59.

- (Q.43h) Those who said they were qualified to teach newswriting and reporting included 93% of those who worked full-time as journalists and 69% of those who said they never worked full-time as journalists.

- (Q.43i) 6% of those who never worked as journalists said they thought anyone who could read well could teach newswriting and reporting, and an additional 8% of them said they did not know if that was true.

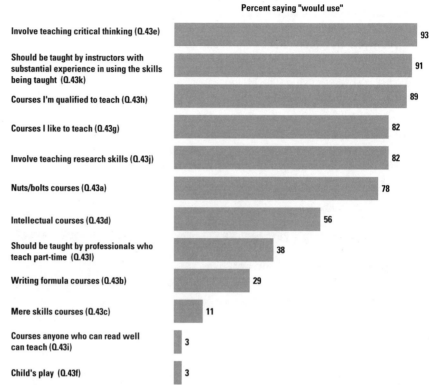

Percent saying "would use"

Involve teaching critical thinking (Q.43e)	93
Should be taught by instructors with substantial experience in using the skills being taught (Q.43k)	91
Courses I'm qualified to teach (Q.43h)	89
Courses I like to teach (Q.43g)	82
Involve teaching research skills (Q.43j)	82
Nuts/bolts courses (Q.43a)	78
Intellectual courses (Q.43d)	56
Should be taught by professionals who teach part-time (Q.43l)	38
Writing formula courses (Q.43b)	29
Mere skills courses (Q.43c)	11
Courses anyone who can read well can teach (Q.43i)	3
Child's play (Q.43f)	3

- (Q.43j) 19% of those who worked as journalists more than 10 years and 13% of those who worked as journalists 10 or fewer years said teaching newswriting and reporting involved teaching research skills.

- The portion who agreed that teaching newswriting and reporting involved teaching research skills declined with age: 27%, 60 and older; 16% 45-59; 11%, 44 and under.

- (Q.43k) 95% of those who worked full-time as journalists, in contrast to 73% of those who have not worked full-time as journalists, agreed that newswriting and reporting should be taught by instructors with substantial experience in using the skills being taught. (This 73% level of opinion about experience being essential in order to teach these courses inevitably included a significant portion, perhaps even all, of the 69% of people who said they had no full-time experience as journalists but said they were qualified to teach these courses [Q.43h].)

Qualifications/requirements for teaching journalism

Please indicate your level of agreement or disagreement with each of the following statements. (Q.29)

- (Q.29a) The highest levels of agreement (strongly and mildly agreed) that journalism educators should have earned doctoral degrees were: 52%, those who never worked full-time as journalists; and 55%, those who have doctoral degrees.

- The highest levels of disagreement (strongly and mildly disagreed) that journalism educators should have earned doctoral degrees were: 60%, those who were journalists for more than 10 years; and 76%, those who were journalists 10 or fewer years.

- 21% of those who worked as journalists 10 or fewer years, in contrast to 5% of those who worked as journalists more than 10 years, strongly agreed that journalism educators should have earned doctoral degrees; 37% of those with more than 10 years experience and 14% of those with 10 or fewer years' experience strongly disagreed.

- 1% of those without doctoral degrees and 22% of those with doctoral degrees strongly agreed that journalism educators should have earned doctoral degrees; 48% of those without doctoral degrees and 6% of those with doctoral degrees strongly disagreed.

- Among those who have doctoral degrees, only 55% agreed, a combination of strongly and mildly, that journalism educators should have earned doctoral degrees. A quarter of them said they neither agreed nor disagreed, 18% disagreed (a combination of mildly and strongly), and 2% said they didn't know.

- 40% of men, in contrast to 30% of women, said they believed journalism educators should have earned doctoral degrees.

- (Q.29b) The highest levels of agreement (strongly and mildly) that journalism educators should have doctoral degrees in mass communication were: 37% of those with doctoral degrees, and 33% of those who were journalists 10 or fewer years.

- The highest levels of opposition to the idea that journalism educators should have doctoral degrees in mass communication were: 82% of those without doctoral degrees, and 67% of those who were journalists more than 10 years.

- 46% of those who were journalists more than 10 years, in contrast to 19% of those who were journalists 10 or fewer years, said they strongly opposed the idea that journalism educators should have doctoral degrees in mass communication.

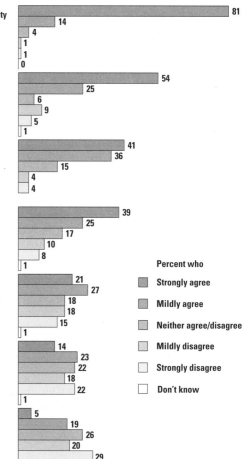

Journalism education units should include faculty members who have extensive professional experience as journalists (Q.29g)
81 / 14 / 4 / 1 / 1 / 0

Either type of research and writing should be accepted for evaluation of candidates in hiring, tenure and promotion procedures (Q.29f)
54 / 25 / 6 / 9 / 5 / 1

Journalism educators should be required to experience the rigorous discipline of depth journalistic research and writing (Q.29d)
41 / 36 / 15 / 4 / 4

Journalism educators should be required to experience either the rigorous discipline of traditional academic or depth journalistic research and writing (Q.29e)
39 / 25 / 17 / 10 / 8 / 1

Journalism educators should be required to experience the rigorous discipline of traditional academic research and writing (Q.29c)
21 / 27 / 18 / 18 / 15 / 1

Journalism educators should have earned doctoral degrees (Q.29a)
14 / 23 / 22 / 18 / 22 / 1

Journalism educators should have a doctorate in mass communication (Q.29b)
5 / 19 / 26 / 20 / 29 / 1

Percent who
- Strongly agree
- Mildly agree
- Neither agree/disagree
- Mildly disagree
- Strongly disagree
- Don't know

- Of those who have doctoral degrees, only 9% of them strongly agreed that journalism educators should have doctorates in mass communication; another 28% mildly agreed; 34% neither agreed nor disagreed; 17% mildly disagreed; 11% strongly disagreed; and 2% said they didn't know.

- 51% of those who have taught 10 or fewer years and 40% of those who have taught 11 or more years strongly opposed the idea that journalism educators should have doctoral degrees in mass communication.

- 47% of men and 52% of women opposed the idea that journalism educators should have doctoral degrees in mass communication.

- (Q.29c) The highest levels of agreement (strongly and mildly) with the statement that journalism educators should be required to experience the rigorous discipline of traditional academic research and writing were: 68%, those who never worked as journalists; 63%, those with doctoral degrees.

- The lowest level of agreement (strongly and mildly) with that statement was 25%, those who did not have doctoral degrees.

- 32% of those who worked as journalists more than 10 years, in contrast to 55% of those who worked as journalists 10 or fewer years, agreed with the idea.
- 58% of those who have been teaching 11 or more years, in contrast with 45% of those who have been teaching 10 or fewer years, agreed with the idea.

- (Q.29d) The highest level of agreement with the idea that journalism educators should be required to experience the rigorous discipline of depth journalistic research and writing was: 81% (strongly and mildly), those who were journalists more than 10 years.
- The lowest level of agreement — combined strongly and mildly — with the idea was: 68%, those who never worked full-time as journalists.
- More than three-fourths of those in all other categories agreed on the importance of journalism educators experiencing the rigorous discipline of depth journalistic research and writing.
- Those with doctoral degrees (78%) and without doctoral degrees (75%) were in close agreement on the importance of journalism educators being required to experience rigorous discipline of depth journalistic research and writing.
- A significantly higher portion (77%) of all educators agreed that journalism educators should be required to experience the rigorous discipline of depth journalistic research and writing than the portion who agreed (49%) that journalism educators should be required to experience the rigorous discipline of traditional academic research and writing.
- The portion of all educators who strongly agreed (41%) that journalism educators should be required to experience the rigorous discipline of depth journalistic research and writing was nearly double the portion who strongly agreed (21%) that journalism educators should be required to experience the rigorous discipline of traditional academic research and writing.

- (Q.29e) The highest levels of agreement (slightly and strongly) on the requirement that educators should experience *either* the rigorous discipline of traditional academic or depth journalistic research and writing were: 70%, those who worked 10 or fewer years as journalists; 69%, women and those with doctoral degrees; 68%, those who taught 11 or more years.
- The lowest level of agreement for this requirement was 58%, those who taught more than 10 years.
- The group that included the highest portion who strongly agreed with this requirement was women, 50% (compared with 36% of men who strongly agreed).
- A majority of those with and without doctoral degrees supported (strongly and mildly) the "either" requirement: 58% of those without a doctoral degree and 69% of those with one.
- When comparing these three research and writing optional requirements for journalism faculty, respondents supported them (strongly and mildly) at the following levels:
  - 76%, depth journalistic research and writing.
  - 64%, *either* traditional academic or depth journalistic

research and writing.
  - 49%, traditional academic research and writing.
- Journalism educators strongly supported these types of research and writing optional requirements at the following levels:
  - 41%, depth journalistic research and writing.
  - 40%, either traditional academic or depth journalistic research and writing.
  - 21%, traditional academic research and writing.
- Journalism educators opposed (strongly and mildly) these three research and writing optional requirements at the following levels:
  - 33%, traditional academic research and writing.
  - 18%, either traditional academic or depth journalistic research and writing.
  - 8%, depth journalistic research and writing.

- (Q.29f) When specifically asked if *either* type of research should be accepted for evaluation of candidates in hiring, tenure and promotion procedures, agreement was even higher than it was on whether faculty should be required to experience either type of research writing:
  - 79%, either type of research should be accepted for evaluation in hiring, tenure and promotion procedures.
  - 64%, faculty should be required to experience either type of research.
- There was close agreement on acceptance of either type of research for hiring, tenure and promotion between groups that had widely differing opinions on some other matters:
  - 79% of those who worked as journalists and 78% of those who never worked as journalists agreed.
  - 79% of those who worked 10 or fewer years as a journalist and 80% of those who worked more than 10 years agreed.
  - 80% of those without doctoral degrees and 78% of those with doctoral degrees agreed.
  - 78% of those who have taught 10 or fewer years and 82% of those who have taught more than 10 years agreed.
- The strongest disagreements — a 10-point spread — on such a policy were between tenured/tenure-track educators and educators from accredited/non-accredited programs:
  - 77% of tenured faculty supported such a policy, but 87% of tenure-track faculty, those who would be affected most immediately by such a policy, supported it;
  - 83% of faculty in accredited programs and 73% from non-accredited programs supported it.

- (Q.29g) The only groups whose agreement was below 75% in strongly agreeing with the idea that journalism education units should include faculty members who have extensive professional experience as journalists: educators who never worked as full-time journalists, 62%; educators with doctoral degrees, 73%.

In the past 10 years, has your university administration required hiring educators with doctoral degrees, or has it been willing to hire educators with extensive experience regardless of their degrees? (Q.31)

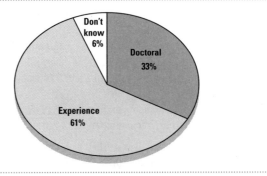

- 21% of faculty from accredited programs, in contrast to 54% of faculty from non-accredited programs, said their university administrators required hiring educators with doctoral degrees.

In recent years, in notices seeking applicants for tenure track positions, has your unit specified … (see choices at right)? (Q.32)

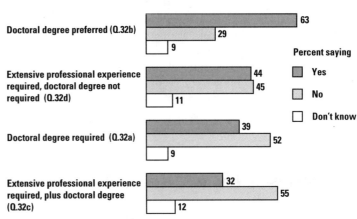

- 35% of faculty from accredited programs and 46% from non-accredited programs said recent notices seeking applicants for tenure-track positions in their programs specified doctoral degree required.

- 43% of faculty age 44 and under said their units had specified doctoral degree required.

- (Q.32) 66% of faculty from accredited programs, in contrast to 57% from non-accredited programs, said their unit had specified doctoral degree preferred.

- The combination of faculty who said their programs specified that a doctoral degree was either required or preferred equals the entire body of respondents.

- While the combination of yes answers to the two questions — doctoral required, doctoral preferred — equals 100%, the portion of faculty who said they "did not know" in response to each question was as high as 10% in some groups.

- (Q.29d) In response to 32c and 32d, a substantial portion of faculty — as high as 17% in some categories — indicated they did not know what specifications their units had made in notices seeking applicants for tenure-track positions.

In the past 10 years, there has been a decline in the number of people hired as journalism professors whose research and writing credentials are based on professional experience. The following is a list of possible reasons for such a decline. Would you please read the list and select statements which come close to your explanation of this decline (see choices at right)? (Q.44)

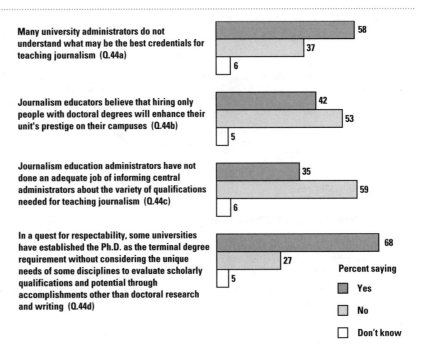

- (Q.44a) 50% of women, in contrast with 60% of men, on journalism faculties, agreed many university administrators do not understand what may be the best credentials for teaching journalism. They believe this contributes to the decline in the number of people hired as journalism professors whose research and writing credentials are based on professional experience.

- 61% of those who have worked as full-time journalists, in contrast to 40% who have never worked as full-time journalists, held that opinion.

- 67% of those who have worked more than 10 years

as journalists, in contrast to 56% of those who have worked 10 or fewer years, held that opinion.

- 64% of those who do not have doctoral degrees, in contrast to 54% of those who have doctoral degrees, held that opinion, as did 53% of those from accredited programs and 64% from non-accredited programs.
- Only 41% of those age 44 and younger, in contrast to 61% of those 45-59 and 67% of those 60 and older, held that opinion.
- (Q.44b) 26% of those who have never worked as journalists, in contrast to 45% who have worked full-time as journalists, agreed that a factor contributing to the decline in hiring as journalism educators people whose research and writing credentials are based on professional experience is the belief among journalism educators that hiring only people with doctoral degrees will enhance their unit's prestige on campus.
- 49% of those without the doctoral degree, in contrast to 37% with the doctoral degree, held that opinion.
- 50% of educators in full-time non-tenured and non-tenure-track positions, in contrast to 41% of educators in tenured or on

tenure track, held that opinion.

- 34% of those age 44 and under, in contrast to 47% of those 45-49, held that opinion.
- (Q.44d) The highest levels of support for the possibility that the decline in the number of journalism professors whose research and writing credentials are based on professional experience has been caused by the imposition at some universities of the doctoral degree as the terminal degree requirement, without considering the unique needs of some disciplines:
  - 79%, educators in full-time non-tenured and non-tenure-track positions; 79%, those who do not have doctoral degrees; 75%, those with more than 10 years' experience as journalists.
- The lowest levels of support for that opinion:
  - 57%, those who have never worked full-time as a journalist.
  - 62%, those who have the doctoral degree.

Philosophy of journalism education

Journalism education involves teaching the skills of critical thinking, research, analysis and clear oral, written and visual expression. It provides instruction in how to develop and use these skills in the ongoing search for truthful and accurate information about people and about developing events, issues and ideas.

Journalism education also conveys the body of ethics, laws and history of the developing profession and an ongoing critique of professional practices. It provides this instruction within the framework of the rights and responsibilities of journalists in a democratic society and within the framework of an extensive liberal arts and sciences education. These elements make the study of journalism, for majors and other students, consistent with and central to the mission of a university.

What do you think about the above statement (Q.34)
80 / 15 / 2 / 1

What do you think the head of your journalism unit would think about the above statement (Q.36)
1 / 82 / 13 / 2 / 1 / 1 / 2

What do you think administrators at your college/university would think about the above statement (Q.35)
32 / 43 / 15 / 7 / 1 / 2

Percent who
- Strongly agree
- Moderately agree
- Neither agree/disagree
- Moderately disagree
- Strongly disagree
- Don't know

What do you think about the above statement? (Q.34)

- The highest level of support by journalism educators for the statement was: 87% who strongly agree, those who have taught 11 or more years.
- The lowest levels of support were: 73% who strongly agree, those 44 and under; 74%, those who have never worked as a journalists.

What do you think administrators at your college/university would think about the above statement? (Q.35)

- The biggest gap in perception about whether university administrators would strongly agree with the statement was between the perceptions of educators from accredited programs (37%) and from non-accredited programs (23%).

What do you think is the most important change needed today in journalism education? (Q.63)

- Though ethnic minorities make up a very small portion of journalism faculties, diversity was mentioned by an extremely small portion as the most important change needed today in journalism education; 1% of all whites listed it.
- 13% of women, in contrast to 4% of men, chose support of journalism education by the journalism profession as the most important change needed today in journalism education. It was chosen by 11% of those who have taught 11 or more years.

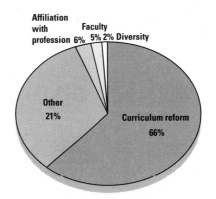

Links with professional development for journalists

Does your department/unit provide an ongoing professional-development program for journalists? (Q.37)

- 35% of accredited programs, in contrast with 14% of non-accredited programs, reported they have ongoing professional development programs for journalists.
- By region, educators reported having such programs: 24% in the South, 26% in the West, 29% in the Midwest and 33% in the Northeast.

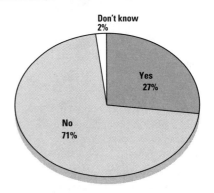

How interested would your journalism education program be in developing a partnership with regional news organizations to create a professional-development program? (Q.38)

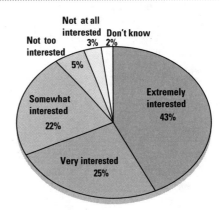

Evaluation of journalism education

Do you agree or disagree with the following statements (see choices below)? (Q.30)

Journalism education programs are this organization's most valuable source of employees (Q.30a)
| 38 | 36 | 18 | 7 | 1 |

Journalism education needs to improve a great deal (Q.30e)
| 35 | 42 | 16 | 4 | 3 |

Recently journalism education has been doing good job preparing students for the profession (Q.30b)
| 11 | 55 | 22 | 9 | 3 |

Journalism professors are on the cutting edge of journalism issues and have a strong influence on change in the profession (Q.30c)
| 3 | 26 | 38 | 23 | 11 |

People at my news organization often ask journalism professors for advice on newsroom issues (Q.30d)
| 3 | 14 | 28 | 54 | 2 |

Percent who:
- Strongly agree
- Mildly agree
- Mildly disagree
- Strongly disagree
- Don't know

- (Q.30a) The largest level of agreement among newsroom recruiters/supervisors with the statement that journalism education programs were the most valuable source of future employees came from small newspapers — 47% who strongly agreed.
- The lowest level of strong agreement was 29%, by those at medium and large newspapers and magazines.
- Belief that journalism education programs were news organizations' most valuable source of future employees increased with age of recruiters/supervisors: 31% of those 35 or younger thought they were the most valuable source, 39% of those 35-49, and 40% of those 50 and older.
- That opinion was held by 44% of recruiters/supervisors who were journalism majors and 32% of those who were not journalism majors.
- (Q.30b) The strongest disagreement with the statement that journalism education programs have been doing a good job of preparing students for the profession was expressed by recruiters/supervisors from broadcast journalism — 40% (combination of mildly, 21%, and strongly, 19%, disagree).
- (Q.30c) The highest level of disagreement with the statement that journalism professors are on the cutting edge of journalism issues and have a strong influence on change in the profession

was expressed by recruiters/supervisors from medium and large newspapers and magazines: 69% disagreed.
- The portion of those who said they did not know if professors were on the cutting edge and had a strong influence on change in the profession was as high as 21%.
- (Q.30d) Though recruiters/supervisors who were journalism majors had higher opinions than non-journalism majors of the quality of journalism education today and of the importance of having an undergraduate journalism degree, majors and non-majors agreed with each other on journalism professors' not being on the cutting edge of journalism issues and not having a strong influence on change in the profession. Only 3% in each of those categories strongly agreed that journalism educators were on the cutting edge and were called on often for advice about newsroom issues. Only 3% of majors and 2% of non-majors strongly agreed journalism educators often were asked for advice about newsroom issues in their news organizations.
- (Q.30e) Recruiters/supervisors who were journalism majors slightly exceeded non-majors in the portion who think journalism education needs to improve a great deal — 79% of majors, 75% of non-majors (combination of strongly and mildly agree).

From your experiences, please rate the importance of the following academic backgrounds in preparing people for a career in journalism (see choices at right): (Q.31)

- (Q.31a)The highest portion who thought an undergraduate degree in journalism was very important was among those who majored in journalism, 45%, and the lowest portion was among those who did not major in journalism, 21%.

- The lowest level of "very important" support among all types of organizations for the undergraduate degree in journalism was 22%, by recruiters/supervisors from medium and large newspapers and magazines.

- (Q.31e)Graduate degrees in journalism received weak support. In fact, a larger portion of some recruiters/supervisors (men and broadcast journalists) gave higher ratings to graduate degrees in journalism being "not at all important" than they did to graduate degrees in fields other than journalism being "not at all important."

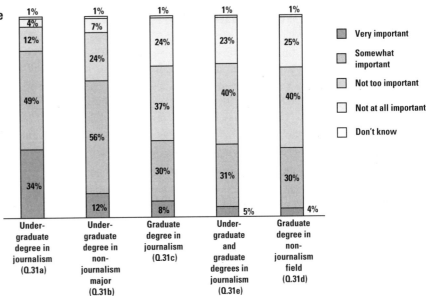

Legend:
- Very important
- Somewhat important
- Not too important
- Not at all important
- Don't know

	Under-graduate degree in journalism (Q.31a)	Under-graduate degree in non-journalism major (Q.31b)	Graduate degree in journalism (Q.31c)	Under-graduate and graduate degrees in journalism (Q.31e)	Graduate degree in non-journalism field (Q.31d)
Don't know	1%	1%	1%	1%	1%
Not at all important	4%	7%			
Not too important	12%	24%	24%	23%	25%
Somewhat important	49%	56%	37%	40%	40%
Very important	34%	12%	30%	31%	30%
(bottom)			8%	5%	4%

Following are some recommendations that have been made for improving journalism education. For each I read, tell me if you think it would improve journalism education a lot, some, a little, or not at all (see choices at right): (Q.42)

- (Q.42c) About three-fourths of all segments of recruiters/supervisors agreed that more full-time faculty focusing their research and writing on issues directly related to journalism would improve journalism education (combination of a lot and some). But the highest level of support for this suggestion was 83%, by women (in contrast to 70% of men).

- (Q.42d) The support for more emphasis on ethics was strongest among recruiters/supervisors from broadcast journalism — 92% of them said it would improve journalism education (48% a lot and 44% some). That was in contrast to 84% of all print recruiters/supervisors (38% a lot and 44% some).

- (Q.42h) The highest support for eliminating journalism as a major and replacing it with a major that would prepare students for communications fields in general was expressed by recruiters/supervisors in broadcast journalism — 14% of them felt it would improve journalism education a lot, in contrast with 5% in print journalism who thought such a change would improve journalism education a lot.

- Those who thought such a change would improve journalism education "not at all" ranged from a high of 73%, among recruiters and supervisors who majored in journalism, to a low of 58%, among recruiters and supervisors who did not major in journalism and those who are 35 or younger.

- (Q.42n)The highest portion of recruiters/supervisors who thought more ethnically diverse graduates would improve journalism

Percent saying it would improve journalism education "a lot"

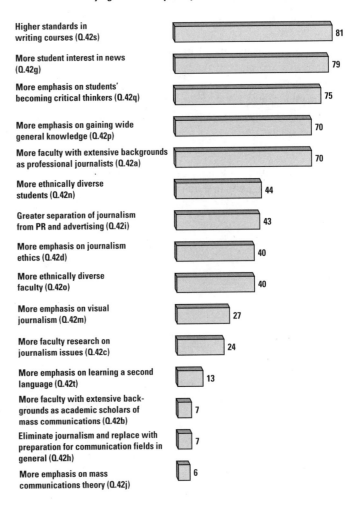

Higher standards in writing courses (Q.42s)	81
More student interest in news (Q.42g)	79
More emphasis on students' becoming critical thinkers (Q.42q)	75
More emphasis on gaining wide general knowledge (Q.42p)	70
More faculty with extensive backgrounds as professional journalists (Q.42a)	70
More ethnically diverse students (Q.42n)	44
Greater separation of journalism from PR and advertising (Q.42i)	43
More emphasis on journalism ethics (Q.42d)	40
More ethnically diverse faculty (Q.42o)	40
More emphasis on visual journalism (Q.42m)	27
More faculty research on journalism issues (Q.42c)	24
More emphasis on learning a second language (Q.42t)	13
More faculty with extensive backgrounds as academic scholars of mass communications (Q.42b)	7
Eliminate journalism and replace with preparation for communication fields in general (Q.42h)	7
More emphasis on mass communications theory (Q.42j)	6

education a lot was 49% — both of women and of medium and large newspapers and magazines.

- (Q.42o) 35% of broadcast recruiters/supervisors and 41% of print recruiters/supervisors expressed the view that more ethnically diverse faculty would improve journalism education a lot.

- The largest portion who thought more ethnically diverse faculty would help "not at all": 15% of recruiters/supervisors over age 50 and the same portion of those who did not major in journalism.

- (Q.42) Among the 15 suggestions considered for improvement of journalism education, recruiters/supervisors from print and broadcast journalism had a high level of agreement. The improvements they regarded as important, beginning with the most important:
  - Higher standards in writing courses.
  - More student interest in news.
  - More emphasis on students becoming critical thinkers, problem-solvers.
  - More emphasis on wide general knowledge base.
  - More full-time faculty with extensive backgrounds as professional journalists.
  - More emphasis on journalism ethics.
  - Greater separation of journalism from public relations and advertising.
  - More ethnically diverse graduates.

- Print and broadcast recruiters/supervisors chose the same three suggestions as the changes that would improve journalism "not at all." They are, beginning with the one disliked most:
  - Eliminate journalism as a major or emphasis and replace it with a major that prepares students for communication fields in general, including public relations and advertising.
  - More emphasis on mass communication theory.
  - More full-time faculty with extensive backgrounds as academic scholars of mass communication.

Newsroom links with journalism education

Do you or other managers in your newsroom maintain contact with any faculty in journalism education programs? (Q.19)

- According to the recruiters/supervisors, a higher portion of broadcast journalism managers than print journalism managers maintained contact with faculty in journalism education programs: 93% of broadcast journalists said yes, 83% of print managers said yes.

- The print category that reported having the most contact with journalism education programs: medium and large newspapers and magazines, 88%.

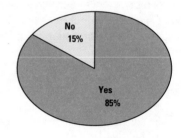

If yes to Q.19, with how many campus journalism education programs do you keep in touch? (Q.20)

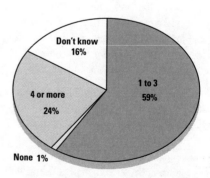

I'd like to know how important different factors are in determining from which journalism education programs your organization recruits students. For each factor I read, tell me whether it is very important, somewhat important, not too important or not at all important (see choices at right): (Q.21)

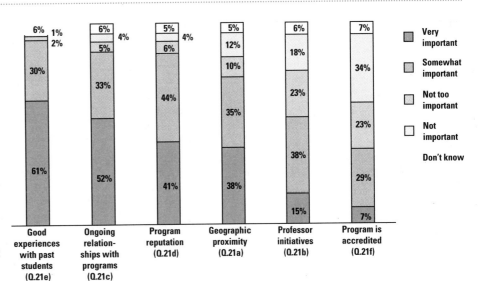

- Recruiters/supervisors from print and broadcast journalism agreed on the factors they considered "very important" in determining from which journalism education programs their organizations will recruit:
  - Good experiences with students from a program in the past received the highest portion of "very important" ratings (63% print, 59% broadcast).
  - Accreditation received, by far, the lowest portion of "very important" ratings (8% print, 10% broadcast).
  - The relatively low regard registered by recruiters/supervisors for accreditation status as a factor in newsroom recruitment

seems not to be reflected in hiring decisions. The survey of new journalists revealed that of those who studied journalism in college, and who entered journalism one to 11 years ago, 89% studied at accredited programs.

What portion of student interns in your newsroom this summer came from programs that are accredited? (Q.22)

- The portion of recruiters/supervisors who said they did not know whether their current interns were from accredited programs was substantial: 40% from broadcast newsrooms, 32% from print newsrooms.

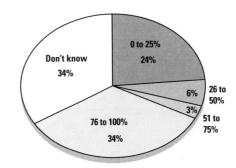

When was the last time you talked with an administrator or other teacher in a journalism education program? (Q.27)

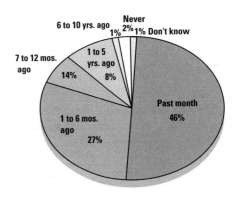

When was the last time you visited a campus journalism education program? (Q.28)

- A larger portion of print (11%) than broadcast (2%) journalism recruiters/supervisors said the last time they visited a journalism education program was 5-10 years ago.
- Those recruiters/supervisors who had never visited a journalism education program included 12% from the print group, 14% from the broadcast group.
- 18% of recruiters/supervisors age 35 or younger reported they had never visited a journalism education program, compared with 10% of those 35-49.

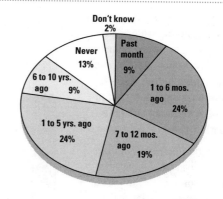

Have you been a guest speaker in a journalism education program in the past three years? (Q.29)

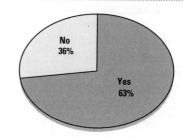

Assessment of recent interns

Of the total number of students you employed in the past year as interns, about what percentage were... (Q.14)

a. Non-journalism majors
b. Undergraduate journalism majors without graduate work in journalism
c. Students studying for a master's degree in journalism

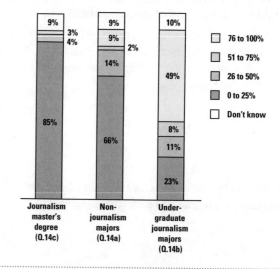

Of the total number of students you employed in the past year as interns, about what percentage of them had worked on either a campus newspaper or campus broadcast news outlet? (Q.15)

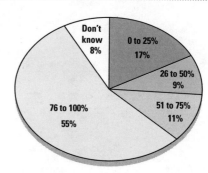

Thinking about the interns in your newsroom in the past year, would you say that the best interns have been students who majored in journalism, students who majored in something other than journalism, or hasn't there been much difference? (Q.16)

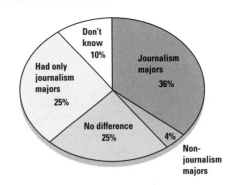

Among the student interns you have hired who studied journalism, do you believe there was generally a qualitative difference between those studying for a bachelor's degree in journalism compared to those studying for a master's degree in journalism? Which were better prepared? (Q.17)

- 54% of broadcast and 32% of print journalism recruiters/supervisors said they did not know whether those who studied for a bachelor's degree in journalism or those who studied for a master's degree in journalism were better prepared.
- There was a significant difference between the portion of print and broadcast newsrooms that hired only journalism majors as interns: 29% of print, 11% of broadcast.
- 46% of recruiters/supervisors age 35 and under, compared with 34% of recruiters/supervisors over age 35, said they did not know if there was a qualitative difference.

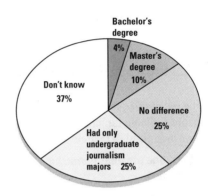

I am going to read a list of experiences that an intern or new journalist might have had. Please tell me how important each is in preparing for an internship or entry-level job in journalism: (Q.18)

a. Working on campus newspaper or broadcast outlet
b. Majoring in journalism
c. Having had a previous internship
d. Having an education that stressed wide general knowledge
e. Having enthusiasm about journalism
f. Obtaining a high grade-point average

- (Q.18a) 56% of print and 46% of broadcast journalism recruiters/supervisors said working on campus newspapers or broadcast outlets was very important.
- Importance of campus journalism experience was regarded as somewhat less important by the youngest group of recruiters. It was regarded as very important by 47% of those 35 or younger, 56% of those over 35.

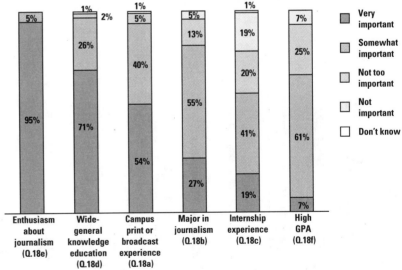

- (Q.18b) 26% of print and 33% of broadcast journalism recruiters/supervisors said majoring in journalism was very important. Those who said it was somewhat important: 57% of those from print, 52% of those from broadcast journalism.

- 23% of recruiters/supervisors from the large and medium newspaper/magazine segment said majoring in journalism was not too important (18%) or not important (5%).
- Those who thought majoring in journalism was very important in each age group of recruiters/supervisors: 53%, those 35 and younger; 60%, those 35-49; 48%, those 50 and older.
- (Q.18c)13% of broadcast and 21% of print recruiters/supervisors said having had a previous internship was very important in preparing for an internship or entry-level job in journalism.
- 35% of those from the medium and large newspapers/magazines segment held that opinion.
- (Q.18f)Importance placed on grade-point average was consistently low but varied somewhat with age of recruiters/supervisors.

The portion who thought it was very important in preparing for internship or entry level job in journalism: 3%, age 35 or younger; 6%, those 35-49; 11%, those 50 or older.

- Print and broadcast journalism recruiters/supervisors agreed in their ranking of the various educational backgrounds and experiences as very important preparation for being hired for an internship or entry-level journalism job, beginning with most important:
  - Enthusiasm for journalism (94% print, 97% broadcast)
  - Wide general knowledge base (69% print, 78% broadcast)
  - Work on campus newspaper or broadcast outlet (56% print, 46% broadcast)
  - Major in journalism (26% print, 33% broadcast)
  - Previous internship (21% print, 13% broadcast)
  - High grade-point average (6% print, 10% broadcast)

Hiring practices/policies for interns

I'm going to read a list of things news organizations may or may not require of people applying for internships. Please tell me whether your news organization requires: (Q.7)

a. Having had at least one previous internship
b. Passing a grammar test
c. Passing a writing test
d. Providing examples of previously published or broadcast work
e. Having an in-person interview
f. Having a phone interview

g. Passing a general knowledge test
h. Demonstrating in an interview that they have wide general knowledge
i. Demonstrating strong basic skills
j. Submitting academic record
k. Meeting a minimum grade-point average
l. Demonstrating high ethical standards
m. Passing a psychological exam
n. Having an on-the-job tryout
o. Having the ability to speak or write a second language

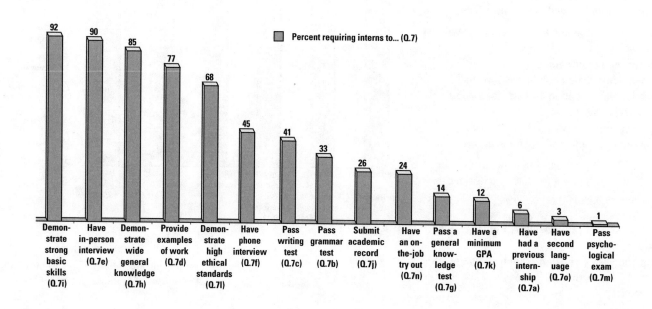

Percent requiring interns to... (Q.7)

Demonstrate strong basic skills (Q.7i)	Have in-person interview (Q.7e)	Demonstrate wide general knowledge (Q.7h)	Provide examples of work (Q.7d)	Demonstrate high ethical standards (Q.7l)	Have phone interview (Q.7f)	Pass writing test (Q.7c)	Pass grammar test (Q.7b)	Submit academic record (Q.7j)	Have an on-the-job try out (Q.7n)	Pass a general knowledge test (Q.7g)	Have a minimum GPA (Q.7k)	Have had a previous internship (Q.7a)	Have second language (Q.7o)	Pass psychological exam (Q.7m)
92	90	85	77	68	45	41	33	26	24	14	12	6	3	1

- (Q.7b)35% of print, compared with 23% of broadcast, recruiters/supervisors said their news organizations required internship applicants to pass a grammar test.
- Passing a grammar test was required by 44% of those 35 or younger, 43% of those 35-49, 19% of those 50 or older.
- (Q.7c)Passing a writing test was more important to broadcast journalism recruiters/supervisors (45%) than it was to those from all print (40%) or those from the medium and large newspapers/magazines segment (37%).
- Passing a writing test was required by 50% of recruiters/supervisors 35 or younger, 41% of those 35-49, 32% of those 50 or older.
- (Q.7d)A much larger portion of print recruiters/supervisors (85%) than those from broadcast journalism (48%) required internship applicants to submit examples of previously published or broadcast work.
- (Q7e)97% of broadcast and 89% of print journalism recruiters/supervisors required internship applicants to have an in-person interview.
- (Q.7f)55% of recruiters/supervisors from medium and large news-

papers/magazines segment, in contrast to 39% from broadcast journalism, required internship applicants to have a phone interview.
- (Q.7g)Passing a general knowledge test was required of internship applicants by: 20% of recruiters/supervisors 35 or younger; 14% of those 35-49; 9% of those 50 or older.
- (Q.7j)22% of recruiters/supervisors from print journalism, in contrast to 38% from broadcast, required internship applicants to submit academic records.
- Submitting academic record was required of internship applicants by: 16% of those 35 or younger; 28% of those 35-49; 29% of those 50 or older.
- (Q.7k)19% of recruiters/supervisors from broadcast journalism, in contrast to 10% from print, required internship applicants to meet a minimum grade-point average.
- (Q.7l)Applicants for internships were required by recruiters/supervisors in various age ranges to demonstrate high ethical standards at the following levels: 77% of those 35 or younger; 65% of those over 35.

Are interns at your news organization assigned a mentor in the newsroom? (Q.9)

- 68% of recruiters/supervisors from the medium and large newspapers/magazines segment said interns in their organizations were assigned a mentor.

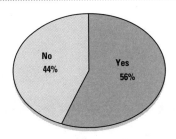

At your organization, would you say that interns are basically expected to sink or swim in the newsroom without much assistance? (Q.10)

- 23% of print journalism recruiters/supervisors, in contrast with 14% from broadcast journalism, said interns in their newsrooms were expected to sink or swim in the newsrooms without much assistance.

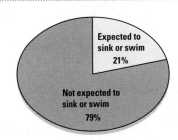

Does your news organization pay interns? (Q.11)

- The portion of broadcast news recruiters/supervisors who reported not paying internships is much higher than the portions of those from print: 79% of broadcast newsrooms didn't pay interns; 16% among all print newsrooms did not pay, and only 6% of those in the medium and large newspapers/magazines segment did not pay.

If yes to Q.11, is the pay for interns about the same as for a beginning reporter, or is it lower? (Q.11a)

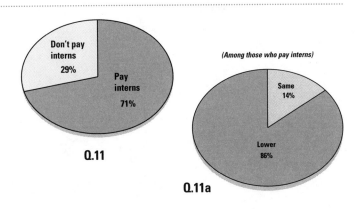

Overall, how actively would you say that your news organization recruits interns? (Q.12)

- Of all people surveyed, 39% said their news organization recruited interns either not very actively (26%) or not at all (13%). The combined portions were nearly the same for print (38%) and broadcast (37%) journalism.
- A larger portion of women (24%) than men (16%) journalism recruiters/supervisors reported their news organizations recruited very actively.

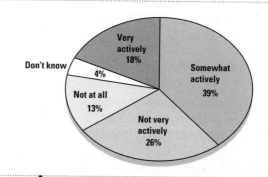

Which one of the following statements best describes the written feedback that your organization gives to its interns (see choices at right)? (Q.13)

- Nearly twice as many print (29%) as broadcast (15%) journalism recruiters/supervisors reported that their news organizations did not give any written feedback to interns.
- Only 29% of print and 39% of broadcast journalism recruiters/supervisors reported that their organizations gave written feedback to interns more than at the end of the internship.
- Written feedback to interns decreased as recruiters/supervisors increased in age: 40% of those 35 or younger, 33% of those 35-49 and 20% of those 50 or older said their news organizations gave written feedback to interns at several points during the internship.

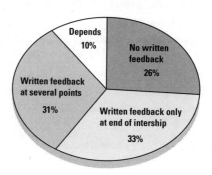

Hiring practices/policies for new journalists

Which one of the following three statements best describes your news organization's hiring of new journalists (see choices at right)? (Q.6)

- The types of news organizations that reported they rarely hired as new journalists people who have had only internship experience: 19% of all newspapers, 15% of small newspapers, 29% of the medium and large newspapers/magazines segment, 21% of all print journalism, 35% of all broadcast journalism.
- 54% of broadcast and 62% of print newsroom recruiters/supervisors reported that their organizations sometimes hired people with only internship experience.

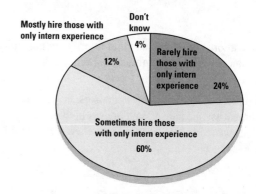

Now think about the hiring of journalists for full-time positions. Please indicate how often your organization uses the following means of finding candidates. Does your organization find candidates this way frequently, sometimes, seldom or never? (Q.23)

a. Applications initiated by candidates
b. Inquiries from agents on behalf of candidates
c. Inquiries from your newsroom to agents
d. Recommendations from current members of the newsroom staff
e. Inquiries from your news organization to journalism education programs about their graduates

f. Inquiries from journalism education programs to your news organization about graduates
g. Notices placed on the Internet
h. Advertisements placed by your organization in trade publications
i. Advertisements in local newspaper classified sections
j. Notices in ethnic-minority journalism newsletters
k. Word-of-mouth to former colleagues at other news organizations

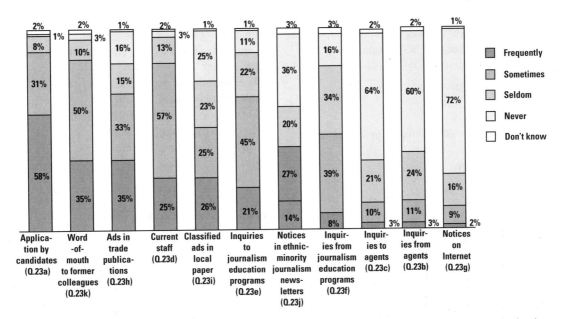

- (Q.23b) Though 47% of broadcast (63% of print) journalism recruiters/supervisors said their news organizations never found candidates by inquiries from agents on behalf of candidates, 7% from broadcast journalism (1% from print) said they frequently found candidates that way and 20% (8% from print) said they sometimes did.

- Response to agents' inquiries varied substantially by age of recruiters/supervisors. Those who said they sometimes found candidates from agents' inquiries: 23%, 35 and under; 9%, 35-49; 5%, 50 and older.

- (Q.23c) Broadcast and print recruiters/supervisors were very close to each other and to the overall pool responses to finding candidates for newsroom jobs by initiating inquiries to agents.

- (Q.23d) Broadcast recruiters/supervisors indicated they frequently relied on recommendations from current newsroom staff somewhat more than those from print journalism did: 33% of broadcast, 24% of print.

- (Q.23h) Broadcast journalism recruiters/supervisors reported their news organizations used advertisements placed in trade publications quite a bit more than those from print organizations used

them — 48% of broadcast journalism organizations used them frequently, 31% of print organizations used them frequently.

- (Q.23l) Ironically, more newspaper (26% of all newspapers) than broadcast (9%) recruiters/supervisors said their organizations never advertised newsroom jobs in local newspaper classified sections.

- (Q.23j) Broadcast journalism recruiters/supervisors reported a much higher placement of notices of their newsroom job openings in ethnic-minority journalists' newsletters — 38% of those from broadcast journalism organizations said they placed ads in them, in contrast to 14% from medium and large newspapers, 8% from all print organizations and 6% from all newspapers.

- By age of recruiters/supervisors, these portions said they never placed job notices in ethnic-minority journalists' newsletters: 29%, 35 and under; 34%, 35-49; 47%, 50 and older.

- (Q.23k) A greater portion of women (46%) than men (31%) newsroom recruiters/supervisors said they frequently used word-of-mouth with former colleagues at other news organizations as a way of finding candidates for newsroom jobs.

Does your news organization prefer to hire journalists who are...(Q.32)

a. **Focused primarily on the processes of journalism, such as getting stories fast and first**

b. **Focused primarily on the substance of their stories such as doing them carefully, accurately and thoroughly**

c. **No preference**

d. **Focus on both**

e. **Don't know**

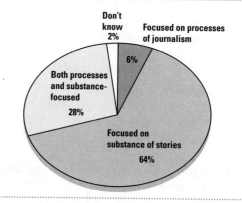

I'm going to read a list of things news organizations may or may not require of people they consider hiring for full-time journalist positions. Please tell me whether your news organization requires: (Q.8)

a. **Having minimum previous experience**

b. **Passing a grammar test**

c. **Passing a writing test**

d. **Providing examples of previously published or broadcast work**

e. **Having an in-person interview**

f. **Having a phone interview**

g. **Passing a general knowledge test**

h. **Demonstrating in an interview that they have wide general knowledge**

i. **Demonstrating strong basic skills**

j. **Submitting academic record**

k. **Demonstrating high ethical standards**

l. **Passing a psychological exam**

m. **Having an on-the-job tryout**

n. **Having the ability to speak or write a second language**

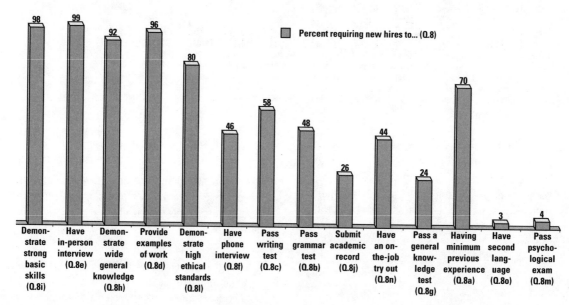

- (Q.8a) 83% of broadcast, compared with 67% of print, recruiters/supervisors said their news organizations required people they consider hiring for full-time journalism positions to have had minimum previous experience.

- (Q.8b) 51% of print and 36% of broadcast recruiters/supervisors reported their news organizations required applicants for full-time positions as journalists to pass a grammar test.

- By age of recruiters/supervisors, a grammar test was required by the following: 58% of those 35 or younger; 51% of those 35-49; 31% of those 50 or older.

- (Q.8c) An equal portion of print and broadcast recruiters/supervisors — 59% — said their news organizations required applicants to pass a writing test.

- A writing test was more likely to be required of applicants by recruiters/supervisors who are younger: 65% of those 35 or younger, 62% of those 35-49, 44% of those 50 or older.

- (Q.8f) 47% of medium and large newspapers/magazines, in contrast to 57% of broadcast organizations, required a phone interview.

- (Q.8g) By age, recruiters/supervisors required applicants to pass a general knowledge test in the following portions: 30%, 35 or younger; 26%, 35-49; 16%, 50 or older.

When hiring a new journalist, how important is it that an applicant have computer research skills? (Q.40)

- Greater emphasis was placed on computer-research skills by older newsroom recruiters. Those who said it was very important that an applicant have computer research skills: 17% of those below age 50 and 27% of those older than 50.

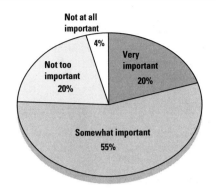

Does the geographic area your news organization covers include communities for which it is helpful to have journalists who speak a second language? (Q.41)

How important is it for a beginning journalists to be able to create stories for both broadcast and print media? (Q.43)

- A larger portion of broadcast (22%) than print (8%) recruiters/supervisors said it was very important for a beginning journalist to be able to create stories for both broadcast and print news media. The portions who said that dual skill was "not at all important" were 38% from print, 17% from broadcast journalism.
- By age of recruiters/supervisors, those who said it was "not at all important" for a beginning journalist to be able to create stories for both broadcast and print — 23%, 35 and under; 35%, 35-49; 41%, 50 and older.

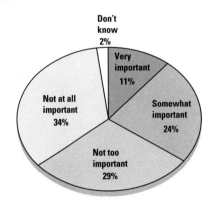

Assessment of newsrooms

When you think of the journalists in your newsroom who have been journalists one to 11 years, on the average how much do you think they like their present jobs? (Q.44)

- 68% of broadcast and 55% of print newsroom recruiters/supervisors said they thought that, on the average, the journalists in their newsrooms who had been journalists one to 11 years liked their jobs a lot.
- By age of recruiters/supervisors, the portion who thought that group of journalists liked their jobs a lot fluctuated: 60% of those 35 and younger, 51% of those 35-49, 70% of those 50 and older.

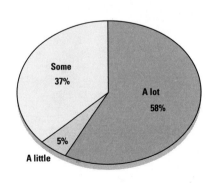

The following are reasons former journalists give for leaving journalism. For each, tell me if it is a major reason, a minor reason or not a reason why journalists whom you know have left the profession: (Q.45)

a. **Low pay**
b. **Long hours**
c. **Not liking where they work**
d. **Boring assignments**
e. **Burnout**
f. **Strong emphasis on the bottom line**

- (Q. 45f) There was substantial agreement among all segments on the causes for people leaving journalism. The only substantial differences were in the portions, by age of recruiters/supervisors, who thought long hours were a major contributing factor: 65%, 35 or under; 55%, 35-49; 46%, 50 and older.

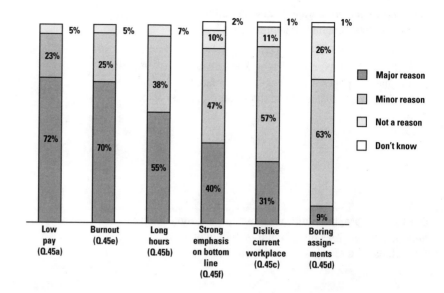

How would you rate the overall quality of newsroom management where you work? (Q.46)

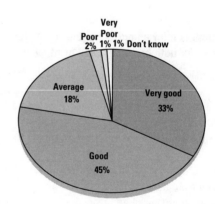

Would you say that most journalists are paid more than they deserve, paid less than they deserve or paid about what they deserve? (Q.47)

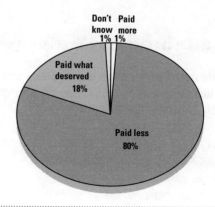

Please indicate whether you agree or disagree with the following statement: I am worried about the impact of sensationalized coverage on the reputation of journalism. (Q.48)

- 92% of broadcast and 88% of print newsroom recruiters/supervisors agreed (combination of strongly and mildly) they were worried about the impact of sensationalized coverage on the reputation of journalism. The intensity of broadcast respondents was much stronger: 72% of them strongly agreed, 58% of print respondents strongly agreed. Responses differed very little when compared by age of respondents.

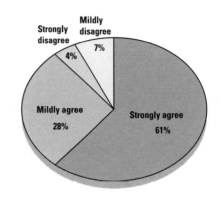

How well do each of the following describe the atmosphere in your newsroom — very well, somewhat well, not too well or not well at all? (Q.49)

a. Cynical
b. Fair
c. Honest
d. Open communication between managers and staff

- (Q.49a) 55% of print and 48% of broadcast newsroom recruiters/supervisors said they agreed that "cynical" described the atmosphere in their newsrooms well (combination of very well and somewhat well). But the intensity of broadcast respondents was stronger: 20% of them, in contrast to 12% of all print and 10% of medium and large newspaper/magazine respondents, thought "cynical" described the atmosphere in their newsrooms very well.

- (Q.49b) 78% of broadcast, in contrast to 65% of print, newsroom recruiters/supervisors said they thought "fair" described their newsrooms very well. When "very well" and "somewhat" responses are combined, 97% of those from both print and broadcast journalism thought their newsrooms were "fair."

- (Q.49c) 93% of broadcast, in contrast to 81% of print, newsroom recruiters/supervisors said they thought "honest" described the atmosphere in their newsrooms very well.

- (Q.49d) Broadcast newsroom recruiters/supervisors, in larger portions than print recruiters/supervisors, said "open communica-

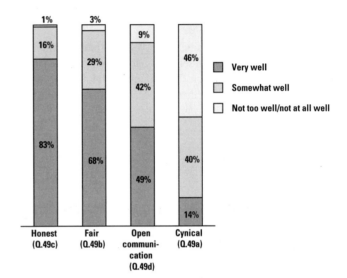

tion between managers and staff" characterized the atmosphere in their newsrooms very well: 63% of those from broadcast journalism, 45% from all print journalism, 36% from medium and large newspapers/magazines. When "very well" and "somewhat" are combined, the ratings are: 96% of those from broadcast journalism, 89% those from all print journalism, 83% of those from medium and large newspapers/magazines.

How well do you think your news organization is preparing staff for the future needs of journalism? (Q.50)

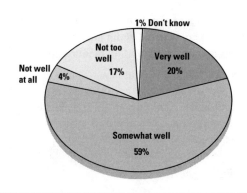

1% Don't know
Not too well 17%
Very well 20%
Not well at all 4%
Somewhat well 59%

How well do you think your news organization does the job of providing people with information they need to be informed citizens? (Q.51)

- Broadcast newsroom recruiters/supervisors had more confidence than their print counterparts that their newsrooms were doing the job very well of providing people with information they need to be informed citizens: 54% of those from broadcast newsrooms, 42% of those from print newsrooms.

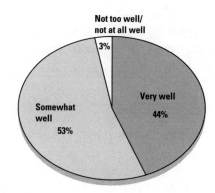

Not too well/ not at all well 3%
Somewhat well 53%
Very well 44%

Characteristics and trends in interns/newsroom staffing

How many journalists are employed in your newsroom? (Q.3)

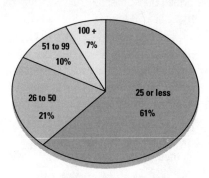

100 + 7%
51 to 99 10%
26 to 50 21%
25 or less 61%

How many interns have worked in your newsroom in the past year? (Q.4)

- While nearly the same portion of print and broadcast newsrooms (17% vs. 16%) employed no interns in the past year, the portions were less similar in other numerical categories of interns — employed 1-4, 58% print and 37% broadcast; employed 5-9, 16% print, 25% broadcast; employed 10 or more, 8% print, 22% broadcast.

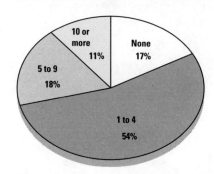

10 or more 11%
None 17%
5 to 9 18%
1 to 4 54%

In the past year, how many journalists has your news organization hired for their first full-time jobs? (Q.5)

- There were significant differences between the percentages of the number of journalists hired for their first full-time jobs by print and broadcast news organizations — none, by 28% of print organizations and by 42% of broadcast organizations; 1-5 journalists, by 63% of print organization and 46% by broadcast organizations; 6 or more journalists, by 7% of print organizations and by 10% of broadcast organizations.

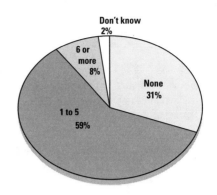

During the last two years, has your news organization's (broadcast time/print space) that is allocated for news and editorial content expanded, shrunk or stayed about the same? (Q.35)

- There were considerable differences between responses from print and broadcast newsroom recruiters/supervisors about whether the space/time allocated in their publications/broadcasts had expanded, shrunk or stayed about the same in the last two years:
  - Expanded — 20% of print, 60% of broadcast.
  - Shrunk — 37% of print, 5% of broadcast.
  - Stayed the same — 42% of print, 33% of broadcast.

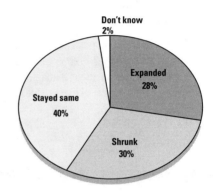

In the last two years, has the size of your newsroom staff increased, decreased or stayed about the same? (Q.36)

- There were considerable differences between responses from print and broadcast newsroom recruiters/supervisors about whether their newsroom staffs increased, decreased or stayed about the same in the last two years:
  - Increased — 32% of print, 54% of broadcast.
  - Decreased — 23% of print, 7% of broadcast.
  - Stayed the same — 46% of print, 37% of broadcast.

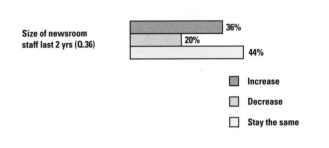

In the next year, do you expect the size of your newsroom staff to increase, decrease or stay about the same? (Q.37)

- Differences between print and broadcast recruiters/supervisors' predictions about change in staff size in next year:
  - Will increase — 23% of print, 47% of broadcast.
  - Will decrease — 7% of print, 0 broadcast.
  - Will stay the same — 69% of print, 51% of broadcast.

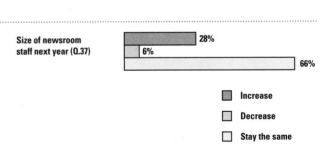

In the next year, do you expect that your news organization's need for beginning journalists will increase, decrease or stay about the same? (Q.38)

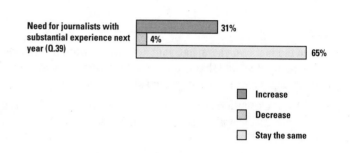

Need for beginning journalists next year (Q.38)
- 19%
- 7%
- 74%

■ Increase
□ Decrease
□ Stay the same

- Differences between print and broadcast recruiters/supervisors' predictions about change in their organizations' need to hire beginning journalists in the next year:
  - Will increase — 18% of print, 21% of broadcast.
  - Will decrease — 7% of print, 6% of broadcast.
  - Will stay the same — 75% of print, 72% of broadcast.

In the next year, do you expect your news organization's need for journalists with substantial experience will increase, decrease or stay about the same? (Q.39)

Need for journalists with substantial experience next year (Q.39)
- 31%
- 4%
- 65%

■ Increase
□ Decrease
□ Stay the same

- Differences between print and broadcast recruiters/supervisors' predictions about change in their organizations' need to hire journalists with substantial experience in the next year:
  - Will increase — 30% of print, 34% of broadcast.
  - Will decrease — 4% of print, 1% of broadcast.
  - Will stay the same — 66% of print, 63% of broadcast.

News organizations' involvement in education

Do you think journalists should take courses in either journalism skills or in areas of study that would increase their expertise in subjects they cover, or do you think this is unnecessary? (Q.52)

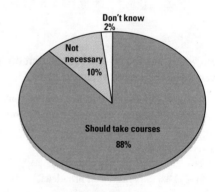

Don't know 2%
Not necessary 10%
Should take courses 88%

Do you think such study would or would not alleviate burnout of individual journalists, or would it not make much difference? (Q.53)

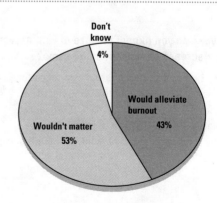

Don't know 4%
Would alleviate burnout 43%
Wouldn't matter 53%

- Broadcast and print newsroom recruiters/supervisors differed by a wide margin on the impact on burnout if journalists took professional development courses: 48% of those from print journalism said they thought it would alleviate burnout, 28% of those from broadcast journalism said it would; 48% of those from print journalism said they thought it would not make much difference, 71% of those from broadcast journalism thought it would not make much difference.

Does your news organization require journalists to take professional-development courses? (Q.54)

Percent saying yes

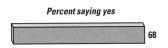 9

Does your news organization encourage its journalists to take professional-development courses? (Q.55)

Percent saying yes

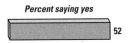 68

- The same portion, 9%, of print and broadcast newsroom recruiters/supervisors said they required (Q.54) journalists in their news organizations to take professional development courses. But the portions of each that said they encouraged staff members to take such courses was not the same: 70% of those from print journalism, 59% from broadcast journalism.

Does your news organization provide professional-development courses in-house? (Q.57)

Percent saying yes

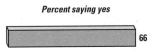 52

- 58% of print newsroom recruiters/supervisors, compared with 31% from broadcast newsrooms, said their news organizations provided professional-development courses in-house.

Do you think your news organization would be interested in creating professional-development courses for journalists in your area in collaboration with other news organizations and journalism education programs in the area? (Q.58)

Percent saying yes

66

- Interest in creating local professional-development courses for journalists in collaboration with other news organizations and journalism education programs varied significantly. Portions of newsroom recruiters/supervisors who said there was interest:
  - 72% of those from all newspapers, 75% from small newspapers, 69% from all print, 53% from broadcast news organizations.
- 23% of those from print newsrooms said no and 7% said they did not know; 37% of those from broadcast newsrooms said no and 10% they did not know.

- Interest varied among recruiters/supervisors when viewed by their age group: 62% of those 35 and under said yes, 73% of those 35-49 said yes, and 53% of those 50 and older yes.
- 28% of those 35 or younger said no and 10% said they did not know; 10% of those 35-49 said no and 8% said they did not know; 42% of those 50 or older said no and 5% said they did not know.

If yes to Q.54 or Q.55: Does your news organization pay tuition for staff members to take courses in either advanced journalism courses or other subjects? (Q.56)

- Among those who said they either required or encouraged staff members to take professional-development courses, 77% of those from print organizations and 64% from broadcast organizations said they paid tuition for staff members to take such courses.

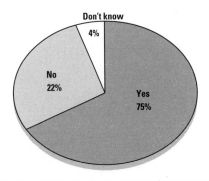

If you had an opportunity to take a course that would help you in your work, what course would you take? (Q.59)

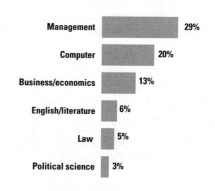

Management	29%
Computer	20%
Business/economics	13%
English/literature	6%
Law	5%
Political science	3%

Does your news organization sponsor or co-sponsor a summer high school journalism program in your area? (Q.33)

- 38% of medium and large newspapers, 28% of print and 10% of broadcast newsroom recruiters/supervisors said their news organizations sponsored or co-sponsored a summer high school journalism program in their communities.

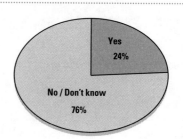

Yes 24%

No / Don't know 76%

If no to Q.33: would your organization be interested in sponsoring or co-sponsoring a summer high school journalism program? (Q.34)

- Print and broadcast newsroom recruiters and supervisors who said they did not sponsor or co-sponsor summer journalism high school programs responded nearly alike when asked if they thought their organization would be interested in doing so: 56% of those from print newsrooms and 52% from broadcast newsrooms said they would be; 32% from print newsrooms and 37% from broadcast newsrooms said they would not be; 12% from print newsrooms and 11% from broadcast newsrooms said they did not know.

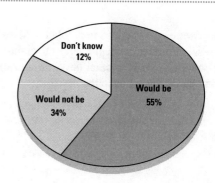

Don't know 12%

Would not be 34%

Would be 55%

Profile

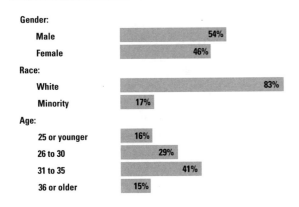

Gender:
- Male — 54%
- Female — 46%

Race:
- White — 83%
- Minority — 17%

Age:
- 25 or younger — 16%
- 26 to 30 — 29%
- 31 to 35 — 41%
- 36 or older — 15%

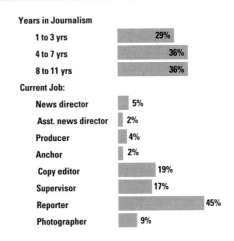

Years in Journalism
- 1 to 3 yrs — 29%
- 4 to 7 yrs — 36%
- 8 to 11 yrs — 36%

Current Job:
- News director — 5%
- Asst. news director — 2%
- Producer — 4%
- Anchor — 2%
- Copy editor — 19%
- Supervisor — 17%
- Reporter — 45%
- Photographer — 9%

Gender

- The overall pool of new journalists became more evenly divided between men and women in the group that entered journalism most recently, 1-3 years. That group was 48% men, 52% women. It represented a significant change from the group that entered journalism 4-11 years ago, which was 56% men, 44% women.
- Within age groups, the proportion of women was significantly higher in the youngest group, age 25 and under. The composition by gender in all age groups was:
  - Age 25 and under — 43% men, 57% women.
  - Age 26-30 — 52% men, 48% women.
  - Age 31-36 — 59% men, 41% women.
  - Age 36-40 — 58% men, 42% women.
  - Over age 40 — 49% men, 51% women.
- The most equal representation of men and women was at weeklies, where the work force is 51% men, 49% women.
- The biggest gap is in broadcast outlets, where the work force is 58% men, 42% women.
- The workforce, by gender, in other types of news organizations: small dailies, 52% men, 48% women; medium dailies, 55% men, 45% women; large dailies, 52% men, 48% women.
- Comparison of gender diversity in overall new journalists' group with diversity among managers who are new journalists:
  - All new journalists — 54% men, 46% women.
  - Managers among new journalists — 55% men, 45% women.
- By educational backgrounds, the largest portion of women — and the only educational background where the portion of women in newsrooms is larger than the portion of men — is among those who earned a journalism master's degree: 40% men, 60% women.
- The situation is reversed in the group that has the highest por-

tion of men, those who have no journalism education: 61% men, 39% women.
- The gender composition in other educational categories: those who studied journalism as undergraduate majors only; 53% men, 47% women; journalism minors, 51% men, 49% women; those who have campus experience as journalists, 54% men, 46% women; those who have no experience as campus journalists, 51% men, 49% women.
- A larger portion of women (83%) than men (70%) who have master's degrees in journalism studied at accredited programs.
- The gender breakdown among those who are considering leaving journalism (54% men, 46% women) and among those who plan to stay in journalism (53% men, 47% women) mirrors the gender composition of the overall pool.
- Enrollment in journalism education programs has been more than 60% women for about 20 years. No type of news organization reflects this composition; men outnumber women in all types.
- Among income levels, the portion of women is larger than the portion of men only at the lowest income level, under $20,000, where the breakdown is 49% men, 51% women. At all other income levels men are proportionally dominant: $20,000-$30,000, 54% men, 46% women; $30,000-$40,000, 59% men, 41% women; over $40,000, 54% men, 46% women.
- In political party identification, men account for a larger portion of Republicans than women (59% men, 41% women); women are a larger portion of Democrats (43% men, 57% women); men are a larger portion of independents (62% men, 38% women); men are a larger portion of those who described themselves politically as "other" (63% men, 37% women).

Race

- The overall pool is 82% white, 7% African-American, 5% Hispanic, 4% Asian-American (1% did not identify ethnicity).
- A larger portion of women than men is ethnic minority: 18% of the women, 13% of the men.
- The gender breakdown by race:
  - Among whites, 55% are men, 45% are women.
  - Among ethnic minorities, 46% are men, 54% are ethnic minorities.
- Those who entered the profession 4-7 years ago include the highest portion of ethnic minorities, 18%. Those who entered journalism 1-3 years ago include 15% ethnic minorities, and those who entered 8-11 years ago include 13% ethnic minorities.
- Consistent with annual surveys by the American Society of Newspaper Editors, this survey of new journalists found that very few ethnic minorities are employed at the traditional beginning points of the print journalism pipeline, weeklies and small dailies.
- The ethnic-minority portion of new journalists at types of news organizations: 1%, weeklies; 2%, small dailies; 20%, medium dailies; 30%, large dailies; 19%, broadcast outlets.
- Comparison of ethnic diversity in the overall new journalists group with diversity among new journalists who are managers:
  - All new journalists: 16% ethnic minority, 83% white.
  - Managers among new journalists: 14% ethnic minority, 86% white.

- By age group, ethnic-minority portions are: of those age 25 and under, 16%; of those age 26-30, 16%; of those age 31-36, 18%; of those age 36-40, 10%; of those age 36-40, 14%.
- A larger portion of ethnic minorities (28%) than whites (19%) graduated from private, parochial high schools.
- The portion of ethnic-minorities is larger in higher income brackets, primarily because larger, higher-paying news organizations are the primary organizations that have recruited ethnic minorities in significant numbers. Ethnic-minority portions of all new journalists by income groups: under $20,000, 7%; $20,000-$30,000, 29%; $30,000-$40,000, 25%; over $40,000, 36%.
- By educational backgrounds of new journalists, ethnic minority portions are: 15% of those who studied journalism as undergraduate majors; 17% of those who were journalism minors; 15% of those who have no journalism education; 20% of those who studied journalism at the master's degree level.
- Ethnic minorities were more likely than whites to get their journalism degrees at accredited programs, with the rate higher for ethnic minorities with master's degrees:
  - Those who graduated from accredited undergraduate programs — 88% of whites, 94% of ethnic minorities.
  - Those who graduated from accredited master's degree programs — 73% of whites, 95% of ethnic minorities.
- Ethnic minorities constitute 15% of those who were campus journalists and 17% of those who were not campus journalists.
- Slightly more ethnic minorities (48%) than whites (42%) are considering leaving journalism.

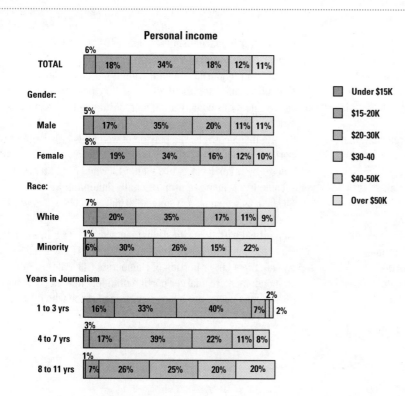

Educational background

Undergraduate journalism major — 47%
Undergraduate journalism minor or several journalism courses — 15%
Master's in journalism — 9%
No journalism study — 27%
Refused to discuss education — 2%

Undergraduate majors

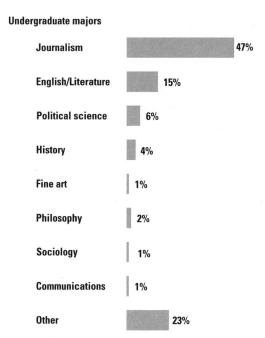

Journalism — 47%
English/Literature — 15%
Political science — 6%
History — 4%
Fine art — 1%
Philosophy — 2%
Sociology — 1%
Communications — 1%
Other — 23%

Public/private high school

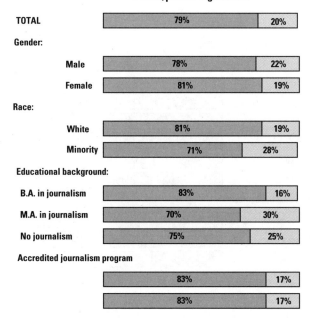

	Public	Private
TOTAL	79%	20%
Gender:		
Male	78%	22%
Female	81%	19%
Race:		
White	81%	19%
Minority	71%	28%
Educational background:		
B.A. in journalism	83%	16%
M.A. in journalism	70%	30%
No journalism	75%	25%
Accredited journalism program		
	83%	17%
	83%	17%

■ Public h.s. graduate
□ Private h.s. graduate

At the time you were in school, was your undergraduate institution accredited by the Accrediting Council on Education in Journalism and Mass Communications? (Q.13)

At the time you were in school, was your graduate institution accredited by the Accrediting Council on Education in Journalism and Mass Communications? (Q.15)

- (Q.13, 15) 94% of ethnic minorities who studied journalism only as undergraduate majors graduated from accredited programs (88% of whites did).
- 95% of ethnic minorities who studied journalism only at the master's degree level graduated from accredited programs (75% of whites did).
- 78% of those who minored in journalism at the undergraduate level studied in accredited programs.
- 94% of those with undergraduate majors in journalism who worked for large dailies and 90% who worked in broadcast journalism graduated from accredited programs.
- By number of years in journalism, among those who have journalism master's degrees are the following portions whose master's degrees were earned at accredited programs: 90% of those who have been in journalism 1-3 years, in contrast to 70% of those who have been in journalism 4-7 years and 78% of those who have been in journalism 8-11 years.

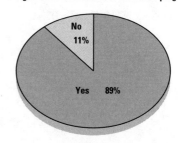

Undergraduates who studied at accredited program

No 11%
Yes 89%

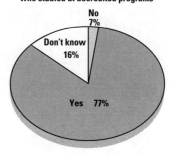

Master's degree graduates who studied at accredited programs

No 7%
Don't know 16%
Yes 77%

In politics, as of today, do you consider yourself a Republican, a Democrat, an Independent or something else? (Q.97)

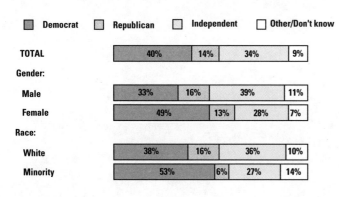

	Democrat	Republican	Independent	Other/Don't know
TOTAL	40%	14%	34%	9%
Gender:				
Male	33%	16%	39%	11%
Female	49%	13%	28%	7%
Race:				
White	38%	16%	36%	10%
Minority	53%	6%	27%	14%

	Democrat	Republican	Independent	Other/Don't know
Age:				
25 or younger	34%	20%	34%	13%
26 to 30	42%	16%	32%	9%
31 to 35	42%	12%	34%	12%
36 to 40	35%	13%	45%	7%
Over 40	45%	13%	31%	11%
Educational Background:				
Undergraduate degree	43%	14%	34%	10%
Master's degree	52%	5%	31%	12%
No journalism degree	36%	14%	38%	11%

What was the single most important factor that made you want to become a journalist? (Q.2)

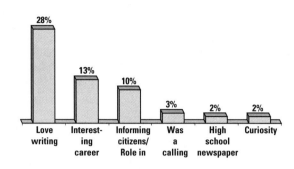

Journalism vs. other majors as best preparation

Do you think that studying journalism was a good decision, or do you think studying something else would have better prepared you for work as a journalist? (Q.18)

- Among those who studied journalism, 11% age 25 and under, 16% age 26-30, 19% age 31 and above thought a major other than journalism would have been better.
- Among those who studied journalism, 87% from small dailies, 66% from large dailies, 69% from broadcast outlets thought journalism was a good major.
- Among those who studied journalism, 83% of those who earn over $20,000, in contrast with 68% of those who earn over $40,000, thought majoring in journalism was a good decision.
- Among those who studied journalism, 20% of those who have been in journalism 8-11 years, in contrast with 11% who have been in journalism 1-3 years, thought a major other than journalism would have been better.
- Among those who studied journalism as undergraduate majors, 79% thought journalism was a good major.

(Among those who studied journalism)

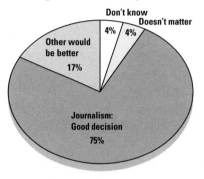

Do you think that NOT studying journalism was a good decision, or do you think that studying journalism would have better prepared you for the work you do? (Q.17)

- Just as those under 25 who were undergraduate journalism majors registered the highest confidence (79%) in journalism as a good major, those under 25 who did not major in journalism expressed the highest confidence (67%) that not majoring in journalism was a good decision.

- Among those who did not major in journalism, 71% on large dailies, in contrast to 38% on weeklies, thought not majoring in journalism was a good idea; 10% on large dailies and 37% from broadcast outlets thought journalism would have been a better major.

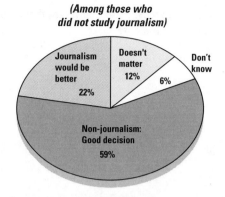

(Among those who did not study journalism)

Journalism would be better 22%

Doesn't matter 12%

Don't know 6%

Non-journalism: Good decision 59%

Journalism experience as part of journalism education

Did you work as a journalist on your campus newspaper? (Q.16a)

Did you work as a journalist on your campus magazine? (Q.16b)

Did you work as a journalist on your campus radio station? (Q.16c)

Did you work as a journalist on your campus television station? (Q.16d)

- (Q16a) Portion who worked on campus newspapers was lowest among those over 36 and among those who had no journalism education — 46% of both groups.

- Among income groups, more of those in the highest income groups worked on campus newspapers — 68%, $30,000-$40,000, and 66%, over $40,000, in contrast to 56% of those who made under $20,000.

- Those who worked on campus newspapers by type of journalism organization: 60% weeklies, 75% small dailies, 82% medium dailies, 74% large dailies, 32% broadcast journalism.

- (Q.16b) Though only 8-15% of respondents said their campus had no magazine, a consistently small percentage in all categories said they worked on campus magazines.

- (Q.16c) 34% of the 25-and-under age group said they worked on the campus radio station, 10-14% higher than any other age group.

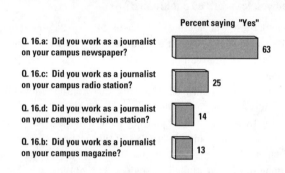

Percent saying "Yes"

Q. 16.a: Did you work as a journalist on your campus newspaper? — 63

Q. 16.c: Did you work as a journalist on your campus radio station? — 25

Q. 16.d: Did you work as a journalist on your campus television station? — 14

Q. 16.b: Did you work as a journalist on your campus magazine? — 13

- The portion who worked on campus radio stations, by type of current journalism employer, ranged from 57% for broadcast journalists to 12% for small dailies and large dailies.

- (Q.16d) 23% of the 25-and-under age group said they worked on their campus television stations, 9 to 14 points higher than any other age group.

- 38% of broadcast journalists worked on their campus television stations, while 5% of print journalists did so.

- Among income groups, the largest portion who worked on campus television stations was the lowest income group, 19% of those who made under $20,000.

- By educational backgrounds, the group with the lowest involvement in every type of campus journalism was made up of those with no journalism education.

While you were studying journalism, were you required to publish or broadcast stories? (Q.19)

- 78% from weeklies and 74% from broadcast outlets were required to publish or broadcast stories, in contrast to 59% from medium dailies.
- 31% of those who were undergraduate journalism majors were not required to publish or broadcast stories as part of their journalism studies.
- 40% of those who earned journalism master's degrees were not required to publish or broadcast stories as part of their journalism studies.

Did you have an internship before you became a professional journalist? (Q.20)

- Among undergraduate journalism majors, a larger portion of women (77%) than men (72%) and a larger portion of ethnic minorities (86%) than whites (72%) had internships.
- The percentage of journalism undergraduate majors who had internships varied insignificantly when compared by number of years they had been in the profession, but did vary within age categories: 85% in the 25-and-under group had internships, 77% in the 26-30 group, 73% in the 31-36 group, 59% in the over-36 group.
- 22% of journalism undergraduate majors did not have internships, and 31% of those who earned journalism master's degrees did not have internships.
- The portion of journalism majors who had internships varied from one type of organization to another: 61% of those on weeklies, 67% of those on small dailies, 76% of those on medium dailies, 85% of those on large dailies, 80% of those at broadcast outlets.
- Among new journalists who have become managers, 75% had internships; 74% of those who are non-managers had interships.

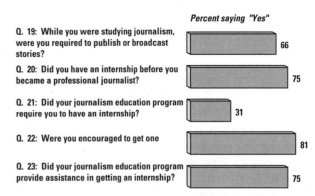

Percent saying "Yes"

Q. 19: While you were studying journalism, were you required to publish or broadcast stories? — 66

Q. 20: Did you have an internship before you became a professional journalist? — 75

Q. 21: Did your journalism education program require you to have an internship? — 31

Q. 22: Were you encouraged to get one — 81

Q. 23: Did your journalism education program provide assistance in getting an internship? — 75

Did your journalism education program require you to have an internship? (Q.21)

- Among those who studied journalism, a larger percentage of women (35%) than men (28%) and ethnic minorities (37%) than whites (30%) were required by their journalism education programs to have internships.
- 34% of those who were undergraduate journalism majors were required to have internships, and 20% of those who earned journalism master's degrees were required to have internships.

Were you encouraged to get one? (Q22)

- Encouragement to get an internship was greater among the youngest journalists. The portion who said they were encouraged: 92% of the 25-and-under group, 82% of the 26-30 group, 81% of the 31-36 group, 68% of the over-36 group.
- Among types of journalism organizations, encouragement to get an internship was highest among those at broadcast outlets — 87%.
- Encouragement to get an internship was experienced by 88% of undergraduate journalism majors, and 68% of those who earned journalism master's degrees.

Did your journalism education program provide assistance in getting an internship? (Q.23)

Nature and impact of the journalism curriculum

All charts in the next four sections (through the first chart on page 126) pertain to those who studied journalism.

Please tell me which of these statements (A, B or C) comes closest to describing your introductory journalism writing class: A) It taught newswriting and was tightly focused on covering news, or B) It was an introduction to writing for various media, including advertising and public relations, or C) Neither of these. (Q.24)

- By age, the largest portion who said their introductory writing class was focused on writing for various media, including advertising and public relations, instead of on journalism was in the 25-and-under group — 25%, compared with 18% in the 26-30 and over-36 groups and 14% in the 31-36 group.
- The group in journalism the longest, 8-11 years, was somewhat more likely to have had an introductory writing class that was

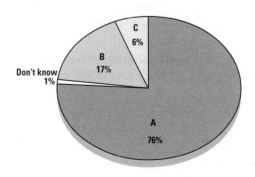

C 6%
B 17%
Don't know 1%
A 76%

focused on journalism rather than communications media in general — 81% did.

- 85% of those who make over $40,000 had introductory courses focused on journalism, in contrast to 70% of those who made under $20,000.
- Among types of news organizations, people who worked at large dailies were the most likely to have had introductory writing courses focused on journalism rather than communications

media in general — 86%. The least likely to have introductory writing courses focused on journalism were the broadcast journalists, 61%.

- 90% who earned journalism master's degrees had introductory writing courses focused on journalism.

Please tell me which of these statements comes closest to describing your journalism education: A) My education focused on preparing me to be ready to enter journalism as a beginning journalist, or B) My education prepared me for a number of different communications professions, or C) My journalism studies did not prepare me for entering any profession. (Q.25)

- Curriculum emphasis was on preparing to enter journalism for 59% of those in journalism 1-3 years, 63% of those in journalism 4-7 years and 66% of those in journalism 8-11 years.
- Incomes in journalism tended to be higher for those whose journalism education focused on preparing them to enter journalism rather than on communications in general. The portion for each income group whose journalism education was focused on preparing them to enter journalism: 52% under $20,000; 61% $20,000-$30,000; 73% $30,000-$40,000; 69% over $40,000.
- Those on weeklies and in broadcast journalism reported the lowest emphasis on being prepared to enter journalism rather

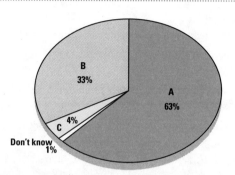

than communications in general: 47% for weeklies and 45% for broadcast journalism — in contrast to 70% for small dailies, 74% for medium dailies, 76% for large dailies.

- Those who studied journalism as undergraduate majors experienced a lower (68%) emphasis on being prepared to enter journalism, rather than communication careers in general, than did those who earned journalism master's degrees (77%).

Did your journalism education prepare you to work in print journalism, broadcast journalism, or both? (Q.26)

- The year people graduated in the last decade did not seem to affect whether their curriculum prepared them to work in both print and broadcast journalism; those who said they were prepared for both included 25% of those in journalism 1-3 years, 30% in journalism 4-7 years, 24% in journalism 8-11 years.
- 75% of the people earning more than $40,000 had educations that prepared them to work in print journalism.
- Broadcast journalists included 13% whose education prepared them to be print journalists, 42% whose education prepared them to be broadcast journalists, and 45% whose education prepared them to be either print or broadcast journalists. Among those on all newspapers, 78% were prepared to be print journalists, 1% of were prepared to work in broadcast journalism, and 21% in either print or broadcast journalism.

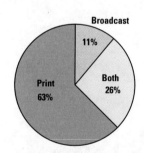

To what extent did your journalism education stress that you have a wide general knowledge base in non-journalism subjects? (Q.27)

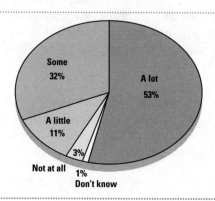

How about curiosity? To what extent did your journalism education program stress the need for curiosity? (Q.28)

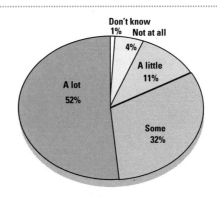

Did you study journalism in a mass communications program that included public relations, advertising and mass communication theory? (Q.29)

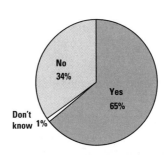

- Ethnic minorities were less likely (58%) than whites (66%) to study journalism in a program that included public relations, advertising and mass communications theory.
- In salary groups, those who made the lowest salaries generally were more likely to have studied journalism in programs that also had emphases in public relations, advertising and mass communications theory — 72% of those who earned under $20,000; 69%, $20,000-$30,000; 55%, $30,000-$40,000; 59%, over $40,000.
- Among types of news organizations, those with the highest number of people who studied in programs that included public relations, advertising and mass communications theory were broadcast outlets, 70%, and weeklies, 76%. The organizations

with the lowest portion were large dailies, 59%.
- 37% of those who earned journalism master's degrees attended programs that included public relations, advertising and mass communications as well as journalism, compared to 68% of those who studied journalism as undergraduate majors.

As you look back on your journalism education, which journalism course was most helpful in preparing you for what you do today? (Q.33)

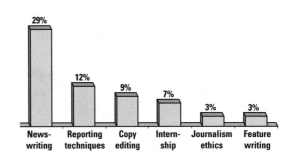

What about outside your major? Which course was most helpful? (Q.34)

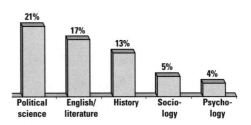

Please tell me whether you strongly agree, mildly agree, mildly disagree or strongly disagree with each of the following statements (see choices at right): (Q.35)

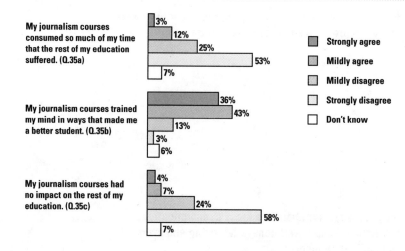

My journalism courses consumed so much of my time that the rest of my education suffered. (Q.35a)
- 3%
- 12%
- 25%
- 53%
- 7%

My journalism courses trained my mind in ways that made me a better student. (Q.35b)
- 36%
- 43%
- 13%
- 3%
- 6%

My journalism courses had no impact on the rest of my education. (Q.35c)
- 4%
- 7%
- 24%
- 58%
- 7%

Legend:
- Strongly agree
- Mildly agree
- Mildly disagree
- Strongly disagree
- Don't know

Approximately what was your average grade in journalism classes? A, B, C, D or F? (Q.36)

- Among all groups surveyed, the greatest variation in "A" grades received in journalism courses was between men (41%) and women (61%); the portions were 52% for whites and 43% for ethnic minorities.

- In income categories, 56% of those who earned over $40,000 were "A" students in journalism courses, compared with 47% of those who earned under $20,000.

- Among types of news organizations, the highest portion of "A" students in journalism courses was among those on large dailies (57%) and the lowest portion was those in broadcast journalism (44%).

- 49% of those who studied journalism as undergraduate majors reported earning "A" averages in journalism courses, while 59% of those who earned journalism master's degrees reported doing so.

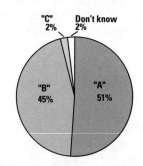

"C" 2% Don't know 2%
"B" 45%
"A" 51%

And, approximately what was your average grade in other classes? A, B, C, D or F? (Q.37)

- The academic accomplishment gap between women and men also existed in non-journalism courses: 36% of women who studied journalism earned "A" averages in non-journalism courses, compared to 21 percent of men; 29% of ethnic minorities compared with 28% of whites.

- People on medium dailies reported the highest non-journalism "A" averages, 38%, and people in broadcast outlets reported the lowest "A" averages, 26%.

- 25% of those who studied journalism as undergraduate majors reported earning "A" averages in non-journalism courses, while 43% of those who earned journalism master's degrees reported doing so.

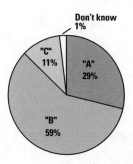

Don't know 1%
"C" 11%
"A" 29%
"B" 59%

- A slightly lower portion (24%) of new journalists who became managers made "A" average grades in non-journalism courses than did those who were non-managers (29%). The two groups' grades in journalism courses were the same.

Did your instruction in journalism education include preparation for communicating with people from racial, cultural, and economic backgrounds different from your own? (Q.38)

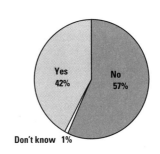

- According to changes measured in two categories, age and number of years in journalism, there has been recent growth in instruction in communicating with people from racial, cultural and economic backgrounds different from their own. Those who said their instruction had included such study: 59%, age 25 and under; 45%, age 26-30; 36%, age 31-36; 34%, over age 36; 59%, in journalism 1-3 years; 41%, in 4-7 years; 30%, in 8-11 years.

- Such instruction was significantly higher among those who earned journalism master's degrees (53%) than among those who were undergraduate journalism majors (43%).

In which journalism courses did such preparation take place? (Q.39)

How would you rate your ability to communicate with people from backgrounds different from your own? (Q.40)

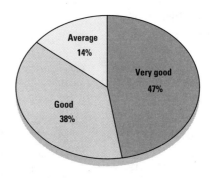

- 98% of ethnic minorities who studied journalism rated as very good or good their ability to communicate with people from backgrounds different from their own, compared with 82% of whites.

- Though more younger than older journalists indicated they had had instruction in communicating with people from various backgrounds, younger journalists rated themselves lower than older journalists rated themselves in their ability to communicate with such people: 43% very good, age 25 and under; 47%, age 26-36; 53%, over age 36.

- Those with higher incomes rated themselves higher: very good, 54%, over $40,000; 51%, $30,000-$40,000; 43%, below $30,000.

- Among types of news organizations, 38% from weeklies rated themselves very good; 56% from large dailies and 54% from broadcast journalism did so.

Attitudes of journalism professors toward journalism

Was it your impression that instructors in the mass communication program as a whole regarded journalism as an important part of the program, or did not regard journalism as important, or was it unclear how important your instructors felt journalism was? (Q.30)

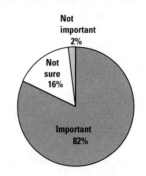

- 22% of ethnic-minority students said it was unclear whether their journalism professors regarded journalism as an important part of the unit's program (compared with 14% whites).

- 25% of those who minored or took a few courses in journalism perceived their journalism professors as being unclear about whether journalism was an important part of the program.

In your journalism classes, how often did professional journalists come in as guest speakers? (Q.31)

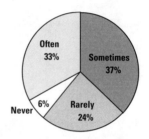

- Approximately a third of all groups (except master's degree graduates) reported that professional journalists rarely or never were guest speakers in their journalism classes; 20% of those who earned a journalism master's degree said journalists rarely or never were guest speakers.

I'm going to read you a list of different attitudes journalism and other mass communication instructors might have about journalism. Please tell me whether most, some, a few or none of your professors expressed the following opinions about the profession (see choices at right). (Q.32)

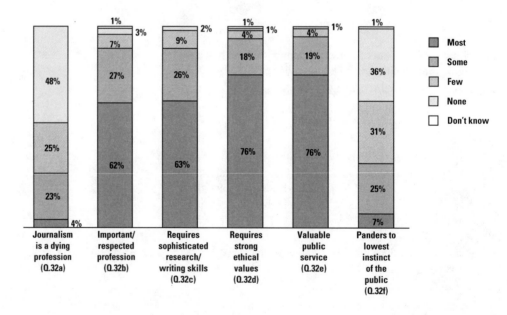

- (Q.32a) More than half of respondents said they had journalism professors who expressed the opinion that journalism was a dying profession.

- This attitude, when measured by length of time new journalists had been in the profession (and, therefore, out of school), had been expressed increasingly by professors in recent years. It was reported by 59% of those who had been in journalism 1-3 years, 52% of those in journalism 4-7 years, 46% of those in journalism 8-11 years.

- The prevalence of this opinion among journalism professors was expressed at nearly the same level by those who studied journalism as undergraduate majors (53%) and by those who earned journalism master's degrees (52%).

- (Q.32b) 10% of respondents had few or no journalism professors who expressed the opinion that journalism was an important and respected profession; the percentage who had such professors was highest among ethnic-minority journalists (15%).

- (Q32c) 11% of respondents said few or none of their journalism professors expressed the opinion that journalism required sophisticated research and writing skills.

- 18% of those who worked on weeklies and 13% of those who made under $20,000, in contrast to 7% of those who earned more than $40,000, said few or none of their professors expressed the opinion that journalism required sophisticated research and writing skills.

- Only 5% of those who earned journalism master's degrees reported that few or none of their professors expressed the opinion that journalism required sophisticated research and writing skills; 11% of those who studied journalism only as undergraduate majors reported that few of none of their profes-

sors expressed that opinion.

- (Q32f) When viewed by age of respondents, the portion of professors who expressed the opinion that journalism panders to the lowest instinct of the public has increased in recent years: 38% of new journalists age 25 and under said most of their journalism professors expressed that opinion. The portion was 33% among those age 26-30; 32% among those age 31-36; 21% among those over age 36.

- The strongest contrast among types of news organizations was between those in broadcast journalism, 38% of whom said most of their journalism professors expressed that opinion, and those on large dailies, 24% of whom said most of their journalism professors expressed that opinion.

Quality of instruction, qualifications of instructors

How would you rate the overall quality of the instruction you received in your journalism education? (Q.46)

- 89% of those who earned journalism master's degrees, 78% of those who studied journalism as undergraduate majors and 67% of undergraduate journalism minors rated the overall quality of their journalism education as very good or good; 22% of those who studied journalism as undergraduate majors rated the quality average or poor, 33% of journalism minors rated it average or poor, and 11% of those who earned journalism master's degrees rated it average or poor.

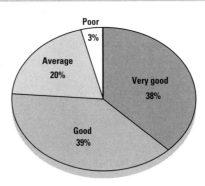

How well did your journalism education prepare you for dealing with the ethical issues in your job? (Q.47)

- The highest satisfaction with instruction in journalism ethics was expressed by those over age 36 (47%), those who worked for weeklies (49%) and those with master's degrees in journalism (52%).

- About 15% percent of most groups thought they had been prepared not very well or not well at all to deal with ethical issues in journalism.

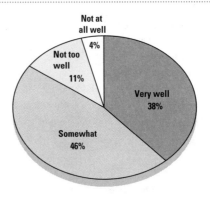

What portion of your journalism instructors, would you say, were very good — all, a majority, about half, a minority or none? (Q.48)

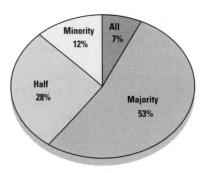

Think of the journalism teacher you thought was the best. Was the teacher full-time or part-time?: (Q.49)

- 82% of whites said their best journalism teachers were full-time and 17% said part-time; 70% of ethnic minorities said their best teachers were full-time and 29% said part-time.
- 86% of those who studied journalism as undergraduate majors said their best journalism teachers were full-time and 14% said part-time; 70% of those who earned journalism master's degrees said their best journalism teachers were full-time and 28% said part-time.

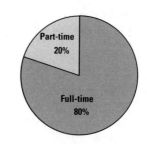

Was the teacher a lecturer, an instructor, an assistant professor, an associate professor or a full professor? (Q.50)

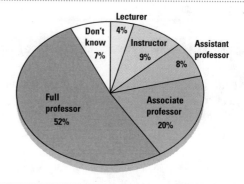

Did that teacher: 1) Have extensive professional experience as a journalist, without a doctoral degree, 2) Have a doctoral degree with little or no professional experience as a journalist, or 3) Have both a doctoral degree and extensive professional experience as a journalist? (Q.51)

- By type of news organizations, the portions who said their best journalism teachers were teachers with extensive professional experience and no Ph.D.: 66%, small dailies; 64%, large dailies; and 40%, broadcast outlets.
- 12% of broadcast journalists — compared with 1% on large dailies — said their best journalism teachers had a Ph.D. and no experience; 39% of broadcast journalists said they were teachers who had a Ph.D. and extensive professional experience.

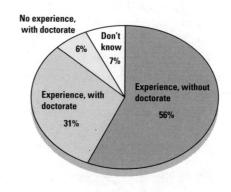

Based on your experience as a journalism student and as a professional journalist, how important is it that... (Q.52)
a. Journalism teachers have professional experience?

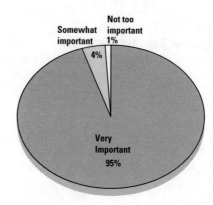

b. And, how important is it that journalism teachers study mass communication theory at the doctoral level?

- (Q52b) The strongest support for journalism teachers' studying mass communication theory at the doctoral level came from those age 25 and under (11%), those who earn under $20,000 (14% compared with 3% from those who earn over $30,000) and broadcast journalists (13% compared with 2% from those on large dailies).
- The strongest opposition — not important at all, they said — to journalism teachers studying mass communication theory at the doctoral level came from those over age 36 (27%), those who make over $40,000 (29%), those who work for large dailies (27%) and graduates of journalism master's degree programs (36%).

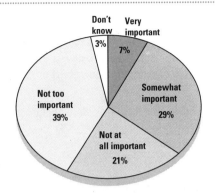

How well journalism education prepares for profession

During your first year as a journalist, did you feel that you were very well prepared for the job, somewhat well-prepared, not too well-prepared or not prepared at all? (Q.53)

- Those who felt very well prepared in the first year on the job: 46% of those who studied journalism as undergraduate majors, 43% of those who earned journalism master's degrees, 25% of those who minored in journalism, and 31% of those who did not study journalism.
- By age, those 25 and under expressed the greatest level of confidence in how well prepared they were their first year on the job: 47% of them said very well-prepared; 34% of those over 40 said they felt well-prepared then.

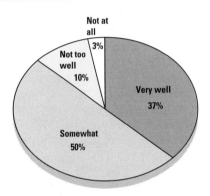

Having been a journalist for a while, do you feel that your education prepared you very well for the job, prepared you somewhat well, not too well or not well at all? (Q.54)

- When asked how they felt now, as opposed to how they felt during their first year on the job, about how well their education prepared them for their first job, the greatest change in perception was reported by those who did not study journalism. In their first year on the job, 31% felt very well-prepared, 13% felt not well-prepared; later, they reported, 46% felt they were very well-prepared when they started to work and 8% felt not well-prepared.
- 46% of those who studied journalism as undergraduate majors said that during their first year on the job they felt they were very well-prepared, and now 43% of them thought they had been very well-prepared; 25% of minors thought they had been

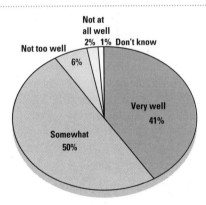

very well-prepared during the first year, and now 32% of them think they were very well-prepared for their first job; there was no change among the 43% of those who earned journalism master's degrees who thought they had been very well-prepared.

Do you think that you would or would not be able to adapt the skills you use in your current job to work in another type of journalism? For example, if you are now a print journalist, would you be able to work as a broadcast or multimedia journalist? (Q.55)

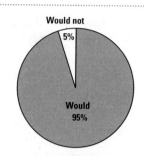

- There was near-unanimity among all segments surveyed that they would be able to adapt their skills to another type of journalism — print, broadcast, multimedia.

Job satisfaction

How much do you like your present job? (Q.56)

- Ethnic minorities expressed a high level of enthusiasm for their jobs: 80% reported liking their jobs a lot, compared with 71% of whites.
- 74% of women said they liked their jobs a lot, compared with 71% of men.
- 79% of those who are managers said they liked their jobs a lot, compared with 70% of non-managers.
- Enthusiasm for jobs increased with age and with length of experience: respondents who said they liked their jobs a lot included 71% of those age 25 and under, 69% age 26-39, 72% age 31-36, 81% age 36-40, 85% over age 40.
- This increase in enthusiasm also was reflected when measured by length of experience: 69% of those who have been in journalism 1-3 years liked their job a lot; 72% of those who have been in journalism 4-7 years; 76% of those who have been in journalism 8-11 years.
- Enthusiasm for their jobs was higher as income increased: 65% of those who made under $20,000 said they liked their jobs a lot, compared with 71% of those who made between $20,000 and $40,000, and 83% of those who made over $40,000.
- Among types of news organizations, those who said they liked their jobs a lot: 86% at large dailies, 82% at broadcast outlets 68% at weeklies, 67% at small dailies, 61% at medium dailies.
- By educational backgrounds, those who said they liked their jobs a lot included 68% of those who studied journalism as undergraduate majors; 71% of those who minored in journalism;

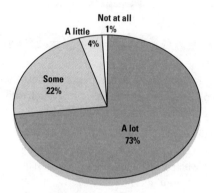

81% of those who have no journalism education; 69% of those who earned journalism master's degrees; 71% of those who were journalists on campus; 79% of those who had no experience as campus journalists.

- 83% of those who said they planned to stay in journalism also said they liked their job a lot, but so did 59% of those who said they might leave the profession.
- Only 5% of all participants said they liked their jobs a little or not at all; the highest dissatisfaction was among those who make under $20,000 (9%).
- Those who were managers and non-managers registered nearly the same responses about whether they planned to stay or might leave: 4% more non-managers than managers said they might leave.

What is it you like most about your current job? Is there anything else? (Q.57)

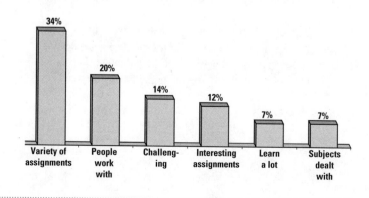

What is it you dislike most about your job? (Q.58)

- There was unanimity across all groups on what was most disliked about their jobs: schedule and pay.
- Whites registered more dissatisfaction than ethnic minorities about pay — 17% whites said it was the thing they disliked most, in contrast to 8% of ethnic minorities.
- Men registered more dissatisfaction about pay and schedule than women did: those who most disliked their schedule — 24% of the men, 18% of the women; those who most disliked their pay — 18% of the men, 12% of the women.
- Those with the least experience expressed the strongest dislike of their pay: 18% of those with 1-3 years experience, 15% with 4-7 years experience, 13% with 8-11 years experience.
- Among types of news organizations, the highest level of dissatisfaction with schedule came from those in broadcast journalism (27%); the highest level of dissatisfaction with pay came from those at weeklies (26%).
- Among all people surveyed, the lowest level of dislike for schedule was 16%, expressed by those who studied journalism only at the master's degree level.

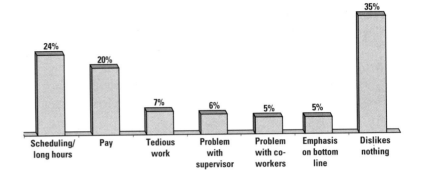

- Pay was the most disliked part of the job for 8% of those who earned journalism master's degrees, a much lower portion than it was among other groups.
- The third highest level of dislike was expressed about supervisors, but that dislike was generally considerably less than for either schedule or pay. The highest level of dislike for supervisors was expressed by: those who made between $30,000 and $40,000, 10%; those who worked on medium dailies, 11%; those who earned journalism master's degrees, 10%.

Would you say that journalism is A) more satisfying and challenging than you expected, B) about as satisfying and challenging as you expected, or C) less satisfying and challenging than you expected? (Q.59)

- Ethnic minorities, whites, men and women expressed close agreement about whether journalism was as satisfying and challenging as they expected: ethnic minorities, 39%; whites, 36%; men, 36%; women, 37%.
- The belief that journalism is more satisfying and challenging than expected increases with age. Those who said journalism was more satisfying and challenging than expected included 31% of those age 25 and under; 38% of those age 26-30; 36% of those age 31-36; 39% of those age 36-40; 44% of those over age 40.
- Those with the least and the most years in journalism registered nearly the same levels of satisfaction: 34% of those in journalism 1-3 years and 35% of those in it 8-11 years said journalism was more satisfying and challenging than expected; the middle group, in the profession 4-7 years, was highest in its satisfaction, 40%.
- Among types of news organizations, the lowest portion to indicate that journalism was more satisfying and challenging than expected was 24% among those on medium dailies; the highest portions were 43%, among those on small dailies, and 41%, among those on large dailies.
- By educational backgrounds, the following portions of each category indicated journalism was more satisfying and challenging than expected: 32% of those who studied journalism as undergraduate majors; 41% of journalism minors; 26% of those who

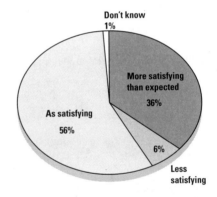

earned journalism master's degrees; 39% of those who had no journalism studies.
- 34% of those who had experience as campus journalists, and 46% of those who did not have experience as campus journalists, regarded journalism as more satisfying and challenging than expected.
- 26% of those who said they might leave journalism said journalism was more satisfying and challenging than expected, in contrast to 44% of those who said they planned to stay in journalism.
- Among all people surveyed, the group with the highest proportion saying journalism was less satisfying and challenging than expected was composed of those who studied journalism only at the master's degree level: 11%.

Do you plan to stay in journalism indefinitely or might you change careers? (Q.60)

- A higher portion of ethnic-minority new journalists (48%) than white new journalists (42%) said they might leave journalism.
- By age group, the largest portion of respondents who indicated they planned to stay in journalism — 65% — was the oldest group, over age 40.
- By educational backgrounds, those who earned journalism master's degrees comprised the largest portion planning to stay: 66%.

What is it that makes you want to stay in journalism? (Q.61)

- The portion of new journalists who said they wanted to stay in journalism primarily because they loved their jobs was substantial but decreased as age increased: 45% of those age 25 and under; 43% age 26-30; 40% age 31-36; 39% over age 40.
- Across types of news organizations, the portions who said loving their jobs made them want to stay: 37% of those at weeklies; 42%, small dailies; 39%, medium dailies; 38%, large dailies, 46%, broadcast outlets.
- By educational backgrounds, the only group that was lower than the average in saying love of job would keep them in the profession was the group with journalism master's degrees —

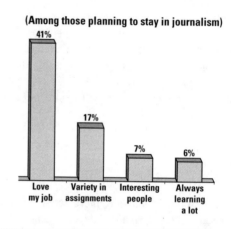

(Among those planning to stay in journalism)

What is it that might make you want to leave journalism? (Q.62)

- A greater portion of men than women said pay might make them want to leave journalism — 34% of the men and 26% of the women.
- A much greater portion of whites than ethnic minorities said pay might make them want to leave — 34% of whites, 11% of ethnic minorities.
- Among types of news organizations, the portions who said pay might make them want to leave journalism were: 36% of those at weeklies, 51% at small dailies, 21% at medium dailies, 19% large dailies, 41% at broadcast outlets.
- By educational backgrounds, the group with the lowest portion indicating pay might make them want to leave journalism was those who earned journalism master's degrees: 10% of them, compared with 27%-33% of other groups.
- Pay decreased as a factor in causing people to consider leaving the profession as respondents' pay increased: 47% of those earning under $20,000 listed it; 32% between $20,000 and $30,000; 24% between $30,000 and $40,000; 14% over $40,000.
- Burnout was more significant among ethnic minorities (14%) than among whites (6%) as a factor that would make them con-

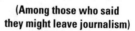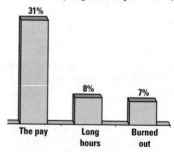

(Among those who said they might leave journalism)

sider leaving journalism. Burnout also was a more significant factor with the youngest group, those age 25 and under (10%), than it was with the oldest group, those over 40 (5%).
- Burnout was much more significant among those who earned journalism master's degrees: 21% said it might cause them to leave, in contrast to 8% of those who were journalism undergraduate majors, 5% of journalism minors and 1% of those with no journalism education.

How soon are you likely to leave journalism? (Q.63)

- The group with the highest portion of people thinking they would leave journalism within a year was the 36-40 age group — 20%.
- A higher portion of whites than ethnic minorities was considering leaving within a year — 13% of whites, 6% of ethnic minorities.
- A slightly higher portion of women than men said they were likely to leave within a year — 13% of women, 10% of men.
- Income was a strong indicator of desire to leave quickly: 27% of those who made under $20,000 reported they were likely to leave within a year; 10% of those who made $20,000-$30,000; 5% of those who made $30,000-$40,000; and 4% of those who made over $40,000. Among types of news organizations, 22% of the new journalists at weeklies and none of those at large dailies said they were likely to leave within a year.
- By education, those who said they might leave within a year: 8% of those who studied journalism as undergraduate majors, 23%

(All charts on this page pertain to those who said they might leave journalism.)

of journalism minors, 16% of those with no journalism studies and 3% of those who earned journalism master's degrees.

If you were to leave, what type of work would you want to do? (Q.64)

- By types of news organizations, the highest interest in going into public relations among those who are considering leaving journalism was: 36% of those from small dailies and 26% from broadcast outlets; the lowest was 11% from both medium and large dailies.
- Interest in entering public relations was in inverse relationship to income: 33% of those who make under $20,000; 28%, $20,000-$30,000; 15%, $30,000-$40,000; 8%, over $40,000.
- Public relations, writer and teaching were the top three alternative jobs of all groups, but in varying ranks.
- By far, the highest level of interest in public relations was expressed by journalism minors (41%), and the lowest interest in public relations was expressed by those who had no journalism studies (11%).
- Becoming a writer (other than journalist) was the first choice of those who have not studied journalism and are considering leaving journalism; their second choice was teaching.

19%	13%	23%	3%
Teaching	Writer	Public relations	Law

- Teaching was the first choice for those who earned journalism master's degrees (24%).
- Among ethnic minorities, teaching (22%) was the top choice for an alternative profession.
- Among whites, public relations (25%) was the top choice.
- The highest interest in law as an alternative profession was only 8%, registered by those age 26-30, by those who have been in journalism 4-7 years and by those in broadcast outlets.

Is there anything that could be done to keep you in journalism? (Q.65)

- Among those who reported they might leave journalism, a slightly larger portion of ethnic minorities than whites said something could be done to keep them in journalism — 77% of ethnic minorities, 72% of whites.
- The group with the smallest portion — 55% — who said something could be done to keep them in journalism was those with journalism master's degrees.
- The desire to leave the profession was slightly stronger among those who have been in it the fewest number of years. While 76% of those who have been in the profession 4 - 7 years said certain changes would keep them in journalism, 70% of those

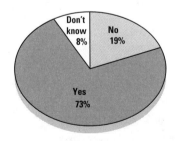

who have been in journalism 1 to 3 years said certain changes would keep them in journalism.
- A smaller portion of non-managers (69%) than managers (79%) said certain changes would keep them in journalism.

What would keep you in journalism? (Q.66)

- More money was much more important to whites as a factor that would keep them in journalism: 57% of whites, 27% of ethnic minorities.
- More money was more important to men (58%) than to women (44%).
- Dissatisfaction with management was more important to ethnic minorities and women than to whites and men. Twelve percent of ethnic minorities and women said working for a different organization could keep them in journalism; 8% of whites and 5% of men said it could.
- More money was more important to conservatives (54%) than to liberals (45%), more important to Republicans (63%) than to Democrats (48%).
- By income groups, more money as a factor that would prevent people from leaving journalism was important to 35% of those who make over $40,000 (the lowest portion) and to 65% of those who make under $20,000 (the largest portion).
- By type of news organizations, the highest level of interest in more money to keep them in journalism was 62% of those at

(Among those who said they might leave journalism.)

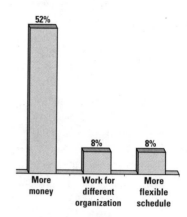

broadcast outlets (only 36% at medium dailies said money would make the difference).
- The group with the largest portion — 25% — who said working for a different organization might keep them in journalism was composed of those who earned journalism master's degrees.

Performance of self and news organization

How would you rate your own performance as a journalist? (Q.67)

- By educational background, those who rated their performance as journalists highest were those with no journalism education (37%) and those who earned journalism master's degrees (36%).
- The self-confidence rating was lowest among those 25 and under: 17% rated themselves very good, 14% rated themselves average.
- The self-confidence rating increased with income. Very good ratings: 23% of those in the under-$20,000 group; 26% in the $20,000-$30,000 group; 36% in the $30,000-$40,000 group; 41% in over-$40,000 group.
- The self-confidence rating also increased with number of years in profession. Very good ratings: 20%, 1-3 years; 34%, 4-7 years; 36%, 8-11 years.
- By type of news organizations, very good self-ratings were given by 24% of these at weeklies, 23% at small dailies, 32% at medium dailies, 44% at large dailies and 27% at broadcast outlets.

How do you think your supervisor would rate your performance as a journalist? (Q.68)

- Of all groups, the group with the largest portion who thought their supervisors rated their work very good: those who earned journalism master's degrees, 60%.
- Portions of other education groups who thought newsroom supervisors rated them very good: those who studied journalism

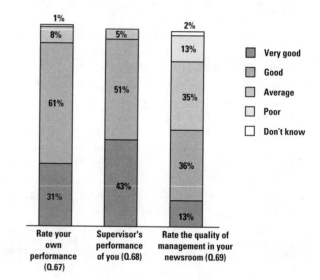

as undergraduate majors, 41%; those who did not study journalism, 48%.
- By type of news organization, the portions who thought their supervisors rated them very good: weeklies, 38%; small dailies, 34%; medium dailies, 47%; large dailies, 59%; broadcast outlets, 41%.
- Slightly more whites than ethnic minorities thought they would get very good ratings: 44% of whites, 40% of ethnic minorities.

- More men than women thought they would get very good ratings: 47% of men, 40% of women.
- Of all groups, the largest portions who thought their superiors would give them only average ratings were: ethnic minorities 11%; those 25 and under, 10%; those in the profession 1-3 years, 10%; those in broadcast journalism, 10%; those who earned less than $20,000, 9%.
- A larger portion of managers (49%) than non-managers (40%) said they thought supervisors would rate their performance as a journalist as very good.

How do you rate the quality of newsroom management where you work? (Q.69)

- Ethnic minorities and whites gave management nearly the same ratings. Very good ratings were given to managers by 15% of ethnic minorities, 13% of whites. Exactly the same portions of each group rated management as poor.
- Those who earned journalism master's degrees gave the lowest portion of very good ratings to management — 1% — and the

highest poor rating — 23%.
- Other poor ratings by educational background: 14% of those who studied journalism as undergraduate majors, 13% of journalism minors and 9% of those with no journalism education.
- Very good management ratings by educational background: 11% of those who studied journalism as undergraduate majors and 21% who had no journalism education.
- Very good management ratings by type of news organization: weeklies 18%, small dailies 8%, medium dailies 5%, large dailies 8%, broadcast outlets 16%.
- Poor management ratings by type of news organization: weeklies 17%, small dailies 15%, medium dailies 16%, large dailies 13%, broadcast outlets 13%.
- Managers had a higher opinion of newsroom management than non-managers did:
  - 57.9% of managers said they thought management was very good or good, compared with 46% of non-managers.
  - 15.6% of non-managers, compared with 8.5% of managers, said they thought management was poor.

Would you say that most journalists are paid more than they deserve, paid less than they deserve or paid about what they deserve? (Q.70)

- The range of support for the proposition that journalists are paid less than they deserve ranged from 69% (those who made more than $40,000) to 93% (those who made under $20,000).

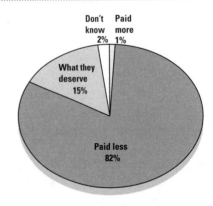

For each of the following (see choices below and on the next page), please tell me whether you strongly agree, mildly agree, mildly disagree, strongly disagree ...

The financial bottom line dominates newsroom decisions. (Q.71)

- 67% to slightly more than 80% within all groups either strongly or mildly agreed that the financial bottom line dominated newsroom decisions.
- The lowest level of agreement was among those with no journalism education, 62%.
- Among age groups, the highest level of agreement was among the youngest and the oldest — 78% of those age 25 and under, and 84% of those over age 40.
- By income levels, the strongest levels of disagreement with the idea the financial bottom line dominated newsroom decisions were expressed by those who made the least, under $20,000 (27%), and those who make the most, over $40,000 (28%).

Idealism dominates newsroom decisions. (Q.72)

- By all groups, the largest portion to agree either strongly or mildly that idealism dominated newsroom decisions too much were those people at broadcast outlets, 28%. The smallest portion was at medium dailies, 10%.
- By educational backgrounds, the group with the smallest portion strongly or mildly agreeing that idealism dominates newsroom decisions too much was composed of those with journalism master's degrees, 9%, twice the portion of those who studied journalism as undergraduate majors (19%), those who were minors (19%) and those who had no journalism education (18%).

I am encouraged to set goals for career advancement. (Q.73)

- The groups with the highest portions who reported being encouraged to set goals for career advancement: those in broadcast journalism, 73%; those who planned to stay in journalism, 73%.

• Those who strongly and mildly disagreed that they were encouraged to set goals for career management: 44% of those who are considering leaving journalism; 42% of those who earned journalism master's degrees; 27% of those who did not study journalism; 38% of those who minored in journalism; and 36% of those who studied journalism as undergraduate majors.

•There was wide disagreement between managers and non-managers on whether they were encouraged to set goals for career management:

■ 25.1% of non-managers and 41.8% of managers strongly agreed they were encouraged.

■ 25.8% of non-managers and 16.4% of managers mildly disagreed.

■ 13.4% of non-managers and 5.6% of managers strongly disagreed.

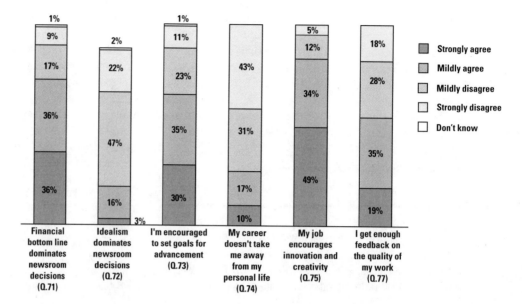

Legend:
- Strongly agree
- Mildly agree
- Mildly disagree
- Strongly disagree
- Don't know

My career as a journalist does not take me away from my personal life. (Q.74)

• A larger portion of managers (49%) than non-managers (40%) disagreed with the statement, "My career as a journalist does not take me away from my personal life."

Innovation and creativity are encouraged in my job. (Q.75)

• 61% of managers, in contrast to 45% of non-managers, strongly agreed with the statement, "Innovation and creativity are encouraged in my job."

• The highest level of agreement that innovation and creativity were encouraged: 63% of those in broadcast outlets strongly agreed.

• Highest levels of disagreement with that statement: 22% strongly and mildly disagreed among those at small dailies, those who earned journalism master's degrees and those who might leave journalism.

In my job I get enough feedback on the quality of my work. (Q.77)

• Portions, by educational background, who mildly or strongly disagreed that they got enough feedback on the quality of their work: did not study journalism, 36%; studied journalism as undergraduate major, 49%; journalism minors and those who earned journalism master's degrees, 53%.

How well is your organization preparing staff for the future needs of journalism? (Q.91)

• 49% of new journalists working on weeklies said they believed their news organizations were preparing staffs for future needs "not too well" or "not at all well" — the highest negative rating; the lowest negative rating was among those who worked at large dailies, 32%.

• 36% of managers, compared with with 46% of non-managers, said they believed their news organizations were preparing staff for future needs of journalism "not too well" or "not at all well."

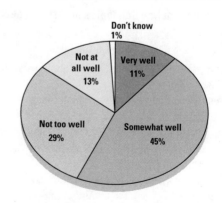

How well do you think your news organization does at providing people with information they need to be informed citizens? (Q.92)

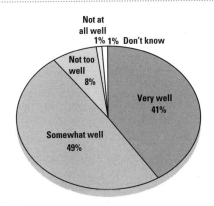

Technology in journalism education and in journalism

Do you use a computer at work? (Q.41)

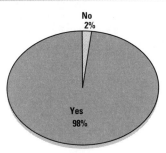

Do you regularly use your office computer to communicate with people outside of your office? (Q.42)

- The use of computers to communicate was greater among ethnic minorities (25%) than among whites (19%) and greater among men (23%) than among women (16%).
- Among all types of news organizations, the portion of new journalists who said they communicated by computer with people outside their offices was: 16% weeklies, 12% small dailies, 18% medium dailies, 31% large dailies, 20% broadcast outlets.
- The lowest levels of computer communication were reported by those who made under $20,000: 10%. For those who worked for small dailies, it was 12%.
- Communication by computer increased with years of experience in the profession: 17% of those in journalism 1-7 years,

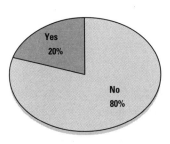

25% of those in journalism 8-11 years.
- 25% of managers, compared with 18% of non-managers, said they regularly used their office computers to communicate with people outside the office.

Do you regularly use your office computer for the collection and analysis of information other than the information found in your organization's library? (Q.43)

- Computers were used for research and analysis of data more by ethnic minorities (49%) than by whites (41%) and more by men (46%) than by women (39%).
- Of all groups surveyed, the highest use of computers for research and analysis of data was at broadcast outlets (55%) and by ethnic minorities (49%); the lowest use was at weekly newspapers, 29%.
- A greater portion of managers (56%) than non-managers (38%)

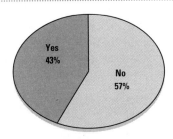

said they used their office computers to collect and analyze information other than information found in the organization's library.

How important is it that journalism education programs teach students how to use computers as communications and research tools? (Q.44)

- When age-group responses were assessed, those in the youngest group, age 25 and under, reported the lowest use of computers. But that group also registered the highest support, 92%, for journalism education programs teaching students how to use computers.

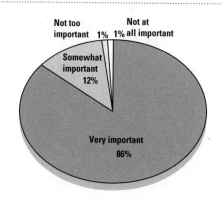

I'm going to read you a set of words that describe how some journalists feel about technological changes taking place in journalism. Please tell me how well each word describes your feelings — very well, somewhat well, not too well or not well at all: Enthusiastic. Threatened. Prepared. Skeptical. Confused. (Q.45)

- (Q.45a) Though women reported using computers less than men do, women reported being more enthusiastic (60%) than men (52%) about technological changes taking place in journalism
- The amount of enthusiasm for technological change also was inverse in relationship to computer use among other groups: age (more use by oldest portion, more enthusiasm for use by youngest portion), income (more use as income increased and more enthusiasm for use as income decreased).
- (Q.45c) A majority of who studied journalism indicated they felt somewhat prepared for technological changes
- Between 20% and 25% of all groups said they felt very prepared.
- The highest ratings of preparedness were from ethnic minorities and those 25 and under — 88% of both said they felt very well-prepared or somewhat well-prepared.

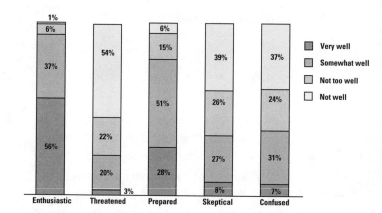

- (Q.45d) The highest level of skepticism about technological changes was expressed by graduates of non-accredited programs (44%).

Atmosphere of newsroom, concern about profession

I am worried about the impact of sensationalized coverage on the reputation of journalism. (Q.76)

- The following portions of people in all types of news organizations said they were either strongly or mildly worried about the impact of sensationalized coverage on the reputation of journalism: weeklies 88%, small dailies 89%, medium dailies 84%, large dailies 88%, broadcast outlets 92%.

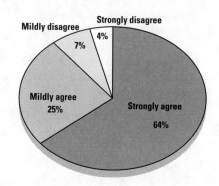

How well do each of the following describe the atmosphere in your newsroom — very well, somewhat well, not too well or not well at all ? (Q.90)

- (Q.90a) Among all groups, the highest portion of new journalists reporting that **"cynical"** characterized their newsrooms was those at medium dailies — 81%.
- Cynicism was reported by all groups to be high; the lowest levels of newsroom cynicism were reported by those age 36-40 (58%) and those who did not study journalism (63%).
- Across types of news organizations, reported levels of newsroom cynicism (very and somewhat cynical) were: at weeklies 61%, small dailies 69%, medium dailies 81%, large dailies 78%, broadcast outlets 63%.
- The lowest level of newsroom cynicism was reported by those who had no journalism education, 63%.

- (Q.90b) Among all groups, ethnic minorities gave "very well" the smallest portion of votes as a description of a **"fair"** atmosphere in their newsrooms — 24%. Their "not too fair" and "not at all fair" combined rating, 21%, was the largest portion among all groups.
- The highest "fair" ratings were given by those who worked in newsrooms at weeklies — 92%.
- The lowest "very fair" rating was given by those who worked at medium dailies, 24%.
- Managers gave their newsrooms a higher "very fair" rating (46%) than non-managers did (34%).

- (Q.90c) The highest "very well" ratings for **"honest"** as a description of their newsroom atmosphere were given by those who worked at weeklies (64%), those with no journalism education (60%) and those in broadcast journalism (59%).
- The lowest "very well" ratings for "honest" were given by those who worked at medium dailies (33%), by ethnic minorities (42%) and by those who worked at large dailies (43%).
- 59% of managers, in contrast to 48% of non-managers, said "honest" described their newsrooms very well.

- (Q.90d) Respondents over age 40 agreed the most — 41% of them — that **"open communication between managers and staff"** described the atmosphere of their newsrooms very well.
- About a third of all groups said "open communication between managers and staff" described their newsrooms not too well or not well at all.

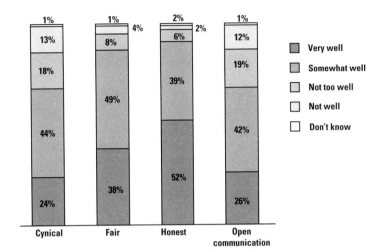

- Among types of news organizations, the highest level of agreement that "open communication between managers and staff" described their newsrooms very well or somewhat well was among weeklies — 80%. The lowest level of agreement was among medium dailies — 55%.
- Among all groups, those who earned journalism master's degrees registered the lowest vote for "open communication" describing their newsrooms very well — 15%.
- By educational backgrounds the greatest contrast was between those with no journalism education and those who earned journalism master's degrees: 21% of those with no journalism study said "open communication" described their newsrooms not too well and not at all well, while 48% of those with journalism master's degrees said that.
- 33% of managers and 23% of non-managers said their newsrooms were characterized by open communication between managers and staff.
- There was also a gap in perception between managers and non-managers on whether "open communication" characterized their newsrooms "not too well" or "not at all":
  - Non-managers — 22% "not too well," 14% "not at all."
  - Managers — 14% "not too well," 7% "not at all."

Education needs, interests of new journalists

Have you taken any college or graduate courses since you received your last degree? (Q.78)

- A larger portion of ethnic minorities than whites have taken undergraduate or graduate courses since they received their last degree: 30% of ethnic minorities, 24% of whites.
- A larger portion of women than men took such courses in that period: 28% women, 23% men.
- 37% of those over age 40 did so, compared with 14% of those 25 and under.
- Viewed by years in journalism, those who took courses were: 1-3 years, 16%; 4-7 years, 28%; 8-11 years, 30%.
- By news organizations, the portions were: those at weeklies 27%; small dailies 20%; medium dailies 30%; large dailies 22%; broadcast outlets 24%.
- By income levels: under $20,000, 20%; $20,000-$30,000, 24%; $30,000-$40,000, 31%; over $40,000, 28%.
- By educational backgrounds: those who studied journalism as undergraduate majors, 18%; journalism minors, 27%; no journalism education, 33%; those who earned journalism master's degrees, 21%.

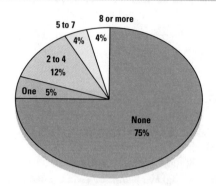

How many classes have you taken? (Q.79)

- Across all educational backgrounds, those who earned journalism master's degrees took the lowest number of courses since receiving their degrees: 10% took up to 5-7 courses, and none took more than that.
- Those with no journalism education took the highest number of courses — 18% of them took more than 10 courses since they received their degrees.

What are some of the classes you have taken?

(Q.80)

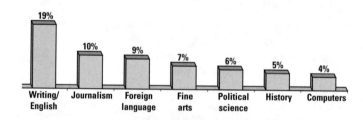

(Among those who have taken classes since receiving bachelor's degree)

How much do you think you might benefit from professional-development courses either in advanced journalism skills or in subjects other than journalism? (Q81)

- The strongest belief that they would benefit "a lot" from professional-development courses was expressed by those who earned journalism master's degrees: 68%.
- Ethnic minorities had a stronger belief than whites that they would benefit "a lot" — 64% vs. 56% — from such courses.
- Women had a stronger belief than men that they would benefit "a lot" — 62% vs. 53%.
- The strongest belief that professional-development courses would benefit them a little or not at all was expressed by those with no journalism education (20%), though they had taken the greatest number of courses.

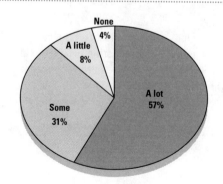

Does your current employer require staff members to take professional-development courses? (Q.82)

- The portion of each type of news organization that required professional-development courses: weeklies 4%, small dailies 5%, medium dailies 6%, large dailies 8%, broadcast outlets 2%.

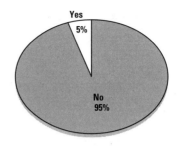

Many professions require ongoing professional-development courses. Do you think journalists should, or should not, be required to participate in ongoing development courses? (Q.83)

- The highest support for journalists' being required to take professional-development courses was from those on medium dailies, 64%.
- Ethnic minorities supported such a requirement more than whites did: 61% vs. 55%.
- Women supported such a requirement more than men: 60% vs. 52%.
- The only groups to support the requirement at less than 50% rates: those who made over $40,000 (49%), and those with no journalism education (48%).

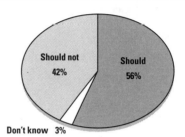

- 61% of those who said they might leave journalism supported the requirement, while 52% those who planned to stay in journalism supported it.

If you had the opportunity to take a course that would help you in your work, what course would you take? (Q.84)

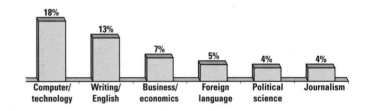

How willing would you be to work as a mentor or writing coach with journalism students at your local high school, community college or university? (Q.85)

- The highest level of enthusiasm for being a mentor or writing coach — very willing — was expressed by the youngest group, those 25 and under, at 71%.
- Ethnic minorities expressed a stronger interest than whites, with 65% of ethnic minorities and 56% of whites saying they were "very willing."

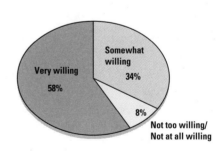

Have you ever worked as a writing coach or mentor? (Q.86)

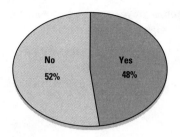

- The group with the largest portion who have worked as coaches and mentors was that of ethnic minorities, 60%, compared with 46% of whites.
- Women expressed a stronger interest than men in becoming mentors or coaches (women 60%, men 56%), but a larger portion of men than women reported they have worked as mentors and coaches (women 46%, men 50%).
- After ethnic minorities, the groups with the largest portions who have worked as mentors and coaches were those over 40 (59%), those who made over $40,000 (58%), those who worked for large dailies (58%), those who have been in journalism 8-11 years (56%), and those who earned journalism master's degrees (55%).

Voices

At the outset of this study, journalists and journalism educators throughout the United States were invited to comment on what they regard as the strengths and weaknesses of journalism education today and to offer insights into how they think journalism education should be improved. They were encouraged to extend the invitation to colleagues.

Many thoughtful responses were received by phone, fax, e-mail and mail. Excerpts are printed here under the title "Voices."

Other "voices" were heard in interviews and at a roundtable discussion held as part of the study. Some are from a telephone survey of individuals responsible for faculty-hiring searches, which were conducted by 117 institutions for the 1995-96 academic year.

Thanks to all who took time to reflect on these important issues.

Voices of journalism educators

" As to the changes that need to be made, I think one of the first is to stop referring to, and talking about, journalism as though it has only one referent — newspapers. I try to live my advocacy by speaking in terms of the journalism function and journalists' roles and by speaking of radio and television news in much the same way I speak of newspapers and magazines. Second, I think taking the results of our research seriously is an absolute necessity. "

R. C. Adams, *professor and chair, Department of Mass Communication and Journalism, California State University, Fresno*

" Changes needed in journalism education:
- Whatever is necessary to have universities agree that journalism/mass communication education is central to the overall university mission.
- Whatever might increase the "real-life" summer opportunities for faculty in newsrooms (print and broadcast) to ensure that the faculty remain current with industry. Add to this development of a system to match industry research needs with faculty availability.

Other observations:
- Would industry consider paying what a beginning school teacher earns to a beginning journalist?
- Media representatives say they want graduates with strong liberal arts backgrounds and then start reeling off technical courses when they explain what they're talking about.
- Wage-and-hour laws apply to media employers who somehow manage to circumvent them in offering unpaid internships to students "

Jo-Ann Huff Albers, *department head, Department of Journalism, Western Kentucky University, Bowling Green*

" A new breed of reporter and editor has emerged and will continue to emerge: a journalist adept at ferreting out valuable information from electronic sources. We have to prepare our students to take full advantage of the technology at their disposal. The emphasis in our courses should not be on the hardware — the nuts and bolts of technology. Rather, our instruction must focus on showing students how to use the technology to make them better reporters and editors, ultimately enabling them to produce better journalism.

This, after all, is what our programs are all about: preparing students to produce better journalism. So, even though newswriting, reporting and editing courses continue to be the heart and soul of our curriculum, the way we teach those courses — particularly in the way we use technology — has changed significantly during the past few years.

Is too much emphasis placed on training our students to enter the media work force? It is the primary goal in our program, for example. I would hope, though, that training our students is not at the expense of better educating them. Journalism educators need to be constantly aware of that possibility. I think that the accreditation criteria go a long way toward ensuring that our students will receive the appropriate blend of skills and conceptual courses in our programs. "

Douglas A. Anderson, *professor and dean, Walter Cronkite School of Journalism and Telecommunication, Arizona State University, Tempe President, Association of Schools of Journalism and Mass Communication*

"

There are too many people teaching journalism and variations of journalism whose own careers and work demonstrate no personal acquaintance with, let alone skill, in high standards. Many teachers have a record of work that reflects little or no respect for the intelligence of the audience, and little ability to deal with serious issues and events in a serious way. There are some whose work has been in other fields, or who may be transplanted from other academic disciplines, whose knowledge of journalism comes almost entirely from reading books about journalism. Occasionally, I get a call from some poor young assistant professor who has been assigned to teach journalism in some distant state and needs to know what book about reporting he can read. I tell them that, like surgery, you cannot learn it from a book. They often seem to be very nice people but in the wrong place.

The idiocy of requiring journalism teachers to have doctoral degrees for appointment and tenure is widespread. One remedy could come from working journalists through a national platform to speak loudly and consistently on this obvious irrationality, addressing direct communication to heads of colleges and universities.

There are too many journalism degrees granted by departments and schools that show too little separation between church and state. Such institutional programs display too little regard for the difference between, on one hand, journalism as a public service, and, on the other, advertising and public relations.

Either make the Association for Education in Journalism and Mass Communication create a separate group for journalism — minus advertising, minus public relations and minus communications theory — or have journalism faculties who hold to high values secede from AEJMC to form their own national body and ask for accrediting powers.

"

Ben H. Bagdikian, *former dean, Graduate School of Journalism, University of California, Berkeley*

"

If I could impress upon professionals any single point, it would be this: We in journalism education do not exist to provide cheap labor for your enterprises.

And, if I could impress upon those of us in journalism education any single point, it would be this: We need our curricula less tied to specific media jobs and more toward general strategies and skills in communicating messages in general.

"

Fred Bales, *associate professor, Department of Communication, University of New Mexico, Albuquerque*

"

As schools and departments with shrinking budgets, we're going to be hard-pressed to serve the traditional and emerging media with anything approaching equal success. A minority of us, I estimate, want traditional media to persist. Whatever the warts, we believe the reporting — or even the threat of reporting — wrongdoing will keep society's power brokers in some balance. The problem is many of the media managers are profit-driven — stockholder-driven — and care less about those roles for the media than their predecessors.

We need to be as current as possible and mix our faculties with academics who are sympathetic and with practitioners recently or still attached to the field. If we want to be accepted more by the academic community, we are going to have to do more academic things. This means scholarship and service on committees and integration in the academic way of life. This is antithetical to daily journalism in many instances.

"

Edward P. Bassett, *professor and director, School of Communications, University of Washington, Seattle*

"

I think the future is so uncertain for journalism/mass communications programs that we are almost back at square one. If I had to make predictions, they would be that only the really strong professional schools will survive and that the rest will become parts of communications departments — and increasingly small parts at that.

The questions we need to ask:
- What is journalism in a world of competing media?
- What is journalism in a world of "competing truths" when the whole idea of journalism — at least as I was taught it — was to find the truth and tell the public about it?

We need to take a hard look at ourselves. We really don't fit well in academic departments and need to model ourselves after professional schools of law, medicine, etc. We can't do that well, however, because we don't have backing from professionals. We need to study our history. We cannot continue in our haphazard way that we have been going. A look at our past may give us insight for the future. At least, let's hope so.

"

Maurine H. Beasley, *professor, College of Journalism, University of Maryland, College Park*

"

One of my goals is to change the attitudes of journalism educators about the value of what we teach. I think that we kill ourselves and undermine our programs each time we say, "Oh, she teaches a skills course," or "We are a trade school."

No one considers that a reporting class is a liberal arts class. If an English composition class, usually taught by a graduate student who knows little about good writing, is a liberal arts class, why not my reporting class? I teach thinking, information-gathering and writing, and I do it a lot better than the typical English teacher.

We should be bragging about our results: students who are trained in clear thinking and writing. Aren't those skills

the heart of a liberal education? To survive we should be selling ourselves as part of the liberal arts and sciences.

"

Glen Bleske, *assistant professor, Department of Journalism, California State University, Chico*

"

How many programs do we need? How should they fit in the university structure? Who will serve the second or third tier of students if j-schools are reduced to the big 20 or 30? I'm talking about good future journalists who start slowly and come from economically or educationally poor backgrounds. Many of them are minorities. Many won't make the entrance cut at big schools, particularly if affirmative action efforts are sliced.

"

Karen F. Brown, *dean of faculty, The Poynter Institute for Media Studies, St. Petersburg, Fla.*

"

As a journalism teacher and a South African, I am often asked why the U.S. press covers South Africa so sporadically. Over the years, editors have not identified South Africa as uniquely worthy of their indifference. Yet South Africa's failure to make the top-10 news stories for 1994 in The Associated Press survey of 357 news and broadcast executives is puzzling. U.S. media had devoted considerable space and time to South Africa in 1994, particularly to the transition from white minority to black majority rule in the April election. Many editorial writers and columnists judged it among the most significant events of the decade, some said of the twentieth century.

What should journalism teachers learn from the collective judgment of news executives at the end of 1994? What news values should we teach that will enable students to impress newspaper and broadcast recruiters? Should we seek instruction from the stories that made the top five — O.J. Simpson, Susan Smith, Kerrigan-Harding, and the baseball and hockey strikes? AP's list mainly of murder, slaughter and sports says something disturbing about journalism and American society. Perhaps news isn't vital to the conversation of self-governance. It's a commodity sold in a marketplace not of information and ideas but of sensation and titillation.

Journalism teachers cannot in good conscience teach those values. We can try only to understand them and to teach about them.

As journalism teachers, we try to balance the call of civics and of commerce. We teach that what journalists decide is news must make its way in an increasingly competitive, fragmented marketplace. But we cannot teach only the values that dominated the selection of the top 10 stories of 1994. We cannot teach that the baseness of human nature in public and private life is all that defines what's newsworthy. We must teach that some stories transcend an allure for large audiences and advertising revenue. Reporting the struggle and triumph that Nelson Mandela represents deserves the best that young journalists can give. History will record that that victory for reason and justice cost thousands of lives across three centuries. Even though the events in April 1994 that fell within the attention span of news killed

only hopelessness and despair, young journalists should know that such stories can grip, inform and inspire. They should know that the Nobel Prize for peace and the Pulitzer Prize for journalism occasionally reward the same values, even though those values may not make the top 10.

"

Trevor R. Brown, *dean, School of Journalism, Indiana University, Bloomington*

"

Our first greatest weakness is not realizing the extent of journalism's potential contribution to meeting human needs. In a word: minding; that is, furnishing whatever capabilities are required to contribute to informing our behavior, individually and collectively. Change needed: Begin journalism education with a thorough functional analysis of informational needs, in the context of behavioral need.

Our second greatest weakness is that we have not advanced to a disciplinary status. Chemistry and physics went through a "practices" stages, but they eventually got some scientific theory and were better able to fulfill their potential for meeting human needs. Change needed: Install a foundation of [scientific] theoretical principles of communicative behavior for journalism education, so students will have a common sense of what they are trying to do — and why.

Our third greatest weakness is relying on intellectual tools from more established academic disciplines — tools which are inappropriate to the nature of journalism (as both science and art). Change needed: Meld art [practice] and behavioral science [principle] together in a research-and-development program. Be more inventive and creative in practice. Have students do a lot more things together as communities, so they will have a fuller appreciation of all that is needed for collective behavior.

"

Richard F. Carter, *professor, School of Communication, University of Washington, Seattle*

"

The most important issue in journalism education today is one that is somewhat invisible: the partnership with the professional. We are entering a new day. Newspapers are in trouble. They are dying. They need research — on how to use the technology, how to capture young readers. Professors can be a great help to them with research.

It's only natural to have the constellation of mass communication in journalism education. The fields in it — advertising and public relations — are very closely related. They are vital parts of the constellation. Public relations has grown in our society. It is proper that it be included.

We can't ignore the new media. The Internet is one of the biggest changes going on. When computers came in, some schools said wait. I said balderdash, we can't wait. With the Internet so pervasive, schools can't wait. We need to hire media futurists. Today there are all these other voices. We are a growth market, not a declining market. Journalism education has never been in such good shape.

"

Richard R. Cole, *dean, School of Journalism and Mass Communication, University of North Carolina, Chapel Hill*

"

We need to decide if we want to remain professional schools, a question which really goes to whether the profession will support us and whether our students can get jobs. If we are to become mass comm. educators — and there is a solid argument for this, as much as it hurts my stomach — then we need to decide what that is.

We need to face the literary problem squarely. Most of our curricula still assume that students come to the j-school already knowing how to write a complete sentence. They can. They just can't do that at the same time they say something in that sentence.

"

Jon Franklin, *professor, School of Journalism and Communication, University of Oregon, Eugene*

"

Are we doing enough to help students/journalists sort out fact from propaganda, fantasy and entertainment? Can we do more to explain the influences behind the media that help determine what news is?

"

Sarah Grimes, *professor, Department of Journalism, University of Massachusetts, Amherst*

"

What evidence is there comparing the effectiveness of sequence-oriented curricula — in which newspaper, broadcast, PR, etc., are on separate tracks — with curricula in which the different parts of journalism are more integrated around a common body of course work?

What are the basic skills now? What do graduating journalism majors need to know?

What are the basic metaskills — that is, motivation, self-direction, ability to take criticism, stress management, learning how to learn — and how are these being specifically taught, practiced and tested in current programs?

"

Gerald Grow, *professor, School of Journalism, Media and Graphic Arts, Florida A&M University, Tallahassee*

" ......

Universities want faculties with doctorates, but having a doctorate does nothing to enhance teaching skills or to certify competence in the areas of professional skills. (I can say this with a fair amount of credibility because I have considerable professional experience and a doctorate.)

How do we make scholarship in our field relevant to the professions in which our graduates work? I think lawyers actually read law reviews. Physicians read medical journals. But I can't recall ever having read *Journalism Quarterly* when I was a working journalist, and I never saw anyone else reading it in news operations where I worked. I fear our "research" very often asks questions that are no more relevant than the "How-many-angels-can-dance-on-the-head-of-a-pin?" question was in an earlier time, or is as obvious as "Roof leaks can be detected in the rain." The articles very often are impenetrable to anyone without a Ph.D. No wonder our scholarship has such a hard time being taken seriously. I think we are guilty of doing and publishing research simply for the sake of fulfilling the expectations of promotion and tenure committees, rather than to advance knowledge in our field.

I think our schools are the only place students can come if they want to work seriously with words and if they want to learn to write. In many ways, I think we are the new home of the "liberal education." I think our curricula offer a coherence in a field of study that is largely unavailable now in colleges or schools of arts and sciences.

We've been largely ineffective in telling our own success stories, which is ironic considering what we purport to teach, but then the media themselves are also ineffective in making cases for their importance to society.

Janet Hill Keefer, *associate professor and dean, School of Journalism and Mass Communication, Drake University, Des Moines, Iowa*

" ......

When journalism educators get together, we don't speak the same language. To assume public relations and journalism are the same study is a perversion of the language. If they take the value out of journalism, the least they can do is take journalism out of the name. History and literature, not public relations and advertising, would be our logical partners.

Writing and reporting are the basis of all good journalism, broadcast and print. Broadcasting is a terribly confused field. It needs writing every bit as much as print journalism does.

The president of the university came to one of our faculty meetings after I became dean. The faculty wanted to know what was expected of them for tenure and promotion. They asked if he wanted them to do the kind of writing that was in *Journalism Quarterly*. His response: "No. We want you to produce outstanding journalism in journalism forums. We want you to contribute to the dialogue of your time, whether in subject areas that journalism treats or in research about journalism."

I sometimes feel as though we at Columbia are lonely monks and scribes preserving the cult of journalism.

Joan Konner, *dean, Graduate School of Journalism, Columbia University, New York City*

" ......

Journalism students need courses in intellectual history. Many of them are bright and facile, but their memories are short, their sense of the flow of historical currents is limited, and they operate without much of an intellectual framework or understanding of the world they will be reporting on. As a result, they are locked into the conventional wisdom of their own times.

Also, in nearly 10 years at *The Chicago Reporter*, we rarely interviewed a job candidate with a sophisticated understanding of statistics. As a result, a lot of apples are getting mixed with a lot of oranges and lemons, not to mention a few pomegranates.

Roy Larson, *director, Garrett-Medill Center for Religion and the News Media, Evanston, Ill.*

"

Let's not dance around the subject. The problem has to do with institutional structure and how that determines who's teaching journalism. I think most of the colleges and universities in this country that have journalism programs require people to have a Ph.D. That means the bulk of those people who are teaching journalism are not people with extensive experience.

The profession keeps wondering why [journalism students] can't think. I think it has something to do with this: If [journalism teachers] don't have strong backgrounds as journalists, they don't understand the thinking involved in doing stories [and] they can't talk about it with their students.

The majority of journalism educators in this country today are not well-educated in journalism; they don't have that strong professional background. One of the things that means is they are more likely to focus on the technology — because they can learn how to push the right buttons — than the thinking, because they didn't experience thinking as a journalist.

Teachers who have never been in the field are told they have to teach newswriting and reporting. We need to look at the structural underpinnings of who teaches journalism in this country. That's a big component of the problems in journalism.

"

Joann Lee, *director of broadcast journalism, Ramapo State College, Northvale, N.J.*

"

The Ph.D. octopus, as William James called it, has been around for a very long time and is clearly related to the mania for credentials that has spanned this century. All professional schools have this problem to some degree. I would not write this off as simply the protective behavior of an entrenched educational bureaucracy, though it is partly that.

The research model has triumphed in higher education since World War II. It has seemed far more important to expand knowledge than to polish students' skills or to nurture them. Even the small, traditional liberal arts

colleges have gone this route. It was inevitable, then, that journalism programs would churn out research. One problem has been that little of this research has impressed folks in other fields. When this goes on long enough, it's a green light for cutbacks. It doesn't help if practitioners are ready to testify that they ignore the research.

Modern universities and colleges just aren't set up to reward the dedicated teaching of fundamentals. There is a powerful argument behind this: a professional's skills and experience may be superb now, but in time they will grow stale. The best guarantee for distinguished teaching over time is continual production that is reviewed and judged by the best people in the field and compared with work in other academic departments.

"

Thomas C. Leonard, *associate dean, Graduate School of Journalism, University of California, Berkeley*

"

Questions that need to be asked:

- To what extent should a more critical stance be taken in the teaching of information-gathering and writing — that is, should our teaching merely reflect existing reporting practices and processes?
- Where does accreditation fit into this model? That is, is it better to offer students more than 50% of their work in journalism and to let some liberal arts context fall to the wayside?
- Should journalism (news-ed) be retained as a definable sequence, or should it be folded into larger comm. study?

"

Duncan McDonald, *professor and dean, School of Journalism and Communication, University of Oregon, Eugene*

"

If we really want to help our students, we should spend more time trying to change the environment into which they are graduating. First, we should abandon the fiction that individual reporters, or even editors, are the key decision-makers in most news media. The journalist's autonomy is almost always sharply bounded by newsroom culture and structures imposed by higher-level managers attempting to maximize return to stockholders or owners. Contrary to the conventional wisdom of reporters as cynical rogues or "vipers," all but the most elite journalists are decision-takers, not makers. If they don't meet expectations set by their employers, they are disciplined or let go. So we need to revise journalism's ethical codes to apply to those who have real power over the product.

"

John McManus, *former assistant professor, Communication Department, Santa Clara University, Santa Clara, Calif.*

"

As a college sophomore in 1947, I decided that telling people what was going on in their world would be rewarding to society and rewarding to me. As a professional journalist in 1967, I decided that teaching others to do the above was the next logical step for me. I've never regretted either decision. Indeed, I currently feel that good journalism will be vital to a healthy society in the decades to come and that practicing journalism will be stimulating and self-fulfilling.

We need to differentiate between the social contract journalists implicitly assume — to adequately inform the public — and the social contracts other communicators assume — i.e., to promote worthy products, services or institutions. One of my fantasies is that AEJMC will become the Association for Education in Mass Communications, and then we can organize the Association for Professional Journalism Education. We are a profession not driven by the marketplace or the seats of power. Our first goal is the education of practitioners.

We need to take the lead in moving away from the technologies of the first half of the 20th century (radio and television) and the technology of the last half of the second mil-

lennium (the printing press) and embrace the technology of academe and of the 21st century. Contemporary mass media are obsolescent and crippled by intense competitive, environmental and social pressures. A digital information medium offers real potential for reducing these pressures and for fulfilling the social contract described above.

"

Harry Marsh, *professor, A.Q. Miller School of Journalism and Mass Communications, Kansas State University, Manhattan*

"

Other professional schools turn out graduates who are so ahead of the curve on technical advancement that mid-career professionals in their fields shudder to see them coming. They know that the kids have useful information that hadn't even been discovered when they were in school.

J-schools should be the same way. We are in a couple of small areas but not in general. That's why we need Ph.D.s — to create the new knowledge that the profession needs in order to cope with change.

For a variety of historical reasons, a Ph.D. in journalism is regarded as just a hoop to jump through in order to qualify for a teaching job. Even The Freedom Forum, in its announcement of the Chapel Hill [Ph.D. program for journalists], treated it as such. But our field — and the demands on it — is changing so much that it desperately needs a continuing source of new knowledge. We have to change the culture that says there is enough knowledge already and we don't need journalism teachers to discover as well as impart the truth.

"

Philip Meyer, *professor and Knight Chair in Journalism, School of Journalism and Mass Communication, University of North Carolina, Chapel Hill*

"

When I was an undergraduate in the early '60s, journalism programs, even good ones, were tolerated, not appreciated, by their fellow academics. And the green-eyeshade/chi-square wars were waging inside journalism education programs. Publishers and editors were regularly taking potshots at journalism education.

Today, although we still have remnants of those problems, I sense that the good programs around the country are generally seen as solid citizens within the academy. Professionals and traditional scholars within journalism/communication programs not only tolerate but often enjoy each other's intellectual company, and the silly and uninformed criticism from the industry is at a minimum.

The (David) Weaver - (G. Cleveland) Wilhoit book showed that, whatever editors said about journalism graduates, they tend to hire them. It's my impression that the "they can't spell" and "they can't do grammar" or, alternatively, "gimme a good liberal arts graduate" arguments have nearly disappeared. And when editors and publishers bring them up these days, they usually have the good taste to be embarrassed about it.

Why are we doing better? Part of it, I suspect, is just age. All disciplines had a period in which they were not accepted as full members of the academy. It took time, and we're not a century old yet. We're now at that stage in our disciplinary history at which folks with journalism/communication degrees play key roles in the industry, in foundations, in academic leadership roles both in the discipline and in higher administration. We have, in other words, more or less arrived.

"

Dean Mills, *professor and dean, School of Journalism, University of Missouri, Columbia*

"

Journalism education followed too closely the culture of the social and behavioral science disciplines at the expense of the humanities and literary fields. Advances in social science have been very helpful to the practice of journalism, but we went overboard. Also, I think the journalism professional culture has been too smug and self-satisfied, rendering its members resistant to essential, field-sustaining, progressive change.

"

Edward Mullins, *professor and dean, College of Communication, University of Alabama, Tuscaloosa*

"

We need to ask: Are journalism students learning how to be tuned in to the world they'll be writing for and about? Are they actually reading newspapers? Good newspapers? I'm afraid many of our students graduate without ever reading any of the nation's leading newspapers. If we don't require that they read *The New York Times*, they don't. I imagine many just read the daily student newspaper, if they read a paper at all. Do they read serious political-cultural magazines like *The Nation, National Review, The New Republic, The Progressive*? My experience is that most of them graduate without even having heard of these magazines.

Are they being introduced to people and groups outside the range of their own class and ethnic group? We could make a deliberate effort to expose students to social worlds they're not familiar with. It's not just the students that don't read major newspapers and serious magazines — not to mention books — who don't talk with people unlike themselves. It's also the faculty. That may be where we need to begin.

"

Carol Polsgrove, *associate professor, School of Journalism, Indiana University, Bloomington*

"

When I left to teach, a lot of people said to me, "Oh, I've always thought about doing that." It was a little more emotional than that. Many of them said that in a tone of desperation: "Would you please drop a trail of bread crumbs on the way out so that we can find our way over the wall, too?"

There is a sense of disenchantment with this calling among many of my colleagues, and I'm talking about all levels, and I'm talking about print and broadcast: the tilt toward the sensational, the lack of respect for the work that we do, the decline in our credibility and, therefore, in our audiences and readership, the poor quality of so much of the work we see, and the poor quality of the leadership that we are asked to follow.

What I found in talking to my colleagues was that it's a daily struggle to keep your job and keep your integrity.

Students hear this, they see this. They say to themselves, "Wait a minute. What am I supposed to think now of this profession I thought I wanted to get into." I think that's the challenge here. How do you deal with the reality of the world of journalism today and the needs of the students who are going to enter that world?

"

Deborah Potter, *faculty member, The Poynter Institute for Media Studies, St. Petersburg, Fla.*

"

University-level journalism education has to address several new areas in the 1990s in order to adequately serve the profession. Special attention needs to be given to learning about public-affairs policy and practice, particularly how government and the economy work and how just about everything these days relates to a global outlook.

"

Frank Quine, *director of development, College of Journalism, University of Maryland, College Park*

"

The main reason for the current spate of mergers under way is that our journalism schools have stressed professional experience of faculty members to such an extent that scholarly ability and accomplishments have often been ignored. This undervaluing of scholarship in journalism faculty members means that journalism schools cannot survive in the research university of today.

Daddy Bleyer, an early leader in journalism education at the University of Wisconsin, foresaw this problem back in the 1930s, and started the first strong doctoral program in journalism and mass communication in order to allow journalism to survive in research universities. Wilbur Schramm was less concerned about the survival of journalism schools, but nevertheless contributed toward the same end as Daddy Bleyer when he founded Ph.D. programs in communication at Illinois and Stanford in the 1940s and 1950s.

"

Everett M. Rogers, *professor and chair, Department of Communication and Journalism, University of New Mexico, Albuquerque*

"

Questions to consider:

- What are the perceptions from different camps and concerns that are lying below the surface, and that we aren't really articulating?
- What does it mean to call it a "professional" field? What are the bargains and trade-offs in that designation?
- What does it mean to "serve the journalism profession more adequately"? Which journalism profession — that of our ideals or that encountered in the newsroom?
- Why do so many in or close to journalism education insist on separating it from the liberal arts? What are the implications of that division, particularly in the academy?

"

Willard D. Rowland Jr., *professor and dean, School of Journalism and Mass Communication, University of Colorado, Boulder*

"

- Our role in society?
- Our role in the academy?
- Ethics?
- How do we address the integration of media?
- How do we communicate with our "publics"?
- Are there ways we can begin to finance our own operations as academic units other than state appropriations and grants?
- What does (the profession) need from us? Are they willing to help?

"

Roger C. Saathoff, *professor and director, School of Mass Communications, Texas Tech University, Lubbock*

"

I think j-schools could benefit from using more adjunct (teachers). At the same time, adjuncts need training as teachers. It's one thing to tell war stories. You can get away with that for a class or two. It's another to teach journalism systematically. We have more experience to offer but having it to offer and being able to apply it are two different things.

"

Berl Schwartz, *general manager and editorial adviser,* The State News, *Michigan State University, East Lansing*

"

As the 21st century approaches, and the most deeply held tenets underlying democratic societies are challenged, the need for the public to understand the issues has never been greater. People must have access to comprehensive, objective information about political, economic and social policies and events, and authoritative analyses of the short- and long-term ramifications of these policies and events that provide them with the opportunity to participate in the formation of public policy. Without access to information, ideas and ways to communicate with and about the government, people will never be able to control the government.

The greatest challenge facing journalism education is to design programs that enable students to develop the critical thinking, research and writing skills to provide the public with the information and channels of communication that people need to participate effectively in a democracy, and the ethical and legal backgrounds to act as advocates in helping the public defend individual rights and liberties.

"

Jacqueline Sharkey, *professor, Department of Journalism, University of Arizona, Tucson*

"

The debate over who should teach journalism — the Ph.D. vs. the professional — is bogus. The Accrediting Council claims a mixture of the two groups makes a fine faculty, but in reality the scale is tipped toward academics. The profession needs to exert more pressure through the Accrediting Council to correct this imbalance.

Journalism schools should be providing more professional-development programs for working journalists. Journalism programs need to set as their top priorities:

- The teaching of critical thinking.
- Not mistaking the computer for the content.
- The role of journalism in a democratic society.
- Teaching how journalism can better reflect the diversity of the publics it serves.

"

Erna Smith, *associate professor and chair, Department of Journalism, San Francisco State University*

"

I'd like for us to lose the old "journalism ain't real learnin' " syndrome that drives us. Journalism ethics, mass media and society, First Amendment law, and other substantive courses should be at least as intellectually legitimate as any other course in the humanities or social sciences. I'd like to see us change the assumptions so courses taught in journalism/mass communications departments carry the same intellectual legitimacy as those in the other academic departments on campus.

[Also] we don't make [students] write enough. Which means we don't make them think enough. At base, I think, a journalism student should be learning to think: to gather information, comprehend it, assess and analyze it, and communicate its essence. We learn to do that and show we can do that by writing. And rewriting. So-called skills courses that require a couple of thumb-suckers a term cheat our students. Reporting classes that require three or four news stories don't do the job. In short, too often we are not demanding enough.

"

Hampden H. Smith III, *professor and head, Department of Journalism and Mass Communications, Washington and Lee University, Lexington, Va.*

"

Some suggestions for improving journalism education:

- A public relations program to show potential graduates that journalism is alive and well. It could also point out career opportunities. Another plus would be to share stories of collegiate journalists who have succeeded in the fourth estate. Feature stories could also be written up about upcoming programs.
- Build rapport with local publications. In my experience, we live in two different worlds. I have had to cultivate a relationship.

"

P. Larry Stahle, *instructor specialist, Weber State University, Ogden, Utah*

"

Instead of wanting to raise hell in the system, most students just want to be part of the system. Very few of my students have any real interest in newspapering as a career. In fact, a good many of my students major in communication studies due to lack of anything else they might have interest in. In my seven years here, I have had only one prospective student come to me and say she "knew" she wanted to be a journalist.

While I believe deeply that students ought to be able to do what they want to do, I ultimately think this trend is bad for the nation and for democracy. With fewer students wanting to be reporters who (in theory) will question and examine the system, and more wanting to be in PR and advertising, most of which is designed to promote the status quo, our democracy suffers.

The late 1970s, the boom period for traditional journalism education, came on the heels of Vietnam and Watergate, when a lot of idealistic young people saw journalism as a way to help the culture make some needed changes. Today, the press is seen as part — or even the biggest cause — of the problems with the world, and who wants to be part of the problem?

Pay is staggeringly low, especially in the lower ranks of weeklies and small dailies where most new grads start. My students, many of whom face $20,000 or more in debt upon graduation, can't be blamed if they're not excited about working for $250 a week.

Workload and stress are, at the same time, staggeringly high. Reporters are asked to work all day and then cover the city council at night and the high school game on the weekend. Publishers, one of the most greedy groups of employers out there, often are able to force these schedules on journalists without paying them overtime.

"

Brian Steffen, *assistant professor, Department of Communication, Simpson College, Indianola, Iowa*

"

After four years of teaching, I believe:
- Many — most? — professionals have no idea of the limits of time actually invested in journalism courses, per se, and the preponderance of liberal arts courses which form the majority of each student's curriculum. A little education for the pros is in order.
- Some schools, I have learned, do not have ethics courses. They all should teach ethics.

"

Paul Steinle, *adjunct associate professor, School of Communication, University of Miami, Miami, Fla.*

"

Changes that need to be made:
- More emphasis on teaching of the best reporting and non-fiction writing.
- More emphasis on writing and reporting and less on specific newsroom skills, all of which change rapidly with the new technologies.
- Remove advertising and public relations from the curriculum. They belong in business schools.
- Increase the separation between the study of mass communication and training in writing and reporting. They are two separate disciplines.

"

Mitchell Stephens, *professor and former chair, Department of Journalism and Mass Communication, New York University, New York City*

"

We need to educate the journalist of the future:
- An information specialist who can figure out anything relating to the universe, who can find, sort, retrieve and organize this information.
- An explanation specialist who can make the world clear, under the premise that the more information there is, the less we understand it.
- A master storyteller, a wordsmith who can turn raw data into something that's compelling for the reader or viewer.

"

Carl Sessions Stepp, *associate professor, College of Journalism, University of Maryland, College Park*

"

I pass long these "macro" conclusions we reached in our discussion during the (Association for Education in Journalism and Mass Communication) Executive Committee meeting (April 1995):

- Journalism education is not broad enough to describe what we will need to provide in the future. It may not be broad enough even now. We must encompass more of communication than just journalism, perhaps more than just mass communication, if we are to serve the professional education needs of emerging industries and students who want to work in an increasingly technology-driven interdisciplinary professional milieu.
- Providing training for students planning professional careers in journalism (and mass communication) is not a broad enough mission for an academic discipline at today's university.
- Relying on the excuse "we're different, we're journalism" to explain why some members of our professorate disdain and refuse to engage in scholarship and research won't cut it on today's campus of higher expectations. And research that's unintelligible to the professions we serve — and even sometimes to academic colleagues — is not fulfilling the potential of the "best" research to both add to a body of knowledge but also to make that body of knowledge applicable to the practice of journalism and mass communication.
- Continuing to study journalism education won't help journalism education as much as developing strategies to make journalism education an indispensable intellectual component of a college or university. Let's quit talking and come up with — and implement — an action plan!

"

Judy VanSlyke Turk, *professor and dean, College of Journalism and Mass Communications, University of South Carolina, Columbia President, Association for Education in Journalism and Mass Communication, 1994-95*

"

How can journalism educators make sure they do not substitute training for education? How can we make certain that training takes place in the context of liberal education? This, I think, is the toughest challenge we face.

Everyone in education must stop suggesting to students that being bad at numbers is almost a guarantee that they will be good at words. Every undergraduate journalism program should require training in statistics, and students should, in a variety of courses, see how knowledge of numbers is critical to responsible journalism. Beyond the issue of being able to critically evaluate information handed to us lies the question of being able to responsibly do computer-assisted reporting tasks with spreadsheets and databases.

We must begin to deal explicitly and in a scholarly way with the relationships between information and ideologies. We need a better appreciation that information is not a neutral product but is, rather, a product of human institutions that have interests and ideologies. When we select some information for a message and omit other information, we are involved in decisions that are at least partly ideological.

Ethical issues should not be confined to the individual practitioner level. The practices the public deplore are, most often, results from decisions at the industry level, corporate policy, and so on.

"

Jean Ward, *professor, School of Journalism and Mass Communication, University of Minnesota, Minneapolis*

"

Questions pertinent to the improvement of journalism education:

- Can we specify our goals versus those of traditional academic disciplines? Are our goals congruent with those of traditional academic disciplines?
- Should journalism be an academic major, or should it be a minor instead?
- Should journalism be strictly a graduate program?
- Should journalism education be more of an apprenticeship? Perhaps a year of apprenticeship between sophomore and junior years, or junior and senior years?
- Should we blatantly draw lines between professional tracks and scholarly tracks and base our hiring and our curriculum on those divisions?

"

Patsy G. Watkins, *professor and chair, Walter J. Lemke Department of Journalism, University of Arkansas, Fayetteville*

"

Will media outlets ever pay a decent starting salary? Why, when rating journalism programs, are the same people from the same universities always asked to rate programs? Why isn't journalism more critical of itself?

Changes needed in journalism education:

- Don't go to a mass media theory way of teaching when skills are still a major requirement for employment.
- Educators must do a better job of research that is meaningful for media and the professions.
- Stop being defensive on campus; go on the offense. Show how our business has a greater daily impact on people day to day than most anything other than air, water, sex and food — and it plays a major role in all of those as well.

"

Richard Wells, *associate professor and chair, Journalism Department, University of North Texas*

"

My concerns are about the course work required outside the journalism curriculum. Having taught journalism at five major institutions, I have seen students wandering through college-course offerings and selecting courses without a structured goal as a driving force. Although I am not particularly an advocate of total specialization, this image of a journalist being "a mile wide and an inch deep" isn't helped by graduates who know very little about anything. I keep getting the feeling those students, in most cases, were looking for the easy way through journalism school. Better advising and tougher requirements would help solve this problem.

Journalism education must never be allowed to become part of "communication arts." When a college basketball player steps to the free-throw line, I cringe when his major is announced as "communication" and hope the viewers do not translate that as "journalism."

"

Kathleen Williams, *adjunct assistant professor, Department of Psychology/Communication Option, Montana State University, Bozeman*

"

Our biggest problem is conveying to the rest of higher education that we can provide the basic skills and theoretical framework of the Information Age for all undergraduate students. This means that instead of threatening to eliminate j-programs as anachronistic relics, universities should be incorporating our approaches to information processing and management into the required general-education curriculum.

"

Clint C. Wilson, *professor and chair, Department of Journalism, Howard University, Washington, D.C.*

"

I see faculty in the same position as linotype operators. Most are not needed. Faculty can have cult followers. Teaching doesn't have to be tied to geography. We could have 7,000 people from all over the world taking a course from one person. I don't believe journalism professors understand what's happening. Technology drives the values, the content of journalism, and it will drive who is going to teach.

"

Jean Gaddy Wilson, *adjunct associate professor, School of Journalism, University of Missouri, Columbia*
Executive director, New Directions for News

Voices of news professionals

"

There has been a lot of talk in journalism in the last couple of years that is highly critical of the way journalists are educated. There's a lot of "I'm getting students who can't write." [or] "I'm getting students who don't have a lot of depth." But there's very little talk about why it is that [industry] standards seem to be no higher than the journalism educators that they criticize. So I don't see what possible incentive students have to go and get the strong, broad liberal arts background that we're talking about. ... It's been my experience that if you have a group of 20 interns that come into a television newsroom, the ones that get the attention, that make the contacts, that are ultimately invited to become desk assistants are the ones that know about makeup and lighting and project their voices.

"

Rose Arce, *producer, WCBS, New York*

"

What needs to be developed is a curriculum that closely mirrors what the profession needs. More emphasis needs to be placed on practical skills rather than theoretical concepts. Interns and recent college graduates lack basic skills, such things as writing, grammar [and] knowledge of how the real world operates. Faculty need to be better acquainted with current media practices.

"

Ed Arke, *FM news director, WITF, Harrisburg, Pa.*

"

Somehow, in some way, people coming into this business must be taught to think critically, to think analytically, and, through that process, ask the right questions. Christopher Lasch, in his last book, "The Revolt of the Elites," phrases it quite well: "We do not know what we need to know until we ask the right questions."

Unfortunately, today's newspapers are filled with stories written by reporters who failed to ask the "right questions." That failure grows out of an inability to think critically. I would

add that the problem is much greater at the editing level, where such "thinking" seems to be non-existent.

The days when reporters could get by merely with facile writing are long gone. It is more necessary now than ever before to be able to take large quantities of information, digest it, analyze it, subject it to critical examination, ask the right questions, and then write the story in a way that will be meaningful both to ordinary readers and specialists in that particular field.

This practice of thinking critically or analytically applies to stories that require months of work, or one or two days of work. In other words, it needs to be part of the daily routine.

"

Don Barlett, *reporter, The Philadelphia Inquirer*

"

"Many of our members say they are unhappy with the product being turned out by journalism schools. At the same time, they recognize that those schools are, for better or worse, an important source of entry-level personnel, especially in the small and medium markets.

There is definitely a prejudice among many of our members against journalism schools, much as there has long been a similar prejudice among old-fashioned newspaper editors. I incline toward the view that a degree in history, political science or some other liberal arts area is generally better preparation for the real work of journalism than an undergraduate journalism degree, even from a very good program.

"

David Bartlett, *president, Radio-Television News Directors Association, Washington, D.C.*

"

Isn't it crucial that all journalism teachers have considerable professional competence? This wouldn't assure us of good or even passable teachers, but it would eliminate some bad ones.

"

James Benet, *former reporter, KQED-TV, San Francisco*

"

My biggest concern about journalism education right now is that our industry is changing at warp speed and that academia may not be able to keep up. Technology, pagination, online, new newsroom structures — teams and the like. It is dizzying right now.

And what seems to be a trend is that j-schools may be turning out 20-something traditionalists. They are versed in the 5 Ws and H — but the definition of those is expanding beyond the traditional narrow meanings. I don't want to lose that emphasis on the basics of newsgathering, but somehow we need to prepare students so they understand this is a business in flux and there is more than one way to do things.

The very important practical journalistic training needs to be expanded to include the new technology and to include new organizational structures. And it needs to make sure that the students coming out are light on their feet and able to work in a changing environment, because that's what we're going to be for the next decade or two. As journalists, we've always been agents of change, but we need to be able to apply that to our own newsrooms as well.

Peter Bhatia, *managing editor,* The Oregonian, *Portland*

"

Our industry has (a problem) in not working closely enough with journalism schools and educators. I know there are challenges to this within the academic community — not wanting j-schools to become trade schools and not allowing those not academically credentialed to be a key part of the students' education.

I would like to see courses (that teach them) how to deal effectively with technology. Kids today are comfortable with and even eager for those ever-newer tools. We need, however, to teach them how to master the tools and not allow the tools to master them. I think here of three aspects:
- How easy it is to become lost in the world of computers and lose the reason we began a search/project.
- How easy it can be to cross some ethical lines in seeking information.
- How easy it is to have half-truth spread quickly across

the country via computer, with anyone now having the ability to become an editor of his/her own "publication."

Mary Kay Blake, *director, recruiting/placement, Gannett Co. Inc., Arlington, Va.*

"

Most journalism graduates will at some career point work for a weekly publication, perhaps in a rural setting. They will need to know more than reporting, writing and editing. The soul of journalism is not in the metropolitan dailies — which is what we teach our young — but in the thousands of small-town or even big-city weeklies. Personally, I never realized newspapers could be so much fun until I got out of the daily newspaper business. Journalism curricula should offer courses on newspaper management, community journalism, print advertising, marketing demographics, and so forth.

Robert C. Bruce, *founding editor,* East Bay Phoenix Journal, *Oakland, Calif.*

"

I am particularly concerned about:

- A shift away from broad-based liberal arts education toward more course work within the journalism major. The result is [that] journalism schools are producing graduates with less general knowledge and less ability to cover a broad base of issues.
- Low starting salaries for journalism graduates.
- Unpaid internships. Many unpaid interns become gofers and do not get real experience. [Also] too few schools require internships. Too many graduates require too much on-the-job training because they have not had solid internships before graduation.
- Graduate programs that place too little emphasis on teaching undergraduates. In too many cases, teaching undergrads is turned over to grad assistants or unqualified adjuncts with little oversight.
- University presidents and deans who place too little emphasis on teaching. Teaching should be given at least as much importance as research. Experience should count for more than research in granting tenure and promotion.

"

Gene Chamberlin, *newspaper consultant, Brookings, S.D.*

"

Journalism education needs both an ethics and a quality/ values component — even more than the business schools.

"

Clare Crawford, *executive producer, CC-M Productions Inc., Washington, D.C.*

"

Teach students how to "hang out" and know people other than themselves. This was less a problem when reporters came from working-class families and knew the communities in which they went to work. [This] shows in terms of not including minorities in stories; not understanding economic classes and the struggles among people who live on the edge; [and] the inability to view people in terms other than them and us — we are them.

Don't let newspapers get away with saying you (journal-

ism educators) don't do a wonderful job because you do. Newspapers must do their share. It would help to debunk the notion that to be a journalist is to work too hard for too little money, etc. Unless we all think it is a proud profession and there are rewards, we all lose.

"

Lucille de View, *writing coach,* The Orange County Register, *Santa Ana, Calif.*

"

It's obvious that the field will change quite a great deal before today's students even leave school. In my mind, learning the fundamentals of writing and reporting must come first. Then adapting those to a range of technologies must be practiced and learned with a great deal of sophistication and ability.

Next, what does it mean to be in the communications field today? Anyone who packages information says they're communicating. But how can we make sure that trained journalists are in a strong position as observers and commentators? How can we hold on to core principles while becoming service-oriented in a constructive way?

"

Sharon Dickman, *deputy editor, editorial page,* Times-Union, *Rochester, N.Y.*

"

The greatest shortfall [in journalism education] is in the area of incorporating lessons of diversity into how reporters and editors as well as artists and photographers should build a mix of people in the community into the news product. The rule book of journalism is being rewritten, and schools should be in on that process.

"

Lewis W. Diuguid, *associate editor,* The Kansas City *(Mo.)* Star

"

Too many students who want journalism careers are not prepared for jobs on graduation because:

- They never worked for their school paper, and, therefore, have no clips. This is the biggest problem I see year-in and year-out. Some professors, especially the theoretical and research types, don't tell the students how important clips are in getting internships and jobs.
- The students did not belong to the right clique and, so, were not in line to get a job on the school paper — sometimes this clique is based on politics, sometimes merely on class, but it always tends to hit hardest those who are poor and those who are minority, and woe to those who are both.
- The school paper is lousy, covering only meetings, etc., or the staff gets no feedback from faculty, and, therefore, the clips are not worth a damn.
- The placement office doesn't inform students about scholarships or other financial aid. That's bad news for poor students, who otherwise might be able to quit a job and work on the school paper to get those important clips.
- The school concentrates on everything except how to write and edit well, the two top requirements for students looking for jobs as reporters or copy editors.
- The school doesn't impress on the students the importance of such other subjects as government, economics, sociology, psychology and, yes, even mathematics.

"

Fernando Dovalina, *assistant managing editor,* Houston Chronicle

"

It is not enough to teach the mechanics, the craft alone. Journalism education cannot be the moral equivalent of auto shop. How do you teach ethics, integrity, vision, mission, trust, taste? I'm not sure, but in trying I would stress assignments that test judgment, that raise issues of fairness, balance, and just plain getting the facts straight. Stimulate analysis of what's being done now and how it affects our understanding and knowledge of events and issues, how it affects society, community, the profession itself. Confront students with choices — news choices, policy decisions, deadline pressures. Make them consider the options and their consequences. Make them defend their methods as well as their facts.

There's the never-ending need to stress the importance of writing — good, clean, clear, structured, unbiased — in broadcasting as well as print.

"

Irv Drasnin, *"Frontline" producer, Drasnin Productions Inc., Los Altos, Calif.*

"

I suspect the term "journalism" tends to derogate the field as a craft, and that stress on "crafts" dominates some j-departments more than necessary. The craftsmanship skills in reporting, writing, editing and even photography are basic and quickly learned. They're best learned by doing, best polished through criticism. It's axiomatic to say that the way to learn to write is to write — right? Any newspaper editor will tell you that "retraining" journalism grads is routine.

"

Thomas Eastham, *vice president and Western director, William Randolph Hearst Foundation, San Francisco*

"

How can journalism education serve the profession better?
By ending academia's focus on advanced degrees. We need to
fill j-schools with genuine practitioners. Real experience is
devalued to such a large measure that most professors can't
help get reporters job-ready because the professors aren't
job-ready. End this stranglehold. Let the best teachers teach
young journalists. Add a new "professional" track in the
tenure ladder if need be. There are humane editors who can
teach. The doors of the university need to be opened to them.

How [can journalism education] become a more
respected academic discipline? It probably won't happen.
Our strength is not in areas regarded by university value systems. The only chance we have is to get more prestigious
practitioners on campus and to get the industry to support j-
schools with more money. We'll have to buy our respect with
external pressure, because it won't work to force journalism
into a cap and gown.

Margaret Engel, *executive director, The Alicia Patterson Foundation,
Washington, D.C.*

"

While I was teaching at one school, it was placed on proba-
tion. An accrediting committee made many recommendations to bring the program up to snuff. Many were on point.
One I thought was misdirected: more full-time professors put
on tenure track and fewer practicing professionals in the
classroom. I have no axe to grind over the fact that my
opportunities to teach evaporated. My concern is whether
students would not be better served by a mixture of working
professionals and professors.

Dennis Foley, *politics/government editor, The Orange County Register,
Santa Ana, Calif.*

"

Though a graduate of a school of journalism, I probably have
spent 10 times as many years as a news source than as a
news reporter. Frankly, I've always breathed a silent sigh of
relief when given a "softball" interview. I am surprised how
few reporters ever ask follow-up questions. Most poor report-

ing that I observe appears to be a result of laziness. It occurs
when reporters take releases at face value, either refusing to
question the "facts" contained therein or research for coun-
tervailing perspectives and opinion.

Not to be completely duplicitous, I can assure you that I
am only too happy when reporters accept my releases without follow-up research or questioning. The newspaper or station becomes our PR organ, albeit lacking my respect, which,
with 50 cents, will buy you coffee in the South.

Barbara Gershman, *equity administrator, Florida Department of
Education, Tallahassee, Fla.*

"

Some questions that need to be considered:

- How do we define quality in journalism education? What are the terms? What are the standards? What are appropriate definitions of quality? Are there any effective measures of quality now? Should standards of quality be created? Would they be different from the current accrediting standards? Should they be part of the accrediting standards and the accrediting process?
- Should units be more involved in directing students toward a more rigorous course of study in the 90-65 portion of their undergraduate requirements?
- To what degree does the influence of the journalism school experience, including the role of the faculty as critics of the press, contribute to the perception today that the press is more cynical and less objective in its coverage?
- How can the values of classroom teaching in journalism/mass communications be strengthened, particularly at institutions that define their mission as a "research university"?

"

Robert H. Giles, *editor and publisher,* The Detroit News
President, Accrediting Council on Education in Journalism and Mass Communications
President, American Society of Newspaper Editors

"

Many of the people we get are lacking basics. They lack basic grammar skills. They don't know a lead from a nut graph. At the other end of the spectrum is lack of awareness of many of the new approaches to journalism [and] trends in reporting. Many new reporters have a blank look when an editor asks what the story means to readers [and] why there is no comment from readers on an issue that will affect them.

"

Linda Green, *city editor,* The Californian, *Salinas, Calif.*

"

This is a trade and not a profession, and many of journalism schools' problems — at least from where I sit — stem from getting this bass ackwards. The journalism educators I most admire from my past — and those I rely on most to send me candidates for my internship program — are the ones who run boot camps that teach folks how to go get tough stories and write them compellingly.

The faculties are already too full of people who have been out of the business too long and haven't the faintest idea of what hiring editors are looking for. And most of them — perhaps out of misplaced kindness, inertia or the need to boost enrollments — don't do anything about weeding out folks who'll probably never make a living in the business.

"

Paul Jablow, *assistant Pennsylvania editor,* The Philadelphia Inquirer

"

I know that educators won't want to hear this, but degrees and grades rarely matter. Instead, I focus on how broad-ranged [students] are (travel, experiences working in the community, etc.) and what kind of practical experiences they have had.

I am very frustrated with the very traditional expectations of the young people we hire. More than their 20-year senior colleagues, they feel like they must cover government, politics, horse races to prove they are talented. They turn their noses up at "success" stories. And yet I am certain that without a new look at the kind of stories we provide, we will lose the franchise we hold so dear.

"

Mindi Keirnan, *assistant vice president, assistant to the president and chief executive officer, Knight-Ridder Inc., Miami*

"

The fundamental question is: Is the role of journalism schools to produce students who are trained to work as competent journalists, or to produce "scholarship" consisting of irrelevant and, in my opinion, bogus "quantitative and qualitative" research?

When I receive an issue of *Journalism Quarterly*, almost invariably there is at least one article that strikes me as so ridiculous that I feel compelled to hurl the journal across the room. I recall one article a few years ago that, as I remember it, attempted to draw a correlation between the number of misspelled words in a newspaper and the number of Pulitzers it had won. This, to me, is suggestive of how far academics will stretch into absurdity to come up with "quantitative" studies. Journalism is not social science, and social science models don't work.

This is not to say that valuable research cannot be performed in journalism schools. For example, an academic could easily have prepared the first comprehensive review of the incidence and impact of subpoenas on the news media. Instead, we did it at the Reporters Committee.

"

Jane E. Kirtley, *executive director, The Reporters Committee for Freedom of the Press, Arlington, Va.*

"

My expectations are simple: I like to find people coming out of journalism schools with a good fundamental education that gives them a broad base for dealing with human beings. If they [have] a journalism degree, I expect they have learned how to spell, write a simple story, and some of the standards and requirements of the profession.

"

Sanders LaMont, *executive editor, The Modesto (Calif.) Bee*

"

Reporters and editors start writing and editing for other reporters and editors, not for real people. They focus on stories that are much less important to readers than they are to the people who put together the paper or newscast — the Whitewater investigation comes to mind. This in-crowd mentality is the least attractive and least useful part of journalism education.

"

John P. McMeel, *president, Universal Press Syndicate, Kansas City, Mo.*

"

If engineering, medicine or law were to become as theoretical as journalism has, I'd be afraid to cross a bridge, be treated for the injuries I receive when it collapses or sue the contractor responsible.

Full tenure-track appointments for M.A.s with substantial — 15-plus years — professional experience would help journalism education. Elimination of the lumping together of communications and journalism would help, as would stressing practical research among faculty.

"

Eric Meyer, *managing director, Newslink, Pewaukee, Wis.*

"

All young journalists should be required to cover fires and write obits. If you get it wrong there, you will never learn to get it right, and no amount of technology is going to save you. I let this position be known to all younger journalists I encounter. Many of them are surprised. They thought deep thinking and mastery of the Web were all they would need.

"

Bob Meyers, *director, Washington Journalism Center, Washington, D.C.*

"

The most compelling question is why the community never seems to be represented in the newsroom. It's a profession-wide problem — and [one] in journalism education. I was probably a junior or senior before I realized I could actually be a sportswriter. There were no role models so it simply never seemed like an option. And no one ever encouraged me in that direction — partly my problem for being so quiet, but there also seemed to be an unspoken bias that sports wasn't really journalism. If we want diversity in the newsroom, which editors all say is true, then we can't be discouraging that diversity in journalism school.

Ann Miller, *sports writer,* The Honolulu Advertiser

"

Journalism education needs to be right on top of changes in the industry so that aspiring students have an accurate and clear-eyed view of what their prospects will be after graduating. There needs to be an emphasis on following the news and knowing the issues. You'd be surprised how many students — and professors — fail to read the news or even follow it on TV, so intent are they on academic concerns.

Linda Wright Moore, *columnist,* Philadelphia Daily News

"

I'd like to see journalism education become much more interactive with the other disciplines the students have to study — politics, philosophy, social studies, sciences, the arts. I'd like to see classroom assignments integrate those things so that, say, there would be a variety of combination courses that would get [students] into the streets to look at important social aspects of the community and, at the same time, force them to find context for what's happening by doing research at the library or on-line.

What I see is that these kids are learning little boxes. That's the social studies course. That's the Journalism 101 course. That's the history course. And they don't seem to put it all together.

I'd like to see them come out thinking more like journal-

ists need to think, be able to gather facts but also know how to gather historical context, understand how to use computers, but use them to look up demographic information of whatever township or place they're covering, and be able to use that to help them ask better questions.

Team teaching with people from other disciplines might be very valuable. I think it would break down some of the walls between the disciplines and in the minds of the students.

Arlene Morgan, *assistant managing editor,* The Philadelphia Inquirer

"

Journalism is different. If you teach someone the journalistic method, you teach them how to think critically, how to investigate, how to synthesize, how to communicate. If you teach them real journalism, you teach them how to think, how to see, how to create — not how to count the brush strokes or copy someone else's work or how to sell an empty canvas. If you teach them real journalism, you teach them an information-gathering and problem-solving method that can be used on everything from how to get the first job to solving child-care problems. You teach them to think — to think and report, think and decide, think and write. If you teach them about journalism, you teach them how to learn about everything else.

Eric Newton, *managing editor,* The Freedom Forum Newseum, Arlington, Va.

"

The sense I get is that a lot more emphasis is going toward having post-graduate degrees than real-world experience in the field. I believe this is a mistake. I believe students need the theory, but they need to hear from the people who have been out there dealing with the questions of libel, ethics, taste — people who have experienced the actual implication of their choices in these matters.

"

Michael J. Parman. *publisher,* The Press Democrat, *Santa Rosa, Calif.*

"

I'd like to see journalism students who, if they know that a politician is putting out an untruth, can get both the fact of the misstatement and the real truth into the story — instead of just repeating what the politician said. In other words, [they should have] critical thinking [ability] and the confidence to correct genuine errors.

"

Eve Pell, *former internship coordinator, Center for Investigative Reporting, San Francisco*

"

Undergraduate journalism schools should be abolished or transformed into institutions that teach bodies of academic knowledge that shape minds into critical instruments able to handle complex problems. If students learn to think, writing well for publication or air will follow with a reasonable amount of guidance. A minimum of production and process techniques should be taught.

Bright graduates should be offered incentives to get advanced degrees, specializing in the substance of coverage areas and learning the basics of daily journalism operations.

"

Douglas A. Ramsey, *senior vice president, Foundation for American Communications, Los Angeles*

"

As a professional journalist, I am ready for some rules about who can call themselves journalists and who can't. I thought I was going to have to shoot the TV when Oliver North started talking about "we in the media" on the strength of running a radio talk show. I think universities could do a great service to journalism and to the public by fostering discussion in pubic and in the professional world on this question.

Advertising and public relations are fine fields of work, and I know many people go from journalism into those jobs at some point. Some television and radio work is journalism. A whole bunch of it is not. In that regard, I am sure it is heresy to talk about further separating advertising/PR sequences from journalism sequences, and further delineating broadcast journalism from learning to be a movie producer. But I think that is what needs to be done.

It seems clear to me that an advanced degree in journalism does one little good in the world of newspapers, magazines and broadcast news. Of much more help is a second degree in some other area: law, urban planning, engineering, business administration. J-schools could perform another valuable service by designing, or somehow cooperating in producing, programs of advanced study for journalists who have been out in the working world for several years and now want to come back and get additional realistic training.

My largest complaint about newspapers is how badly editors are prepared to do their jobs. They don't know enough about their job and never get any training for it. Very few of them have any preparation for one very important part of their job: managing people. J-schools could offer, in their undergraduate programs, at least one course in people-management skills. If j-schools also offered a course in the business side of newspapers (or broadcast stations), reporters and editors would go out into the world a little more cognizant of the pressures that publishers and top managers face.

"

Gayle Reaves, *reporter,* The Dallas Morning News

❝

I think our journalism schools need:

- To impress on students that they are to be servants of the truth and of the public, and that they need to act like servants.
- To impress on students that many important jobs in journalism carry little glory or individual recognition.
- To impress on students that they need "to bleed some" over their errors, not shrug them off as unimportant.
- To impress on students that our credibility is earned by the inch but lost by the mile.
- To teach students there is no substitute for accuracy.

❞

Phil J. Record, *ombudsman,* Fort Worth *(Texas)* Star-Telegram

❝

Here is (what I want from graduates):

- Good page designers and graphic artists who understand how the newspaper readers of today and tomorrow absorb information.
- Reporters who have an eye for enterprise and know how to dig to get it. We're a growing newspaper group in a growing market, and after all is said and done about the need for newspapers to be relevant, "coffee spitters" get more reader response than anything we do. In some cases, "relevant" has become a code word for soft and for stories that tell readers what they already know. News is what they don't know.
- Reporters who know how to present the news they've gathered in tightly written stories with glance boxes and graphics.
- Journalists who are well-schooled in technological advances, whether the Internet or computer-assisted reporting and readership studies.

❞

Jim Ripley, *managing editor, Tribune Newspapers, Mesa, Ariz.*

❝

I'm sort of a radical on this subject. I think journalism education took some sort of wrong turn and went into communications esoterica instead of taking a turn into history. I think history would have been a much better partnership for journalism. I think if it had broken that way, if we had a reservoir of history professors, as opposed to communications professors, in journalism schools, I think we would be exploring other paths and looking for answers to the future.

More and more there is an insistence that journalism faculty have Ph.D.s, that more and more of the faculty members have communication degrees, as opposed to history degrees and economics degrees and political science degrees — the backgrounds I think would have some real bearing and application on journalism schools. But we don't seem to be going in that direction.

Meanwhile, I think real journalism education is contracting, and I think in a way that is an opportunity for pushing for some change.

❞

Gene Roberts, *managing editor,* The New York Times

❝

I worry about whether students understand professionalism. We now ask interns to accept in writing because of two instances in which students said yes and then no when they got what they considered better offers. I know competition for good interns is intense, but I wonder if these students have any sense of personal or professional ethics. The two cases came from the same school, so I wrote to the dean who did not reply. I can tell you where we won't be recruiting next year.

I like students who come to us with practical skills, even if they're not advanced. We expect an internship to be a learning experience for us and for the students. If they have the basics, they can and will learn. Too many don't have the basics. Too many don't get hard news, don't understand business. It is very unusual to find students who have any idea of what goes on in a newsroom.

❞

Sharon Rosenhause, *managing editor,* San Francisco Examiner

"

Journalism education must place even more emphasis on ethical behavior among journalists. Particular attention must be paid to accuracy in newsgathering and writing. This would help improve the quality of journalism and bolster the public's confidence in our work.

"

Edward Russo, *political reporter,* Journal-Star, *Lincoln, Neb.*

"

Out here, miles — literally and figuratively — from our j-school educations, we seem to have forgotten the follow-up question. Students need to know about it. We are left with he-said/she-said journalism, unable to triangulate into that neighboring dimension which can allow us glimpses of understanding, or even truth.

"

Paul Shaffer, *free-lance writer, Boise, Idaho*

"

Journalism students need a much better grounding in subjects such as history, sociology, psychology, art and the sciences than they have now. Many j-school graduates are technically capable but lack any depth in areas which would add context to their reporting.

Too many j-school grads have no feel for what the job is actually like, versus what they think it will be. They are the ones who sour on the job in a few years, drifting off into other fields.

I'd hire a graduate of a good liberal arts college with two years of working journalism experience over a top journalism school grad with no real-world experience any day, all else being equal.

"

Kevin Shelly, *assistant city editor,* The Press, *Atlantic City, N.J.*

"

I have mixed feelings about journalism and the whole on-line development scene. Right now the journalism opportunities (in on-line) are primarily design and layout type of jobs. A lot of organizations want to leverage their copy from other sources. It's like all the shoestring radio news shows that

read the morning paper. On-line seems to be another avenue for existing material. The greatest thing that on-line, and digital publishing in general, has to offer is the whole concept of immediate access to archived information. Regardless of whether original material is done on-line, what's going to matter for journalists, wherever they work [is that] strong writing skills will always be essential.

"

Eric Sinclair, *Grafica Multimedia Inc., Belmont, Calif.*

"

We place journalism educators in a real conflict. I've been to many of these meetings (about journalism educators), and we always say pretty nobly that we want a good liberal arts background. I think in many newsrooms, though, the new applicant that gets the job is the one who comes with skills ready to plug in. I don't know if that's good or bad, but I think it's a practical matter that sends pressure back against the educators to equip people to be employed. I can tell you that as I talk to AP executives, the theme I heard again and again was: Send us people who understand the world and who make some sense out of it.

Our people have very little interest in skills training. Will we hire them without skills training? I talked to our photo director, whose operation has won Pulitzers for three out of the last four years. He said, too, that when he goes to campuses he tells students to get out of photo courses. "Forget them," he said. "Learn how to run a camera and go study anthropology or history." The theory being that someone has to bring real passion to covering a story, bring a fire to it, a real interest and curiosity, whether they're using words or making pictures. And a narrowly focused person is much less likely to do that than someone who's been thinking and attacking things critically in other subjects.

The main missing skill is clear writing. I've found it to be lacking consistently over the years in graduates. I think clear writing results from clear thinking, and muddy writing is the result of muddy thinking. I'm not sure writing can be taught, but I think clear thinking can be taught, good analytical thinking can be taught.

"

Rick Sprattling, *general executive, The Associated Press, New York*

"

Journalism education, I hope, will lead the way in returning universities to teaching, which they have abandoned in favor of academic research. If they led universities in this way, journalism schools would achieve a very high degree of respect within the university. This would be earthshaking. J-schools could save universities from the pending public wrath that is about to descend with a fury as more and more demands are made for more emphasis on teaching as university budgets get pinched.

There's a regrettable trend in journalism education to require the Ph.D., and this comes at the expense of professional experience among the faculty. J-schools are being tempted by a faulty anti-teaching, research-dominated mindset that has permeated university thinking and corrupted its values.

The research that's come out of journalism schools, with very few notable exceptions, has little value to the profession. That's not true for medical research, or law, or economics, I think. My solution would be to de-emphasize research in journalism schools rather than try to improve it.

"

Lee Stinnett, *executive director, American Society of Newspaper Editors, Reston, Va.*

"

I would encourage any department which hired me as a consultant to have as few Ph.D.s as possible. I would recommend getting as many working journalists as I could into the school. When framing the graduation requirements for journalism majors, I would require a second major in a field proposed by the student as complementary to professional preparation to be a reporter. It would be my goal to build a journalism graduate who is ready from the day she walks into your newsroom to research, write, edit and report. She would have the practical training to practice the craft of journalism and a demonstrated knowledge of an area of knowledge that it profits a journalist to know.

"

Ray Suarez, *host, "Talk of the Nation," National Public Radio, Washington, D.C.*

"

I have the impression that journalism majors are asked at some point to pick print or broadcast. Why does that happen? The print students seem to have the advantage of being forced to write and rewrite. But what seems to happen to the broadcast major is they get a smattering of writing and then they learn to edit tape. They learn how to point the camera, they learn lighting, they learn what foot candles are. They learn all these things that are completely useless to me. When I'm going to hire a production coordinator or a technician, I can hire someone from a school of broadcast technology.

When I hire a journalist, I want them to be able to take the city budget I hand them and, based on what they've read, analyze it, tell me what they think. I don't see much of that in the students from broadcast journalism education. I guess I lay it at the feet of journalism education, but I also agree that as broadcasters we have rewarded superficial backgrounds.

The reason why we're here — no matter what our income level, our race or our sex — we are supposed to represent the interests of the community. We are in the business of giving people options. By what we do, we say, "Here's information that may help you decide what you want to do. We're not making the decision for you, but we are giving you the information." If journalists don't realize that's what journalism is all about, they should get outta here. Maybe the professors can't say that, but we can.

"

Paula Walker, *producer, WCBS, New York*

University Policies

Model policies governing appointment, promotion and tenure of faculty

Some universities have adopted effective policies that accept journalistic research and writing as meeting faculty research and writing requirements and have also established criteria for evaluating such material. The following 10 pages contain excerpts of policies from:

University of California, Berkeley
University-wide policy governing appointment and promotion of faculty

University of Colorado, Boulder
School of Journalism and Mass Communication
Personnel policies and procedures

Kansas State University
A.Q. Miller School of Journalism and Mass Communications
Criteria for appointment, evaluation, tenure and promotion

Ohio University
E.W. Scripps School of Journalism
Tenure and promotion policy

University of Oregon
Eric W. Allen School of Journalism and Communication
Policy for faculty tenure and promotion

University of California, Berkeley
University-wide policy governing appointment and promotion of faculty

Criteria for Appointment, Promotion, and Appraisal

The review committee shall judge the candidate with respect to the proposed rank and duties, considering the record of the candidate's performance in (1) teaching, (2) research and other creative work, (3) professional activity, and (4) University and public service. Mentoring and advising of students or new faculty members are to be encouraged and given recognition in the teaching or service categories of academic personnel actions. In evaluating the candidate's qualification within these areas, the review committee shall exercise reasonable flexibility, balancing when the case requires, heavier commitments and responsibilities in one area against lighter commitments and responsibilities in another. The review committee must judge whether the candidate is engaging in a program of work that is both sound and productive. As the University enters new fields of endeavor and refocuses its ongoing activities, cases will arise in which the proper work of faculty members departs markedly from established academic patterns. In such cases, the review committees must take exceptional care to apply the criteria with sufficient flexibility. However, flexibility does not entail a relaxation of high standards. Superior intellectual attainment, as evidenced both in teaching and in research or other creative achievement, is an indispensable qualification for appointment or promotion to tenure positions. Insistence upon this standard for holders of the professorship is necessary for maintenance of the quality of the University as an institution dedicated to the discovery and transmission of knowledge. Consideration should be given to changes in emphasis and interest that may occur in an academic career. The candidate may submit for the review file a presentation of his or her activity in all four areas.

The criteria set forth below are intended to serve as guides for minimum standards in judging the candidate, not to set boundaries to exclude other elements of performance that may be considered.

(1) **Teaching.** Clearly demonstrated evidence of high quality in teaching is an essential criterion for appointment, advancement, or promotion. Under no circumstances will a tenure commitment be made unless there is a clear documentation of ability and diligence in the teaching role. In judging the effectiveness of a candidate's teaching, the committee should consider such points as the following: the candidate's command of the subject; continuous growth in the subject field; ability to organize material and to present it with force and logic; capacity to awaken in students an awareness of the relationship of the subject to other fields of knowledge; fostering of student independence and capability to reason; spirit and enthusiasm which vitalize the candidate's learning and teaching; abili-

ty to arouse curiosity in beginning students, to encourage high standards, and to stimulate advanced students to creative work; personal attributes as they affect teaching and students; extent and skill of the candidate's participation in the general guidance, mentoring, and advising of students; effectiveness in creating an academic environment that is open and encouraging to all students. The committee should pay due attention to the variety of demands placed on instructors by the types of teaching called for in various disciplines and at various levels, and should judge the total performance of the candidate with proper reference to assigned teaching responsibilities. The committee should clearly indicate the sources of evidence on which its appraisal of teaching competence has been based. In those exceptional cases when no such evidence is available, the candidate's potentialities as a teacher may be indicated in closely analogous activities. In preparing its recommendation, the review committee should keep in mind that a redacted copy of its report may be an important means of informing the candidate of the evaluation of his or her teaching and of the basis for that evaluation.

It is the responsibility of the department chair to submit meaningful statements, accompanied by evidence, of the candidate's teaching effectiveness at lower-division, upper-division, and graduate levels of instruction. More than one kind of evidence shall accompany each review file. Among significant types of evidence of teaching effectiveness are the following: (a) opinions of other faculty members knowledgeable in the candidate's field, particularly if based on class visitations, on attendance at public lectures or lectures before professional societies given by the candidate, or on the performance of students in courses taught by the candidate that are prerequisite to those of the informant; (b) opinions of students; (c) opinions of graduates who have achieved notable professional success since leaving the University; (d) number and caliber of students guided in research by the candidate and of those attracted to the campus by the candidate's repute as a teacher; and (e) development of new and effective techniques of instruction.

All cases for advancement and promotion normally will include:
(a) evaluations and comments solicited from students for most, if not all, courses taught since the candidate's last review; (b) a quarter-by-quarter or semester-by-semester enumeration of the number and types of courses and tutorials taught since the candidate's last review; (c) their

level; (d) their enrollments; (e) the percentage of students represented by student course evaluations for each course; (f) brief explanations for abnormal course loads; (g) identification of any new courses taught or of old courses when there was substantial reorganization of approach or content; (h) notice of any awards or formal mentions for distinguished teaching; (i) when the faculty member under review wishes, a self-evaluation of his or her teaching; and (j) evaluation by other faculty members of teaching effectiveness. When any of the information specified in this paragraph is not provided, the department chair will include an explanation for that omission in the candidate's dossier. If such information is not included with the letter of recommendation and its absence is not adequately accounted for, it is the review committee chair's responsibility to request it through the Chancellor.

(2) **Research and Creative Work.** Evidence of a productive and creative mind should be sought in the candidate's published research or recognized artistic production in original architectural or engineering designs, or the like.

Publications in research and other creative accomplishment should be evaluated, not merely enumerated. There should be evidence that the candidate is continuously and effectively engaged in creative activity of high quality and significance. Work in progress should be assessed whenever possible. When published work in joint authorship (or other product of joint effort) is presented as evidence, it is the responsibility of the department chair to establish as clearly as possible the role of the candidate in the joint effort. It should be recognized that special cases of collaboration occur in the performing arts and that the contribution of a particular collaborator may not be readily discernible by those viewing the finished work. When the candidate is such a collaborator, it is the responsibility of the department chair to make a separate evaluation of the candidate's contribution and to provide outside opinions based on observation of the work while in progress. Account should be taken of the type and quality of creative activity normally expected in the candidate's field. Appraisals of publications or other works in the scholarly and critical literature provide important testimony. Due consideration should be given to variations among fields and specialties and to new genres and fields of inquiry.

Textbooks, reports, circulars, and similar publications normally are considered evidence of teaching ability or public service. However, contributions by faculty members to the professional literature or to the advancement of profes-

sional practice or professional education should be judged creative work when they present new ideas or original scholarly research.

In certain fields such as art, architecture, dance, music, literature, and drama, distinguished creation should receive consideration equivalent to that accorded to distinction attained in research. In evaluating artistic creativity, an attempt should be made to define the candidate's merit in the light of such criteria as originality, scope, richness, and depth of creative expressions. It should be recognized that in music, drama, and dance, distinguished performance, including conducting and directing, is evidence of a candidate's creativity.

(3) **Professional Competence and Activity.** In certain positions in the professional schools and colleges, such as architecture, business administration, dentistry, engineering, law, medicine, etc., a demonstrated distinction in the special competencies appropriate to the field and its characteristic activities should be recognized as a criterion for appointment or promotion. The candidate's professional activities should be scrutinized for evidence of achievement and leadership in the field and of demonstrated progressiveness in the development or utilization of new approaches and techniques for the solution of professional problems. It is the responsibility of the department chair to provide evidence that the position in question is of the type described above and that the candidate is qualified to fill it.

(4) **University and Public Service.** The faculty plays an important role in the administration of the University and in the formulation of its policies. Recognition should therefore be given to scholars who prove themselves to be able administrators and who participate effectively and imaginatively in faculty government and the formulation of departmental, college, and University policies. Services by members of the faculty to the community, State, and nation, both in their special capacities as scholars and in areas beyond those special capacities when the work done is at a sufficiently high level and of sufficiently high quality, should likewise be recognized as evidence for promotion. Faculty service activities related to the improvement of elementary and secondary education represent one example of this kind of service. Similarly, contributions to student welfare through service on student-faculty committees and as advisers to student organizations should be recognized as evidence.

University of Colorado, Boulder
School of Journalism and Mass Communication
Personnel policies and procedures

MISSION OF THE SCHOOL

The philosophy that guides the School is a vision of professional education as a discourse that is deeply embedded in an interdisciplinary liberal arts heritage. That perspective does not accept the conventional distinctions between professional skills and liberal scholarship. It is a view that recognizes that all liberal disciplines have historically been concerned with attributes of skill and vocationalism and that journalism and communication studies are no less legitimate pathways to understanding and insight. This is why the School sees the skills portion of its curriculum as a basic element of liberal education — as tools through which one learns the discipline of determined information gathering, careful reasoning and analysis, critical thinking, and clear, articulate expression in writing, speech and other media. That philosophy is also why the School has always insisted on a well-rounded education for its students, one that leads them to a sophisticated understanding of the media in society by infusing their curriculum with the study of history, economics, law and policy, ethics, international aspects, behavioral and social processes, and textual criticism and interpretation. This emphasis is an essential element of professional media education. It has also served as the base upon which the School has built the research orientation of its graduate programs.

In keeping with this philosophy, and in line with the best of its counterparts across the country, this School has a dual mission. It must provide good, solid instruction in the fundamental aspects of media practice while also conducting advanced, rigorous inquiry into the important questions about media performance and the role of communication generally in society. It must continue to provide the highest quality, broadly defined professional programs for those intending to become responsible, well-informed, and skilled media practitioners. Yet it must also become a leading center for study, commentary and debate about the communication media.

FACULTY MIX

In view of its dual mission, the School of Journalism and Mass Communication must seek an appropriate faculty, one capable of meeting its various instructional, research and creative work obligations. As an accredited program the School is subject to the twelve standards of the [Accrediting] Council on Education in Journalism and Mass Communications. One of those standards is of direct relevance to policies for building faculties in programs such as the School's, with particular significance for the evaluation of faculty in appointment, promotion, and tenure decisions. According to ACEJMC Standard #6:

All faculty must be academically and professionally qualified for their respective responsibilities. Practical expertise is highly valued for those teaching skills courses. Appropriate academic expertise is most desirable for those teaching cours-

es such as law, history, public opinion, media effects, etc.

In other words, to maintain accreditation the School has to meet the requirement for a faculty with both professional credentials and scholarly skills. Ideally it seeks individuals with both sorts of backgrounds, including high level media experience and the best doctorates in appropriate fields. However, finding that ideal mix is rare. Consequently, the School — as with its counterparts at Stanford, Northwestern, Illinois, North Carolina, Missouri and elsewhere — meets its accreditation requirements by also seeking colleagues who represent excellence and a high level of achievement in at least one or the other of the two major areas and then striking a balance between them.

A. Academic Role

The role the faculty member is to play determines which credentials are more important. Most academic areas accept the possession of a doctorate as an obvious prerequisite for entry into university teaching, a practice established by decades of tradition. However, doctorates in communication research or other fields providing expertise for advanced inquiry into journalism and the media typically lead to the teaching of theoretical courses rather than the skill and practice courses so necessary for a reputable professional program.

1. The Scholar/Professional

Journalism, by its nature is an analytical, even scholarly, activity and those who have practiced it with distinction should be recognized as having experience equivalent to those who have earned Ph.D.s. it is expected that such people will contribute to the national dialog associated with issues in the field and that such contributions are equivalent to scholarly work published in research journals. Furthermore, it is expected that such faculty will participate as legitimate members of the senior faculty councils of the university with contributions respected for their insights based on such experience.

Typically, master's degrees (MA, MS, MBA, MFA, MOA) are the appropriate terminal degrees for faculty members with significant professional experience who teach professional courses and continue to practice or publish professionally in some mass communication area. Typically this type of faculty member concentrates on:
a) teaching professional (performance/skill) courses
b) producing work that commands respect through professional publications and creative productions
c) maintaining close relationships with the mass media and professional associations.

2. **The Scholar**

Extensive journalistic experience; while valuable, may not be necessary for a faculty member whose primary roles are research and teaching in areas that are more traditionally theoretical than professional. A doctorate is the terminal degree for such a person. This type of faculty member typically concentrates on:

a) teaching theoretical or academic courses

b) conducting research and producing reports that are accepted for presentation through a refereed process

c) participating in appropriate scholarly associations

While it is expected that most faculty members will be stronger in one category than the other, the concept of the professional/scholar who does both is still the ideal. The School would like to encourage practice-oriented and research-oriented faculty members to work together in an environment that would nurture both types of contributions.

FACULTY EVALUATION

C. **Performance Indicators**

2. **Research and/or Creative Work**

All faculty members tenured or in the tenure track must maintain a continuing program of scholarship and/or creative work. Whether a faculty member is pursuing scholarship, creative work, or both, it is expected that the work will be subject to peer review and will be of sufficient quality to be highly regarded nationally. The quality and quantity of the work are judged together, although quality is more important than quantity. For initial reappointment, a faculty member is expected to have begun a promising research or creative program. Before tenure can be recommended, the program must be productive and significant.

a) **Research**

Research activity and critical analysis are the traditional routes to achievement in mass communication scholarship. Achievement in research and scholarship is expressed in journal articles, books, research programs, grants and fellowships, and presentations to professional organizations. In simple terms, the research and scholarship indicators are the quality of research as judged by peers, plus the quantity of such activities. It is easier to count than to judge, but the School does both, attempting to determine if the work represents meritorious or excellent performance.

The following factors are considered in evaluating the candidate's qualifications:

- a vigorous, organized, systematic research program
- a selection of research questions which are judged significant by experts in the field as evidenced by publication in respected journals and by external reference letters

- an ongoing research and publication record at this University and in previous positions
  - the candidate's scholarly reputation at other universities, in the industry, government and other appropriate institutions
  - contributions to group efforts in the initiation and development of grants and research projects

Scholarship will be evaluated based on judgment by peers, taking into account the competitiveness of the organizations and publications, as well as critical reactions to the articles and presentations.

(i) **Indicators of Meritorious Performance**

Active pursuit of scholarly activities resulting in publication of a minimum of one article a year on the average in a peer-judged or refereed publication. These publications should not be in-house and should have an editorial screening or peer review process. Articles vary in importance, amount of effort represented in their development, and impact on the field and these differences should be considered in evaluating the work. Encyclopedia entries, for example, will generally be considered as short articles but not representing the same level of effort as a report on a research project. Published articles or articles confirmed for publication will weigh more heavily than articles "under review," which will be given little consideration, other than as an indication of continuing productivity.

Scholarly achievements can take a variety of forms; among them:

- Analytical, critical, and interpretive books
- Monographs that are reviewed
- Book chapters
- Articles in refereed journals
- Reviews in refereed journals
- Refereed papers presented at scholarly meetings
- Funded grant proposals and research reports

(ii) **Indicators of Excellence and Outstanding Work**

Work that moves beyond the standards of meritorious performance and represents advanced research and critical commentary on significant issues leading to national recognition of the faculty member. The work will be recognized as contributing to the perception of the candidate as an expert or leader in some area or discipline.

b) **Creative Work**

A professional in mass communications is expected to maintain his or her professional credentials by developing a program of critical commentary on professional practices and/or continuing a program of professional work that represents the highest standards of professional performance. In the same way that a music or fine arts professor, for example, is expected to perform or exhibit, a journalism professor should be rewarded for the public practice of journalism.

Creative work — i.e. professional practice — can take a variety of forms:

- professional work such as radio, television and film productions, or newspaper and magazine articles in the mass media;
- photographic or graphic arts publications or exhibitions;
- publication of commentaries and critical reviews about the field and related subjects in popular media, including television and radio, magazines, major newspapers, trade publications, and journalism reviews;
- professional writing, designing and producing: including scripts, documentary narratives, columns and editorials, investigative reports, news features and analyses, and advertising and public communication campaigns;
- speeches to public and community groups about mass communication issues and education
- making invited presentations as well as organizing meetings, seminars and conferences on media trends and issues;
- professional work of a demanding nature in responsible positions with the media;
- primary involvement in the production of a program of work accepted for exhibition, electronic distribution, or acceptance by archives.

(i) Indicators of Meritorious Performance

Like research and scholarship, creative work should also be deemed meritorious, meaning that the effort represents the active pursuit of an organized body of creative or professional work. Generally, it is expected that an average of one substantive piece of work a year is expected as a minimum. This performance is to be evaluated in terms of the scope of effort — consideration will be given to the differences in effort and impact between creative works. For example, writ-

ing and producing a 20-minute documentary or a 3-part investigative series may represent much more effort than a 300-word column. Impact and importance of the piece will also be considered.

(ii) Indicators of Excellence and Outstanding Work

Work that moves beyond the standards of meritorious performance and represents advancements in professional performance and critical commentary on significant professional issues leading to national recognition of the faculty member.

(iii) Criteria

Creative work will be evaluated based on judgment by peers, taking into account the competitiveness of the organizations and publications, as well as reactions to the articles and presentations. While the editor's function in most journalistic environments guarantees professional peer review, it is also advisable to accumulate other types of scholarly review on the work produced or accomplished.

Criteria include:

- whether the work breaks new ground and successfully advances state-of-the-art concepts, ideas and approaches that transcend ordinary professional practices;
- whether work is published, juried or competitively recognized. Evaluation of these works should consider not only the competitiveness of the forum, but also critical reaction to the work;
- whether professional work experience demonstrably enhances the faculty member's teaching, service, and professionalism.

Candidates must submit additional documentation which includes:

- evaluation of work submitted for competitions;
- reviews of the work by competent critics;
- articles, slides, video tapes, photographs, story boards and other supporting material used in production;
- letters from conference organizers, the public and other testimonials;
- awards, honors and other accolades.

Kansas State University
A.Q. Miller School of Journalism and Mass Communications
Criteria for appointment, evaluation, tenure and promotion

The professorate is more than a singular pursuit. It requires a mosaic of contributions through quality teaching, meaningful research and creative endeavors, and dedicated service.

The A.Q. Miller School of Journalism and Mass Communications serves a variety of constituencies — students who need competent instruction, media organization that benefit from public service, a university community that recognizes the centrality of communications, and a society-at-large that becomes better informed through the creation and application of knowledge in the discipline.

These responsibilities require a faculty with an appropriate balance of professional experience, academic credentials, teaching excellence, and a commitment to extend knowledge beyond the campus through scholarly publication, creative endeavors, and public service.

A faculty must match a program's goals. As an academic unit with a strong professional component, the School of Journalism and Mass Communications seeks to impart to students:

- Critical thinking about the role and impact of mass communication in society.
- Writing and other communication skills necessary to enter and advance in careers.
- Problem-solving abilities to serve the public in a socially responsible manner.

Beyond the classroom, the School expects its faculty to contribute in these areas:

- Scholarly research and creative endeavors that extend and apply knowledge.
- Service to the media and public, in keeping with the university's land-grant heritage.
- Advancing the reputation and impact of Kansas State University in the state and beyond.

The School seeks to appoint, tenure and promote those candidates whose quality and diversity of talents best serve these goals. A professor cannot be measured simply by the articles published, to the exclusion of the lives inspired. Similarly, a record of service is not sufficient in itself. The School seeks an appropriate balance — and an aggregate quality — among these expectations.

Initial Appointments

Candidates are recommended for initial appointment only after the School's tenured faculty has assessed the candidate's level and quality of academic preparation, professional experience, and potential contributions as a faculty member.

For all initial faculty appointments, it must be made clear from the outset if the position is to be a traditional academic appointment or a professional appointment. During the search for a new faculty member, starting with the job description that is circulated nationally, the expected credentials must be clearly stated. If professional experience is accepted in lieu of the doctorate at the time of appointment, then it will be so considered when tenure and promotions are recommended.

Traditional Academic Appointment

A doctoral degree is the usual prerequisite for appointment to one of the professorial ranks in the School. An appointment at the rank of instructor may be made in anticipation of obtaining the terminal degree. When such an appointment is made, it will be with the written agreement that the doctorate must be obtained within a specified time to qualify for retention.

Professional Appointment

The Faculty Handbook recognizes that accomplishments or experience other than the terminal degree may qualify a candidate for appointment to one of the professorial ranks (C130). In an academic unit with a strong professional component, practitioners who bring valuable mass communication experience to the faculty are essential to the School's mission.

Therefore, professional accomplishment will be considered in lieu of the terminal degree in determining the suitability of a candidate for a professional appointment. For a professional appointment, the following qualifications may be considered in lieu of a terminal degree: The master's degree and seven or more years of full-time experience deemed by the faculty of the School to be professional and appropriate.

In addition, nationally recognized mass communicators may be granted nontenure-track appointments at any appropriate rank with the approval of the School's faculty, the dean and the provost (C15).

Tenure and Promotion

Once the initial appointment has been made, whether as a traditional academic appointment or as a professional appointment, theoretical and professional orientations are equally appropriate in making tenure and promotion decisions. Excellence in performance and the expectation of continued professional growth are the criteria for making such decisions.

Traditional Academic Appointment

For faculty with a traditional academic appointment, tenure and promotion standards require evidence of outstanding achievement in teaching, service and scholarship, with the quality and significance of research submitted to peer evaluation in the discipline and with creative endeavors judged by standards of professional accomplishment.

Scholarship emphasizes original research in peer-reviewed academic journals and books, peer-reviewed and invited scholarly papers, and research disseminated in other media forms. Scholarship also encompasses professional work in trade publications and popular media, if the work demonstrates high standards in the practice of the discipline. Recognition is given to significant creative works in the visual arts, electronic media, multimedia, and other forms of media and technology related to the School's mission, as well as to textbooks and instructional materials that contribute in fresh ways to the discipline. While the discipline has few traditional extramural funding sources, grants are encouraged and will be rewarded.

Professional Appointment

For faculty on a professional appointment, tenure and promotion standards require evidence of outstanding achievement in teaching, service and scholarship, with the quality and significance of creative endeavors evaluated in terms of professional accomplishment.

Scholarship includes books, articles, commentaries, reviews and analyses of subjects through trade publications, newspapers, magazines and other professional and popular media, if the work demonstrates high standards in the practice of the discipline. Scholarship also encompasses the production of programs, segments, scripts, commentaries, reviews, articles and other creative works in the visual arts, electronic media, multimedia, and other forms of media and technology related to the School's mission. Recognition is given to textbooks and instructional materials that contribute in fresh ways to the discipline. While not mandated for professional appointments, traditional academic research is encouraged and will be rewarded.

Ohio University
E.W. Scripps School of Journalism
Tenure and promotion policy

Principles

The school believes satisfaction of its mission is reflected in contributions of individual members of its faculty in four broad areas: (1) teaching, to their students through professional direction provided in the classroom; (2) advising and professional counseling in the classroom, office and other settings; (3) publication and research, to the school by extending its academic and professional capabilities, its service to its profession and community and, through such endeavors, its prestige among its peers; and (4) service, to the university through normal academic service and acceptance of such special assignments at college and university committees, and to the profession through active participation in professional organizations and through leadership roles in school-sponsored professional development programs.

Specific means of implementing these contributions are numerous and varied. It is unreasonable to expect any individual to participate equally among all the possible activities or for faculty members to share equally in all tasks. The evaluation of any individual must be made on the basis of both the individual's expertise and performance and the expectations and needs of the school.

A reasonable approach to academic advancement, therefore, requires some weighting of the criteria. Demonstrated excellence in teaching and advising is crucial to the school's mission and is required. Beyond that, discretion is necessary. For example, a superior, award-winning teacher with an impressive array of service missions may be awarded tenure or promoted even though the publication record is adequate but not extensive. conversely, a highly productive researcher who is a fine teacher may be promoted despite little indication of service.

The intent of this document is to open avenues for promotion and tenure for faculty members whose backgrounds are professional, academic or a combination of the two.

Publication and Research

Continuing scholarship, including publication of the results of such scholarship, is an essential part of the academic environment. Academic service to students, the school, university and the profession depends upon analysis, originality and meaningful demonstration of journalistic practices. Although this work is expected to be predominantly journalistic, the nature of the School of Journalism is such that scholarship and publication will take many forms. The Promotion and Tenure Committee, therefore, will consider the following:

- Publication of a sufficient body of work in journalism, advertising, marketing or communication scholarly journals to demonstrate productivity and an intellectual focus over time.
- Publication of refereed books in any of the disciplines encompassed by the school.
- Publication, in print or by electronic means, or broadcast of analyses, critical reviews or other informal scholarship of depth and significance in professional publications, in newspapers, magazines or broadcast and telecommunications outlets.
- Publication of significant works in popular, literary or technical publications or in book form.
- Publication of articles, reviews and commentaries on other subject in newspapers, computer databases, on-line information systems, broadcast or other popular media, if they demonstrate high standards in the practice of journalism.
- Publication of textbooks or other books in journalism and mass communication if the books break new ground and successfully advance concepts, ideas and approaches that transcend ordinary instructional material.
- Proprietary research within disciplines encompassed by the school.
- Professional achievement in the graphics-visual arts area and in other professional disciplines represented by the journalism faculty. The work should be original and should advance the state of the art or profession.
- Consultations within the disciplines encompassed by the school.
- Presentation of papers at scholarly or professional meetings, invitations to participate in professional meetings, editorial positions with major professional journals, testimony before governmental committees and professional honors and awards.

The candidate will provide a complete listing of scholarly and professional publications, which will be evaluated by the Promotion and Tenure Committee. Consideration will be given to these questions, among others:

- Has the work been regular, continuous and focused?
- Has the work been perceived as significant in the discipline?
- Is the work appropriate for the intended audience?

University of Oregon
Eric W. Allen School of Journalism and Communication
Policy for faculty tenure and promotion

Philosophy of the School

The School's philosophy of education is one that is deeply rooted in the liberal arts. Professionally oriented courses in the School are based upon, and in many instances, extensions of, the preparation students receive in the liberal arts including their coursework in English, literature, economics, history and other liberal arts and social sciences. In their course work in the School, students are not only introduced to media organizations, practices and conventions, but are required to develop and to demonstrate the same habits of mind, analytical thinking, clear written and verbal expression and abstract reasoning that are fundamental to liberal arts disciplines.

Thus the School's programs serve two simultaneous functions, that of providing up-to-date instruction in the fundamental aspects of media practice, while at the same time engaging in rigorous examination of media performance and the role of communication in society.

Faculty Mix

To carry out this dual function requires a faculty with a different mix of backgrounds than that found in a traditional liberal arts department. The School seeks, and national accrediting standards require, a balanced faculty composed both of those with doctoral degrees in the field, and of those with significant attainments in the media professions.

Regardless of the backgrounds of individual faculty members, they are expected to contribute to the School's mission through meritorious teaching, continuing analytical contribution to the understanding of media practices, and service to the University, the School and professional and scholarly organizations, as well as media industries.

Special Role of Service to the Media Community

Because close ties to the media community are not only desirable, but indispensable to a professional school, service takes on a special importance beyond the normal expectation of a liberal arts department. The faculty are regularly called upon to share their knowledge and expertise with media groups, and to organize and conduct professional development programs. These time-consuming demands enrich the School in many ways. They provide contact with potential funding sources, enrich teaching through first-hand experiences, and often present research opportunities. However, they place considerable time demands on the faculty over and above the normal expectation of School/University and scholarly service.

Scholarship/Research

Scholarship, from the point of view of the School of Journalism and Communication, is an expansive term.

It may mean the original quantitative or qualitative research for the purpose of developing theory and knowledge about the field. Such scholarship may find expression in traditional academic journals and books. Candidates following this track are encouraged to seek publication in the most appropriate and significant outlets available in their fields.

In other instances, scholarship may mean the assembling and evaluation of findings of applied research and of existing practices. Such scholarship may find avenues in professional journals and reports, university textbooks and in other forms of non-academic/professional publication.

It must be emphasized that the School of Journalism and Communication does not place different values on the academic publication route and the professional publication or production route.

Variations in publication/production are vital to the assembling of a mix of journalism faculty members who reflect the broadest spectrum of knowledge about mass communications. In all cases, the scholarship and research activities of journalism faculty members ultimately are designed to advance knowledge and to refine professional practices. Such a mix of approaches is of great value to the School of Journalism and Communication.

Scholarship/research within the School of Journalism and Communication is of two primary types: academic-orientation and professional orientation.

The following are among the special indicators of achievement in scholarship/research for faculty of the School of Journalism and Communication, and are not in any priority ranking. Significant achievement is more important than the number of indicators engaged.

TYPE	EVALUATION

Academic Orientation

TYPE	EVALUATION
refereed articles	article publication article citations
scholarly paper presentation	refereed or invited
published scholarly proceedings	refereed or invited
scholarly books (authored or edited)	reviews in journals
book chapters in edited works	peer researchers
research projects	grants received published results

Professional Orientation

TYPE	EVALUATION
text books	peer acceptance and use reviews in journals
professional books on history, criticism, or application in the field, non-fiction "trade books"	invited publication reviews
book chapters	invited publication industry acceptance
articles in professional magazines	peer response
publication of work within a faculty member's specialty: • ad copy, design, planning • newspaper articles • magazine articles • radio/TV programs or specials • public relations campaigns • photo, graphic arts exhibitions • publication design	industry recognition re-publication of original work
addresses at other universities and to professional societies	invited
professional competitions	award-winning entries
professional consulting	prepared materials (e.g., portfolios, strategic plans, testimonials)

Bibliography

"A Special Report on Journalism Education: What Makes a Great Journalism School," American Journalism Review, May 1995.

Accrediting Council on Education in Journalism and Mass Communications (1995). "Accredited Journalism and Mass Communications Education, 1995-96," University of Kansas, Lawrence.

Accrediting Council on Education in Journalism and Mass Communications. Visiting committee reports and other files, 1989-96, University of Kansas, Lawrence.

Adam, G. Stuart. "Notes Toward a Definition of Journalism – Understanding an Old Craft as an Art Form," The Poynter Papers: No. 2, The Poynter Institute for Media Studies, St. Petersburg, Fla., 1993.

AEJMC (Association for Education in Journalism and Mass Communication). "Challenges and Opportunities in Journalism and Mass Communication Education," a report of the Task Force on the Future of Journalism and Mass Communication Education, 1989.

AEJMC. "Vision 2000 Task Force," presidential report presented at AEJMC convention, August 1994.

AEJMC. Curriculum Task Force report, "JMC Education: Responding to the Challenge of Change." A presidential task report presented at the AEJMC convention, August 1995.

American Society of Newspaper Editors. "Minority Newsroom Employment Shows Small Gain," news releases, 1995, 1996.

American Society of Newspaper Editors. Education for Journalism Committee annual reports, 1970-1994.

American Society of Newspaper Editors Committee on Education. "Journalism Education: Facing Up to the Challenge of Change," report, 1990.

American Society of Newspaper Editors. "The Changing Face of the Newsroom: A Human Resources Report," May 1989.

Associated Press Managing Editors. "Journalism Schools: Who, What, When, Where and Why Not," APME News, September 1984.

Associated Press Managing Editors. Journalism Education Committee Report, 1995.

Associated Press Managing Editors. Journalism Education Committee Report, 1995.

ASJMC (Association of Schools of Journalism and Mass Communication) Insights. "Journalism/Mass Communications Agenda for the '90's," William G. Christ, Ruth S. Holmberg, Vernon A. Keel, Del Brinkman, Winter 1995.

ASJMC Insights. "ASJMC Roundtable No. 3 – Administering J/MC Units in the 1990s: Problems, Issues, and Opportunities," Summer 1991.

ASJMC report. "1994-95 Faculty/Administrator Demographic Survey," June 1995.

Auletta, Ken. "The Wages of Synergy," The New Yorker, November 1995.

Bagdikian, Ben H. "Woodstein U. – Notes on the Mass Production and Questionable Education of Journalists," The Atlantic, March 1977.

Balk, Alfred. "Showdown at Communicology Gap," Nieman Reports, Winter 1994.

Bartlett, David, and Matthew Winkler. "Preparing the Next Generation," speeches at the Leadership Institute for Journalism and Mass Communication Education," The Freedom Forum Media Studies Center, New York, June 1995.

Becker, Lee B., and Joseph D Graf. "Myths and Trends: What the Real Numbers Say about Journalism Education," The Freedom Forum, Arlington, Va., 1995.

Berdahl, Robert M. "The University in the New Information Age," lecture at the Leadership Institute for Journalism and Mass Communication Education, The Freedom Forum Media Studies Center, New York, June 1994.

Black, Creed C. "Educating Our Successors," Sky Dunlap Memorial Address, convention of California Newspaper Publishers Association, San Francisco, 1979.

Black, Creed C. "Remember Where You Came From," remarks to the Accrediting Council on Education in Journalism and Mass Communications, Chicago, Sept. 11, 1995.

Blanchard, Robert O., and William G. Christ. "Media Education and the Liberal Arts: A Blueprint for the New Professionalism." Hillsdale: Lawrence Erlbaum, 1993.

Blanchard, Robert O., and William G. Christ. "The New Professionalism and the Iron Triangles," Feedback, Winter 1993.

Bleyer, Willard G. Collected speeches, articles, letters. University Archives, University of Wisconsin, Madison.

Bonner, Alice, and Judith Hines. "Death by Cheeseburger: High School Journalism in the 1990s and Beyond," The Freedom Forum, Arlington, Va., 1994.

Bogue, Allan G., and Robert Taylor. "The University of Wisconsin: One Hundred and Twenty-Five Years." Madison: The University of Wisconsin Press, 1975.

Boyer, Ernest L. "College: The Undergraduate Experience in America." New York: Harper & Row, 1987.

Brinkman, Del. "Notes Towards a Statement on Educating Journalists for the 21st Century," paper, John S. and James L. Knight Foundation, September 1994.

Buchanan, Brian J., editor. "No Train, No Gain: Continuing Training for Newspaper Journalists in the 1990s." The Freedom Forum, Arlington, Va., 1993.

Carey, James W. "A Plea for the University Tradition," *Journalism Quarterly*, Winter 1978.

Carey, James W. "Where Journalism Education Went Wrong," remarks, Oct. 14, 1992, Columbia University, New York, 1992.

Carey, James W. "The Press and The Public Discourse," *Kettering Review*, Winter 1992.

Carter, Richard F. "On the Essential Contributions of Mass Communications Programs," *Journalism Educator*, Winter 1995.

Christ, William G., editor. "Assessing Communication Education: A Handbook for Media, Speech and Theatre Educators." Hillsdale: Lawrence Erlbaum, 1994.

Cleghorn, Reese. "A Credo for the '90s," acceptance speech for The Freedom Forum Journalism Administrator of the Year Award, Washington, D.C., August 1995.

DeFleur, Melvin L. "The Forthcoming Shortage of Communications Ph.Ds: Trends That Will Influence Recruiting," paper, The Freedom Forum Media Studies Center, New York, May 1993.

Dennis, Everette E. "Commentaries on Journalism Education," The Freedom Forum Media Studies Center, New York, June 1986.

Dennis, Everette E. "Reshaping the Media: Mass Communication in an Information Age." Newbury Park: Sage Publications, 1989.

Dennis, Everette E. "Educating the University," lecture, October 1990, University of Michigan, 1990.

Dennis, Everette E., and Ellen Wartella, editors. "American Communication Research – The Remembered History." Mahwah, N.J.: Lawrence Erlbaum, 1996.

Dickson, Thomas V., and Ralph L. Sellmeyer. "Responses to Proposals for Curricular Change," *Journalism Educator*, Autumn 1992.

Easterbrook, Gregg. "Covering the Winnetka Schools in August," *The Washington Monthly*, May 1986.

Fallows, James. "Breaking the News: How the Media Undermine American Democracy." New York: Pantheon Books, 1996.

Farrar, Ronald T. "J-Schools: A Nouveau Riche Environment?" *Nieman Reports*, Autumn-Winter 1975.

Fibich, Linda. "Under Siege," *American Journalism Review*, September 1995.

Friendly, Jonathan. "Journalism Schools Are Long on Students, Short on Respect," *The New York Times*, June 3, 1984.

Fulton, Katherine. "Future Tense: The Anxious Journey of a Technophobe," *Columbia Journalism Review*, November/December 1993.

Fulton, Katherine. "A Tour of Our Uncertain Future," *Columbia Journalism Review*, March/April 1996.

Gannett Center Journal. "The Making of Journalists," Gannett Center for Media Studies (now The Freedom Forum Media Studies Center), New York, Spring 1988.

Gaunt, Philip. "Making the Newsmakers: International Handbook on Journalism Training." Westport: Greenwood Press, 1992.

Giles, Robert H. "Notes on Accreditation for the Journalism Roundtable," lecture, University of Maryland, February 1995.

Giles, Robert H. "Journalism Education: Facing Up to the Challenge," American Society of Newspaper Editors Committee on Education for Journalism, April 1990.

Gopnik, Adam. "Read All About It," *The New Yorker*, Dec. 12, 1994.

Gremillion, Jeff. "On the Fast Track to Network News – Star School," *Columbia Journalism Review*, January/February 1995.

Grimes, Sara L. "A 'Literary Gentleman' Introduced Journalism to the Campus," *The Campus Chronicle* (University of Massachusetts at Amherst), Oct. 28, 1988.

Halberstam, David. "The Education of a Journalist," *Columbia Journalism Review*, November/December 1994.

Hardt, Hanno, and Bonnie Brennen, editors. "Newsworkers: Toward a History of the Rank and File." Minneapolis: University of Minnesota Press, 1995.

Hume, Ellen. "Tabloids, Talk Radio, and the Future of News: Technology's Impact on Journalism," Washington, D.C.: Annenberg Washington Program, 1995.

Jacobson, Gianna. "For Journalism Graduates, Opportunities in New Media," *The New York Times*, May 20, 1996.

Johnson, J. T. "New Journalism Education for Journalists," *Nieman Reports*, Fall 1995.

Katz, Jon. "Reinventing the Media: Beyond Broadcast Journalism," *Columbia Journalism Review*, March/April 1992.

Katz, Jon. "Rock, Rap and Movies Bring You the News," *Rolling Stone*, March 5, 1992.

Kurtz, Howard. "Hot Air." New York: Times Books, 1996.

Lambeth, Edmund B. "Media Leadership: What Business of Academe?" *ASJMC Insights*, Winter 1992.

Leonard, Thomas C. "News for All: America's Coming-of-Age with the Press." New York: Oxford University Press, 1995.

Levine, Art. "J-School Memories #2: 'Psst, Wanna Read Some Hot Narrative?'" *The Washington Monthly*, May 1986.

Lewis, Carolyn. "The $19,000 Press Pass – A Former Journalism School Dean Asks, Is It Worth It?" *The Washington Monthly*, May 1986.

Lewis, Michael. "J-School Ate My Brain," *The New Republic*, April 19, 1993.

Ludwick, Jim. "The Great Equalizer," *Montana Journalism Review*, October 1993.

Massy, William F., Andrea K. Wilger, and Carol Colbeck. "Overcoming 'Hollowed' Collegiality," *Change*, July/August 1994.

McKenna, Kate. "The Future Is Now," *American Journalism Review*, October 1993.

Media Studies Journal. "Media Critics," The Freedom Forum Media Studies Center, New York, Spring 1995.

Mintz, Morton. "Stories the Media," *The Washington Monthly*, March 1995.

Mirando, Joseph A. "The First College Journalism Students: Answering Robert E. Lee's Offer of a Higher Education," History Division paper at the AEJMC convention, Washington, D.C., August 1995.

Nelson, Joyce. "Sultans of Sleaze: Public Relations and the Media." Monroe, Maine: Common Courage Press, 1989.

New York Herald Tribune, "Willard Bleyer Dies; Teacher of Journalism," Nov. 1, 1935.

Papper, Bob, and Andrew Sharma. "Diversity Remains an Elusive Goal," *Communicator*, October 1995.

Pease, Ted. "Professional Orientation Still Equals Second-Class Status in Some J Schools." Paper prepared at The Freedom Forum Media Studies Center, New York, 1993.

Peters, Charles. "But I'd Really Rather You Didn't Go At All," *The Washington Monthly*, May 1986.

Pitts, Alice Fox. "Read All About It!" Washington: American Society of Newspaper Editors, 1974.

"Planning for Curricular Change in Journalism Education: Project on the Future of Journalism and Mass Communication Education." Second edition. Eugene: School of Journalism, University of Oregon, 1987.

Polsgrove, Carol. "It Wasn't Pretty, Folks, But Didn't We Have Fun – Esquire in the Sixties." New York: W. W. Norton & Company, 1995.

Postman, Neil. "Amusing Ourselves to Death: Public Discourse in the Age of Show Business." New York: Viking Penguin, 1985.

Pulitzer, Joseph. "Planning a School of Journalism – The Basic Concept in 1904," *North American Review*, 1904.

Radio and Television News Directors Foundation report. "A Seat at the Table: The Role of Journalism in the Digital Era," "News in the Next Century," 1995.

Radio and Television News Directors Foundation. "The Future of News, Defining the Issues," report, 1995.

Rogers, Everett M. "A History of Communication Study: A Biographical Approach." New York: The Free Press, 1994.

Rogers, Everett M., and Steven H. Chaffee. "Communication and Journalism from 'Daddy' Bleyer to Wilbur Schramm," *Journalism Monographs*, 148/December 1994.

Rosen, Jay. "Community Connectedness Passwords for Public Journalism," *The Poynter Papers: No.3*, The Poynter Institute for Media Studies, 1993.

Rowland, Willard D. Jr. "The Role of Journalism and Communication Studies in the Liberal Arts: A Place of Honor," *ASJMC Insights*, 1991.

Ryan, Michael, and David L. Martinson. "An Analysis of Faculty Recruiting in Schools and Departments," *Journalism & Mass Communication Educator*, Winter 1996.

Seigenthaler, John. "The First Amendment – Rewind and Fast Forward," lecture at the Leadership Institute for Journalism and Mass Communication Education, The Freedom Forum Media Studies Center, New York, June 1994.

Simpson, Christopher. "Science of Coercion: Communication Research and Psychological Warfare 1945-1960." New York: Oxford University Press, 1994.

Smith, Page. "Killing the Spirit: Higher Education in America." New York: Viking, 1990.

"State of the Field: Academic Leaders in Journalism, Mass Communication and Speech Communication Look to the Future at the University of Texas at Austin," a summary, 1994.

Stauber, John, and Sheldon Rampton. "Toxic Sludge Is Good for You: Lies, Damn Lies and the Public Relations Industry." Monroe, Maine: Common Courage Press, 1995.

Steffens, Lincoln. "The New School of Journalism," *The Bookman*, XVIII, October 1903.

Stepp, Carl Sessions. "The Thrill Is Gone," *American Journalism Review*, October 1995.

Tan, Alexis. "Communication Studies in a Global Village," Robison Lecture, Department of Communication, College of Communications and Fine Arts, Bradley University, 1995.

Tan, Alexis. "Journalism and Mass Communication Programs in the University As Seen by Heads of J/MC Programs and University Administrators," *ASJMC Insights*, Spring 1991.

Taylor, Donna S. Interview with Scott Cutlip, University of Wisconsin University Archives Oral History Project, 1977.

Terry, Carolyn. "J-School Crunch: Defending Your Life," *Presstime*, March 1993.

Waldman, Steven. "If We Must Have J-Schools …" *The Washington Monthly*, May 1986.

Weaver, David H., and G. Cleveland Wilhoit. "The American Journalist: A Portrait of U.S. News People and Their Work." Bloomington: Indiana University Press, 1986.

Weaver, David H., and G. Cleveland Wilhoit. "The American Journalist in the 1990s: U.S. News People at the End of an Era." Mahwah, N.J.: Lawrence Erlbaum, 1996.

Weinberg, Steve. "Bridging the Chasm: Dark Thoughts and Sparks of Hope about Journalism Education," *The Quill*, October 1990.

"Who Should Teach Journalism? – Letters to San Francisco State." Department of Journalism, San Francisco State University, December 1989.

Whitelaw, Kevin. "Is J-school Worth It?" *U.S. News & World Report*, March 18, 1996.

Wicklein, John. "No Experience Required," *Columbia Journalism*

Review, September/October 1994.

Wingspread Project for the Future of Newsroom/Classroom Relations. Report, "We've Got to Talk to Each Other: Journalists and Journalism Educators," Racine, Wis., February 1987.

Williams, Sara Lockwood. "Twenty Years of Education for Journalism – A History of the School of Journalism of the University of Missouri." Columbia: The E. W. Stephens Publishing Company, 1929.

Wyatt, Robert O., and David P. Badger. "A New Typology for Journalism and Mass Communication Writing," *Journalism Educator*, Spring 1993.